BACKPACKER
THE OUTDOORS AT YOUR DOORSTEP

More Backcountry Cooking

MOVEABLE
FEASTS
FROM THE
EXPERTS

Dorcas Miller

THE MOUNTAINEERS BOOKS

Published by
The Mountaineers
1001 SW Klickitat Way, Suite 201
Seattle, WA 98134

BACKPACKER
THE OUTDOORS AT YOUR DOORSTEP

33 East Minor Street
Emmaus, PA 18098

Published simultaneously in Great Britain by Cordee, 3a DeMontfort Street, Leicester, England, LE1 7HD

Manufactured in the United States of America

Editor: Riverbend Publishing
Cover design: The Mountaineers Books
Book design: Ani Rucki
Layout: Riverbend Publishing
Photographer: All photographs are by the author (or are from her collection) unless otherwise noted.
Illustrator: Dawn Peterson
Cover photograph: Photo © Rob Bossi

Library of Congress Cataloging-in-Publication Data
Miller, Dorcas S., 1949–
More backcountry cooking : moveable feasts by the experts / by Dorcas
Miller.— 1st ed.
      p. cm.
  ISBN 0-89886-900-5 (pbk.)
  1. Outdoor cookery. 2. Quick and easy cookery. 3. Camping—Equipment
and supplies. I. Title.
  TX823 .M5424 2002
  641.5'78—dc21
                                                                2002013026

♻ Printed on recycled paper
ISBN 10: 0-89886-900-5
ISBN 13: 978-0-89886-900-2

Dedication

To Jean Spangenberg,
  fellow foodie and backcountry chef extraordinaire

Contents

NUTRITION AND DIETARY NEEDS

Appendices

Introduction

What's your favorite outdoor activity—backpacking, canoeing, river kayaking, skiing, snowshoeing, biking, sea kayaking, rock climbing?

"Eating," says my friend Deb Sugarman. "Eating is my favorite outdoor activity."

I've certainly had lots of practice. I've been eating in the backcountry for more than thirty years. In one of my early jobs as an outdoor instructor, I lived on not very good freeze-dried food. A few summers later I dined for seven weeks on a rotation of four dinners: rice, split peas, lentils, and millet (I've never since been enthusiastic about split peas).

Since then, I've come to appreciate eating as a time to chow down on tasty, fulfilling food that provides nourishment when a hard-working body needs it the most. It's also an opportunity to appreciate the splendor of the outdoors, to complain about trail trials, to pause and refresh, to look back at what you have accomplished, and to prepare for what's ahead. Eating is good for the soul as well as the body.

These days I'd rather do the work at home and watch the sunset while my easy-to-prepare meal simmers away. I use box meals with a few gourmet ingredients such as ginger and coconut cream powder to make taste buds sing. I take advantage of dehydrated foods now available in supermarkets—mushrooms, tomatoes, and all kinds of exotic fruit—to give meals flavor and depth. I have a dehydrator and use it for items that I can't buy at the store: I dry kidney beans, then add them and dried tomatoes to a chili box mix. I make sure that there are comfort foods, whatever they may be: Earl Grey tea, French roast, good chocolate, homemade granola. I include a trail baker and cake mix whenever there's a birthday or any other excuse for a celebration. And I'm willing to spend a few extra dollars to make mundane meals memorable.

Because I care about eating well, I usually volunteer to plan and pack food. It's a responsibility, for the right amount of good food doesn't appear magically. If I get something wrong, I'll hear about it immediately and perhaps for years.

I do not, however, want to be the camp cook. Every meal that goes into the pack has complete directions so that anyone—even the most cooking impaired—can take a turn at the campstove.

What recipes stand out as favorites over the years? Fried Bulgur with Cheese is an unlikely but excellent breakfast that provides lots of firepower. Buckwheat pancakes with real maple syrup were a hit on the last day of a challenging canoe trip down the Harracanaw River in Quebec. My fellow Outward Bounders and I scarfed down flapjacks (the original granola bars) slathered with peanut butter and jelly to fuel us across lakes and over portages in northern Minnesota and southern Canada; my students in Maine later called them Golden Bricks of the North. A climbing buddy recently said that he's been making Logan Bread for winter trips for years. Homemade beef jerky is popular whenever it appears.

Chicken stew with ginger and toasted nuts is an all-time favorite, whether in the Sierras or along the shores of the St. John River. Lemon squares from the bakery (I'm not a purist) were pretty darn good on a sea kayaking outing in Maine. And calorie-drenched fruitcake served on a skiing trip saved us from the deep freeze when an Arctic high tipped the thermometer at -32°, Fahrenheit.

Two of the most important aspects of a trip are the weather and the food. You can't control the weather, but you can control the food. Bad food—or not enough food—can put a sour end to an otherwise enjoyable day. Good food—in sufficient quantity—can make up for a pile of adversity and leave you with pleasant memories.

Good Food has Three Qualities

- It supplies an adequate—even generous—cache of calories.
- It tastes good.
- It offers variety in flavor, texture, and eye appeal.

PART 1

Meal by Meal

Chapter 1

Breakfast

Before we launch into recipes, here's a short quiz. Choose the answer that best matches your view of this meal:

a) Breakfast is simply an infusion of caffeine and calories. I'm not fussy about taste, only about quantity.

b) I want to get on trail promptly, but I want to be properly fed, which means an adequate amount of something tasty to keep me going until snack time.

c) I don't want to be rushed at breakfast. I like to get up, have a cup of coffee, talk with other people on the trip, watch birds, and enjoy a leisurely meal.

There's no right or wrong, but if you don't identify your style, and especially if you are not in sync with your partners, breakfast can be a time of friction rather than simply breaking the fast.

The foods here run the gamut from gorp laced with chocolate-coated coffee beans to make-ahead bars, hot cereals (with lots of alternatives to oatmeal), breakfast burritos, and biscuits. It's important to look at the nutritional information. If you are aiming for 3500 or 4000 calories a day, and you want to get 30 percent of them at breakfast (and 40 percent at lunch and another 30 percent at dinner), then you need 1050 or 1200 calories before you hit the trail.

Because a lot of folks can't or don't want to eat the three cups of cereal that would provide enough calories, most of these recipes are scaled to smaller portions. If a single recipe isn't adequate to your needs, either scale it up or add something—such as a bagel or a cup of cocoa—to boost the numbers.

© Marypat Zitzer

›› *Breakfast Gorp*

No time for coffee? Grab a handful of this mix. That's the verdict from Backpacker testers, who praised this simple but imaginative concoction.

At home, combine:

½ cup cashews

½ cup flaked coconut

½ cup chocolate-covered coffee beans

Recipe from: Sharon Burrer, Backpacker

Servings: Makes six servings of ¼ cup each.

Nutritional information: 164 calories, 12 grams fat, 15 grams carbohydrate, and 3 grams protein per serving.

›› *Lemon-Raisin Breakfast Bars*

Laurie Gullion, a long-time outdoorsperson who found that she could no longer face another bowl of oatmeal or granola, now makes these bars, allotting one bar at the beginning of a trip and two bars as she gets hungrier.

At home, combine in saucepan:

2 cups raisins or diced dried apricots

14 ounces condensed, sweetened milk

1 tablespoon lemon juice

1 tablespoon grated lemon rind

Heat and stir until bubbly; cool slightly; set aside.

In a bowl, combine and stir well:

1 cup flour   ½ teaspoon baking soda

½ teaspoon salt

In a separate bowl, beat together:

1 cup butter   1⅓ cups brown sugar

1½ teaspoons vanilla

Stir in flour mixture and add:

1½ cups oats

1 cup chopped walnuts or sliced almonds

Reserve 2 cups of batter and press the remainder into a 9 x 13-inch greased pan. Spread raisin mixture to within ½ inch of edges. Sprinkle with small pieces of reserved batter; press lightly. Bake 25 to 30 minutes or until golden brown. Slice into 12 bars.

The key ingredient in Breakfast Gorp: chocolate-covered coffee beans.

Servings: Twelve servings of 1 bar each or six servings of 2 bars each.

Nutritional information: 498 calories, 16 grams fat, 84 grams carbohydrate, and 9 grams protein per bar.

›› Granola

Even though it's possible to buy many types of granola, I still make my own because it's fresher, it tastes better, and it has just the right amount of sweetness. Here's my tried-and-true recipe.

At home, combine in a large, flat pan:

10 cups instant rolled oats   1 cup sunflower seeds

½ cup sesame seeds   1 cup chopped almonds

1 cup chopped walnuts   ¾ cup oil

½ cup honey (more to taste)

Stir well. Bake at 350 degrees, stirring after 15 or 20 minutes. Continue baking until golden brown, about 20 more minutes. Remove from oven and stir in:

2 cups raisins or other chopped dried fruit

2 cups wheat germ

Let cool. Add:

6 cups powdered milk

Stir well. If you don't plan to use the granola within a week, store it in the refrigerator.

›› Muesli

Granola is baked, muesli is not. In this recipe, sour cream powder provides an unusual twist. Combine the dry mix and water the night before and greet the day with a breakfast that's ready to be eaten.

At home, combine and stir well:

1¼ cups rolled oats, wheat, or rye   2 tablespoons sunflower seeds

2 tablespoons chopped nuts   ¼ cup raisins

¼ cup chopped dried fruit   1 teaspoon cinnamon

½ cup sour cream powder   ¼ cup powdered milk

⅛ teaspoon salt, or to taste

On trail, pour dry mix into a pot and add:

2¼ cups water

Let stand overnight.

Servings: Seventeen servings of 1 cup each.

Nutritional information: 607 calories, 29 grams fat, 71 grams carbohydrate, and 27 grams protein per cup.

The Best No-Cook Breakfast

After years of experimentation, Diane Hiener of Dorset, Ohio, has found her perfect no-cook breakfast: cinnamon rolls from the bakery. "Too heavy for long trips, but just right for weekends," she says. "Pack them in a sealed container and don't forget the hot chocolate!"

—*Backpacker*

Servings: Two servings of 1½ cups each.

Nutritional information: 459 calories, 24 grams fat, 81 grams carbohydrate, and 18 grams protein per serving.

›› *Hot Cereal*

Rolled oats, rolled wheat, rolled rye, bulgur, and any combination of these grains make excellent hot cereals. For the fastest breakfast, use instant rolled oats or the finest-grain bulgur. To shorten cooking time break up rolled grains by chopping them briefly in a food processor. Honey, sugar, nuts, sesame seeds, sunflower seeds, margarine, butter, or dried fruit pep up the flavor and pump up the calories.

One-half cup rolled grain will make 1 cup cooked cereal. While honey, sugar, powdered milk, margarine, or butter does not increase the overall volume; nuts, seeds, and dried fruit do.

Servings: One serving of slightly more than 1 cup, depending on ingredients.

Nutritional information: See sidebar page 14.

At home, pack in a zipper-lock bag:
½ cup rolled cereal
additional ingredients to taste

On trail, if you are using instant rolled oats or fine-grained bulgur, place dry mix in bowl and add:
1 cup boiling water (slightly more if using dried fruit)

Stir and let stand 10 minutes.

If you are using a grain that needs to be cooked, combine dry mix and water in a pot, bring to a boil, reduce heat, and simmer several minutes until done; the exact time depends on the grain.

›› *Creamy Rice Cereal*

Servings: Two servings of 1¼ cups each.

Nutritional information: 442 calories, 13 grams fat, 70 grams carbohydrate, and 16 grams protein per serving.

Even people who dislike hot cereal have enjoyed this recipe. Chopping the nuts and dates as fine as possible gives the dish a smooth texture. The dates serve as a sweetener, so try it first before you add sugar or honey.

At home, pack in a zipper-lock bag:

½ cup creamed rice, quick-cooking   ⅓ cup almonds, chopped very fine

6 dates, sliced very thin   ⅔ cup powdered milk

dash salt, or to taste

On trail, slowly add ingredients to:

2 cups boiling water

Cook for 30 seconds, stirring; cover; remove from heat; and let stand 3 minutes.

Hot Cereal Nutritional Information					
	AMOUNT	**CALORIES**	**FAT**	**CARBOHYDRATE**	**PROTEIN**
Almonds	2 scant T	84	8g	3g	3g
Apples, dried	2 rings	31	0g	8g	0g
Apricots, dried	5 halves	70	0g	18g	1g
Bulgur	½ c dry	227	1g	47g	8g
Honey	1 T	65	0g	17g	0g
Margarine	1 T	100	12g	0g	0g
Milk, instant	⅓ c	82	0g	12g	8g
Oats, rolled	½ c	150	3g	27g	8g
Raisins	2 T	60	0g	16g	0g
Sesame seeds	2 T	160	9g	5g	3g
Sugar, brown	1 T	40	0g	11g	0g
Sunflower seeds	2 T	83	7g	4g	3g
Walnuts	2 scant T	90	9g	2g	3g
Abbreviations: T = tablespoon; c = cup; g = gram Trace amounts and no amount have both been recorded as "0"					

›› Pecan Rice Cereal

Be patient when making this recipe, as it requires a lot of stirring.

At home, pack these items individually:

1 cup instant long-grain rice   ½ cup pecans

¼ cup honey

On trail, toast the pecans over medium heat for 3 to 4 minutes. Just before removing the pot from the heat, sprinkle the pecans with:

¼ teaspoon salt

Pour the pecans into a small dish and crumble with a spoon. Put the rice in a pot and add:

2 cups water

½ teaspoon salt

Cover and bring to a boil, then simmer uncovered over medium heat for about 10 minutes or until the water is nearly absorbed. Add:

½ cup water

and continue boiling until the additional water is also nearly absorbed. Then add:

½ cup water

Bring rice to one last boil and simmer until it reaches the consistency of oatmeal. Remove pan from the heat, serve rice into bowls, and top with toasted pecans and honey.

Recipe from: Stern Dixon, Backpacker

Servings: Two servings of about 1¼ cups each.

Nutritional information: 512 calories, 16 grams fat, 83 grams carbohydrate, and 10 grams protein per serving.

© *Marypat Zitzer*

›› Backpacker *Rice Pudding*

With the addition of vanilla pudding, this dish is creamier than the Rice Pudding in the dessert section. It also has twice as many raisins and an extra-large portion of powdered milk—all the better to help you launch the day.

At home, combine in a zipper-lock bag:

⅔ cup powdered milk   1 cup instant rice

½ cup instant vanilla pudding   1 cup raisins

½ teaspoon cinnamon   Pinch nutmeg

On trail, place ingredients in a pot and add:

2 cups water

Stir well. Bring to a light boil over medium heat. Cover, remove from heat, and let stand for 5 minutes.

Recipe from: *Tim Randall,* Backpacker

Servings: Four.

Nutritional information: 335 calories, 2 grams fat, 77 grams carbohydrate, and 7 grams protein.

›› *Hangdog Oatmeal*

When Drew Ross headed out on an 18-day backpacking trip in Canada's remote Mackenzie Mountains, he rotated through Grapenuts, granola, Malt O' Meal, oatmeal, and Cream of Rice. Here's his recipe for oatmeal, one that chocaholics will appreciate. Drew grinds his dried bananas in a coffee grinder.

At home, mix these ingredients in a zipper-lock bag:

2½ cups instant oatmeal   2 tablespoons brown sugar, or to taste

½ cup dried bananas, ground   ¾ cup chocolate chips, or to taste

On trail, boil:

4 cups water, or more as necessary

Add contents of bag, stir, bring to boil, remove from stove, and set aside until it is cool enough to eat.

Recipe from: *Drew Ross,* Backpacker

Servings: Two servings of about 3 cups each.

Nutritional information: 1056 calories, 40 grams fat, 161 grams carbohydrate, and 13 grams protein per serving.

›› *Fruity Breakfast Porridge*

If you're organized enough, make a meal with brown rice the night before and save a cup for this super oatmeal substitute; long-cooking brown rice has more nutrients than the instant variety.

At home, combine in a zipper-lock bag:

¼ cup powdered milk   ⅛ teaspoon cinnamon

⅛ teaspoon nutmeg   ¼ cup chopped walnuts

2 tablespoons brown sugar   2 tablespoons raisins

2 tablespoons dried berries (cherries, blueberries, etc.)

½ cup instant brown rice

On trail, combine all dry ingredients in a pot with:

1¼ cups water

Cook over low heat for 8 to 12 minutes, stirring frequently. As the porridge simmers, add water until it reaches the desired consistency.

Recipe from: *Liz Rusch,* Backpacker

Servings: Two.

Nutritional information: 322 calories, 10 grams fat, 53 grams carbohydrate, and 9 grams protein per serving.

Cooking Times and Yields for 1 Cup (Dry) Hot Cereal			
DRY CEREAL	**WATER**	**COOKING TIME**	**YIELD**
Oats, rolled, instant	2 cups	Add boiling water	2 cups
Oats, rolled, quick	2 cups	1 minute, let stand 2 to 3 minutes	2 cups
Oats, rolled, regular	2 cups	5 to 15 minutes	2 cups
Oats, steel-cut	3⅓ cups	15 to 20 minutes	3⅓ cups
Rice, creamed, quick	4 cups	30 seconds, let stand 3 minutes	4 cups
Wheat, creamed, quick	5 cups	30 seconds, let stand 3 minutes	5 cups

›› Hot Buckwheat Cereal with Bananas, Nuts, and Honey

Servings: Two.

Nutritional information: Including nuts, 346 calories, 17 grams fat, 49 grams carbohydrate, and 6 grams protein per serving.

If you are heading out with someone who has food allergies (including yourself), see what backpacker Carol Steinberg has to share on this subject in Hot Topic 17. This recipe and the next are two of her favorite morning-starters. Substitute cream of rye or amaranth for the buckwheat if you like; just check the directions on the box.

At home, pack in a zipper-lock bag:

¼ cup cream of buckwheat

½ cup dried banana slices

Pack these items individually:

¼ cup raisins or dates

⅓ cup chopped almonds, walnuts, or pecans (optional)

2 tablespoons honey, or to taste

On trail, add cereal and banana slices to:

1¼ cups boiling water

Reduce heat and simmer to desired consistency, stirring often. Add dried fruit, nuts, and honey before serving.

Recipe from: *Carol Steinberg,* Backpacker

›› Couscous and Fruit

This recipe, slightly modified, is from Claudine Martin's cookbook The Trekking Chef, *which is now out of print. If you can't buy couscous by the cup or pound, check your supermarket for boxed couscous. A 12-ounce package contains about 1 1/2 cups.*

Servings: Four servings of about 1+ cup each.

Nutritional information: 478 calories, 6 grams fat, 96 grams carbohydrate, and 9 grams protein per serving.

At home, place in a zipper-lock bag:

- 1½ cups couscous
- ¼ cup dried bananas, ground
- ¼ cup sugar
- Dash salt
- ½ cup dried berries, ground
- ½ cup dried pineapple bits
- ½ teaspoon cinnamon

Pack separately:

- 2 tablespoons butter or margarine

On the trail, put butter in a pot and add:

- 4 cups water

Bring to a boil, then add contents of couscous bag. Stir well, cover, and turn off the heat. Let stand for 5 minutes. Fluff the couscous and serve.

Alas, most backcountry water must now be purified. Bring water to a rolling boil; use a water filter with an iodine component. © Marypat Zitzer

›› *Fried Bulgur with Cheese*

Servings: Two servings of 1¼ cups each.

Nutritional information: 486 calories, 24 grams fat, 53 grams carbohydrate, and 16 grams protein.

This breakfast is an all-time favorite and provides a vast change from sweetened cereal. On a 49-day canoe trip with no resupply, we carried an onion for every day, so even at the end of the trip, the aroma of frying onion drew everyone to the camp kitchen.

At home, pack these items individually:

1 cup bulgur	1 small onion
2 to 3 tablespoons oil	2 ounces Cheddar cheese
Garlic powder or fresh garlic to taste	

On trail, the night before, place bulgur in a pot and add:

2 cups water

Let stand overnight. In the morning, dice the onion (and slice the garlic if using fresh), then sauté in oil. Add rehydrated bulgur to skillet and fry until golden brown and crispy. Season with salt, pepper, and garlic powder. Meanwhile, dice the cheese and fold into the bulgur just before you are ready to serve the meal. (If you serve the bulgur first and then divide the cheese, the cheese won't melt as well, but the pan will be easier to clean.)

>> Breakfast Burritos

This hearty meal works as well for dinner as it does for breakfast.

At home, combine in a zipper-lock bag:

2 cups dried hash browns

2 tablespoons dried onion

1 tablespoon dried tomato, finely cut

1 tablespoon dried red or green bell pepper

1 tablespoon dried mushrooms

In another zipper-lock bag, combine:

9 tablespoons (equal to 6 eggs) powdered eggs

2 tablespoons powdered Cheddar cheese

Pack individually:

2 tablespoons oil

6 flour tortillas

On trail, place dried hash browns and veggies in a pot or bowl, cover with boiling water, and let stand 5 to 8 minutes. Drain any excess water, using the liquid to reconstitute the eggs. Heat the oil in a frying pan and add the potato mixture. Cook undisturbed for 3 to 7 minutes until brown and crispy; a nonstick pan is useful here. Turn with a spatula and fry the other side for about a minute. Pour the egg mixture right in with the potatoes and cook until the eggs set. Briefly warm tortillas in a covered pan. Fill each tortilla with about 1/2 cup of filling and roll into a burrito. Serve with salsa or hot sauce.

> **Servings:** Two hefty servings of 3 burritos each.
>
> **Nutritional information:** 913 calories, 40 grams fat, 141 grams carbohydrate, and 35 grams protein per serving.

›› Eggs Bandolier

Read about eggs in Hot Topic 2, How to—.

Servings: Two.

Nutritional information: 588 calories, 37 grams fat, 38 grams carbohydrate, and 26 grams protein per serving.

At home, pack these ingredients individually:

2 English muffins

2 pieces Canadian bacon

2 slices Cheddar cheese

4 tablespoons (equal to 2 eggs) powdered eggs

10-ounce package Hollandaise sauce mix

2 teaspoons lemon juice

1 tablespoon butter

On trail, melt the butter in a nonstick skillet. Slice and toast the muffins, then set each pair in its own bowl. Cover now and with each addition to maintain warmth. Fry Canadian bacon until slightly brown, then place bacon and a piece of cheese on a muffin half. Scramble eggs, then place equal portions on top of each cheese slice. Make the Hollandaise sauce according to package directions and pour over eggs. Season with salt and pepper and top with remaining half of muffin.

Recipe from: *www.backpacker.com/technique*

Strategizing on the Dubawnt River, Canada

›› Wheat Bagel with Mushroom Omelette

At home, combine:

¼ teaspoon onion flakes

¼ teaspoon parsley flakes

Pack these items individually:

6 tablespoons (equal to 3 eggs) powdered eggs

¼ cup dried mushrooms, sliced

1 small wheat bagel

2 teaspoons vegetable oil

On trail, cover mushrooms with water to rehydrate and set aside.

Combine the egg powder, parsley, and onion and add:

⅓ cup plus 2 tablespoons water

Heat the oil in the pan, then add the egg mixture and cook until the bottom is golden brown. Flip, if desired, to brown the other side. Spread the rehydrated mushrooms over the top, fold the omelette in half, and serve with the bagel.

Recipe from: Michele Morris, Backpacker

Servings: One.

Nutritional information: 591 calories, 28 grams fat, 50 grams carbohydrates, and 29 grams protein.

›› Ersatz Eggs and Cheese

This tofu-based dish contains no dairy yet looks remarkably like eggs with cheese because the carrot turns the tofu the color of scrambled eggs.

At home, pack:

2 large carrots, finely grated   16 ounces firm tofu

3 single-serving packets soy sauce   Dash sesame oil

In camp, cook carrots over low heat until soft. Crumble tofu and add to pan. Add soy sauce and sesame oil and simmer until hot.

Recipe from: Stern Dixon, Backpacker

Servings: Four.

Nutritional information: 121 calories, 5 grams fat, 5 grams carbohydrate, and 10 grams protein per serving.

›› Pancakes

Servings: One serving of 6 pancakes.

Nutritional information: 576 calories, 16 grams fat, 93 grams carbohydrate, and 18 grams protein per serving.

Servings: One serving of ⅓ cup syrup.

Nutritional information: 604 calories, 24 grams fat, 52 grams carbohydrate, and 0 grams protein per serving.

Serve pancakes with syrup, butter, jam, confectioners sugar, fruit compote (see Desserts), or other topping of your choice. To perk up the batter, add a tablespoon poppy seeds and 1 or 2 teaspoons dried orange rind; 2 tablespoons minced walnuts; or 3 tablespoons buttermilk powder. Or substitute 1 cup buckwheat flour for 1 cup whole wheat flour in biscuit mix.

At home, pack in a zipper-lock bag:

1 cup Biscuit Mix (page 31)

On trail, add:

½ cup plus 2 tablespoons water

Grease and warm the pan; it is at the right temperature when a drop of water dances in place. Drop or pour batter onto the surface to form a 4-inch pancake. Let the batter cook for 2 to 3 minutes. When bubbles have risen to the surface but have not broken, turn the pancake and cook the other side 1 to 1 ½ minutes.

›› Syrup

Having worked at a sugaring operation in Vermont one spring, I'm partial to maple syrup and carry the real thing when I'm canoeing. For a lighter alternative, pack maple granules that can be reconstituted on trail (see Resources). Or, try this non-maple recipe.

At home, combine in a leakproof container:

¼ cup brown sugar or honey

2 tablespoons butter or margarine

On trail, heat these ingredients and add:

2 tablespoons water

›› Teff Pancakes with Applesauce

People who cannot eat wheat products often use teff flour, tapioca flour, amaranth flour, or buckwheat flour. (Teff is a grain.)

At home, combine in a zipper-lock bag and mix well:

1 cup teff flour

1 tablespoon baking soda

½ teaspoon salt

1¼ cups water

½ cup tapioca flour

½ teaspoon cream of tartar

2 teaspoons canola oil

In another bag, pack:

2½ oz dried applesauce

On trail, place applesauce in a bowl and add about 1 ½ times as much water as there is applesauce; add more as needed to reach desired consistency. Cover and let stand. To the pancake mixture, add:

1¼ cups water

Mix well. Warm a lightly greased pan over the camp stove. Drop batter by tablespoons into the pan to make 2-inch rounds. Hold pan 2 to 3 inches above the flame to avoid scorching the cakes. Serve with applesauce.

Recipe from: *Carol Steinberg,* Backpacker

Servings: Two servings of 13 pancakes each.

Nutritional information: 468 calories, 6 grams fat, 132 grams carbohydrate, and 6 grams protein per serving.

›› Spiced Breakfast Bannock

At home, combine in a zipper-lock bag:

1 cup Biscuit Mix (page 31)

½ teaspoon cinnamon

3 tablespoons raisins or chopped dried fruit

4 teaspoons sugar

3 tablespoons chopped nuts

On trail, add to dry ingredients:

⅔ cup water

Stir slowly. Add more water as needed to achieve a batter that is thicker than pancake batter and thinner than biscuit dough. Spoon into greased, warmed pan over low heat. Cook 10 minutes on one side, flip, and cook as needed on the other side. Eat as is or drizzle with honey.

Recipe adapted from: *Terry Krautwurst,* Backpacker

Servings: Two servings of 1 medium bannock each.

Nutritional information: 437 calories, 15 grams fat, 69 grams carbohydrate, and 11 grams protein per serving.

›› Breakfast Tofu Scramble

Servings: Two.

Nutritional information: 250 calories, 16 grams fat, 5 grams carbohydrate, and 18 grams protein per serving.

This tasty dish has lots of protein. For a little extra weight—and lots of extra punch—use 1 tablespoon finely chopped fresh garlic and half a small onion instead of their dried counterparts. Sauté and set aside until the tofu has been browned, then add along with the other vegetables. Serve with a bagel or tortilla.

At home, combine in a zipper-lock bag:

1 teaspoon basil	½ teaspoon cumin
½ teaspoon turmeric	1 dash cayenne pepper
1 teaspoon garlic powder	Pinch salt

Tie off that corner of the bag. Then add:

1 tablespoon chopped dried tomatoes

1 tablespoon bell pepper flakes

2 teaspoons onion flakes

Pack individually:

1 package raw tofu (12 to 16 ounces)

1 tablespoon vegetable oil

On trail, rehydrate dried vegetables by covering with boiling water; let stand; when rehydrated, drain liquid. Meanwhile, crumble the tofu and sauté it in oil until slightly browned. Add the vegetables and spices, mix well, and cook a few more minutes until heated. Add salt to taste.

Recipe from: *Allison Carroll*, Backpacker

›› Breakfast Potatoes

Use this recipe on a paddling trip when the boat (not your back) is carrying the weight. For a first-morning-out breakfast, prep the spuds at home. Otherwise, cut morning chores by boiling the potatoes the night before. Either way, though, allow plenty of time for frying. If you do not have a nonstick pan, take extra oil. If you prefer fresh to dry, pack a small onion and two cloves of garlic.

Servings: Four servings of 1½ potatoes each.

Nutritional information: 354 calories, 3 grams fat, 78 grams carbohydrate, and 7 grams protein per serving.

At home, combine in a zipper-lock bag:

½ teaspoon ground coriander

½ tablespoon chili powder

1 teaspoon onion flakes

1 teaspoon ground cumin

½ teaspoon salt

½ teaspoon garlic powder

Also pack individually:

6 medium potatoes

4 ounces green chilies (optional)

2 teaspoons olive oil

On trail, scrub the potatoes, pare the eyes and damaged spots, and dice into ¹/₂-inch cubes. Cover with water, bring to a boil, then remove from heat. Let sit until tender (approximately 15 minutes), then drain. Meanwhile, if you are using fresh onions and garlic, sauté them in olive oil for 5 minutes using a nonstick pan. Stir in the potatoes, spices, and minced green chilies. Cook on high heat, turning often, until golden brown and crispy.

Recipe from: *Jasmine Star,* Backpacker

›› Heavenly Hash Browns

Servings: Two servings of about 1⅓+ cups each.

Nutritional information: 401 calories, 4 grams fat, 79 grams carbohydrate, and 19 grams protein per serving.

This recipe is more suited to traveling light. The textured vegetable protein (TVP) does not have much taste, but it adds protein to this heavily carbohydrate dish. For that wonderful smell of frying onions, take a small onion instead of dried flakes.

At home, pack in a zipper-lock bag:
½ cup textured vegetable protein granules

3 tablespoons onion flakes

1 package (10 ounces) dried shredded potatoes or hash browns

Also pack:
½ tablespoon oil

On trail, add to the potato mix:
1⅓ cups boiling water

Stir and let stand for 5 to 10 minutes. Then, heat half the oil in a frying pan. Add onions, TVP, potatoes, and remaining oil. Mix and pat down, then cook on low heat 10 to 15 minutes. Cook the other side. Cut, season, and serve.

Recipe from: *Josh Coen*, Backpacker

Exploring new turf in the Russian River Watershed, Alaska © Marypat Zitzer

›› Doughnuts I

On a lay-over day on a long canoeing trip, I rustled up Biscuit Mix, shortening, honey, and cinnamon to make finger-sized doughnuts that were hot and crispy. If you try this recipe, be extremely careful with the hot fat, which can cause severe burns if it gets spilled on your skin. Should you have leftover fat, let it cool and return it to the original container or place it in several layers of zipper-lock bags, then put it with your carry-out trash.

Servings: Three servings of 4 small doughnuts each.

Nutritional information: 432 calories, 28 grams fat, 42 grams carbohydrate, and 6 grams protein per serving.

At home, combine in a zipper-lock bag:

1 cup Biscuit Mix (page 31)   2 tablespoons honey

1 teaspoon cinnamon

Pack separately:

1 cup vegetable shortening

On trail, add to Biscuit Mix:

⅓ cup water or more as needed

Stir well and knead dough until smooth. Pat into a ¹/₂-inch-thick slab four inches deep. Cut doughnuts ¹/₂ inch wide. Fry in hot fat, removing when golden brown. If the fat is too cool, the doughnuts will be greasy; if it is too hot, the doughnuts will burn. When the dough hits the grease, sinks to the bottom, and then bounces back to the surface—bubbling all the while—you'll get crispy, tender doughnuts.

›› Doughnuts II

I was introduced to these doughnuts on a spring canoeing trip in northern Maine. They are properly made with an outsize frying pan and a fire, but a stove will do in a pinch. Look for ready-made biscuits in the refrigerator section of the supermarket. Again, be extremely careful with the hot grease.

Servings: Four servings of 2 doughnuts each.

Nutritional information: 995 calories, 69 grams fat, 80 grams carbohydrate, and 9 grams protein per serving.

At home, combine:

   1 cup sugar

   2 tablespoons cinnamon

Pack individually:

   1 cylinder ready-made biscuits   2 cups vegetable shortening

   1 medium-sized paper bag

On trail, break open the cylinder, make a hole in each biscuit, and fry (see instructions for preparing Doughnuts I). Remove from pan and drain on paper towels. Drop into a paper bag with sugar and cinnamon and shake well.

Recipe from: *Steve Cobb*

Doughnuts the Maine Guide way.

›› Biscuit Mix

Use this mix for pancakes, biscuits, pie dough, coffee cake, dumplings, and any other flour-based food. If you opt for using only whole wheat flour, the baked goods will be heavier and denser.

At home, combine:

- 1 cup unbleached white flour
- 2 teaspoons baking powder
- 2 tablespoons oil
- 1 cup whole wheat flour
- ½ teaspoon salt
- ⅓ cup powdered milk

Nutritional information: 576 calories, 16 grams fat, 93 grams carbohydrate, and 18 grams protein per 1 cup mix.

Making it through the Fast

Breakfast is so named because it's a break in the longest fast of the day—nighttime. How do you keep your belly from grumbling and your body from getting cold in the middle of the night? Dr. Frank Cerny, an exercise physiologist at State University of New York at Buffalo, offers the answer: Eat more fat before you go to bed. Dr. Cerny says your last meal of the day should contain 25 to 30 percent fat so you'll stay warm and comfortable through the night, especially in winter, but at other times of the year, too. So chow down on some nuts before bedtime and you won't be so ravenous when you wake the next morning.

—Backpacker

›› Coffee Cake

If you're an early riser, whip up this coffee cake while the others are getting up, and you'll earn high points all around.

At home, combine in a zipper-lock bag:

2 cups Biscuit Mix (page 31)

2 tablespoons brown sugar

In a leakproof container, combine:

⅓ cup oatmeal

1 teaspoon cinnamon

¼ cup plus 2 tablespoons brown sugar

¼ cup margarine or clarified butter

On trail, add to Biscuit Mix and sugar:

⅔ cup water, or more as needed

Stir to make a spreadable dough. Spoon into greased pan. Sprinkle the oatmeal mixture on top.

For the Ultralight BakePacker (5 ½ inches in diameter): Use half the recipe, bake/boil in an oven bag 15 minutes or until done, and let stand 3 minutes.

For the Standard BakePacker (7 ½ inches in diameter): Bake/boil in an oven bag 25 minutes or until done and let stand 3 minutes.

For the Alpine Banks Fry-Bake Pan: Bake in greased pan for 18 to 20 minutes or until done.

For the Outback Oven (6 or 7 inches in diameter): Bring thermometer into bake zone and then bake 20 to 22 minutes or until done.

For the Outback Oven (8 inches in diameter): Bring thermometer into bake zone and then bake 18 to 20 minutes or until done.

›› *Coffee Cake for the Banks Fry-Bake Pan*

If the coffee cake rises too high in a backpacking Dutch oven, it will get too near the lid and burn. For a 7-inch-diameter pan, use this slightly smaller recipe:

At home, combine in a zipper-lock bag

1⅓ cups Biscuit Mix (page 31)

1 tablespoon and 1 teaspoon brown sugar

In another bag, combine:

3 tablespoons oatmeal

⅔ teaspoon cinnamon

¼ cup brown sugar

2½ tablespoons margarine or clarified butter

On trail, add to Biscuit Mix and sugar:

½ cup minus 1 tablespoon water, or more as necessary

Spread in greased pan and top with oatmeal mixture. Bake 18 to 20 minutes or until done.

<aside>
Servings: Three.

Nutritional information: 434 calories, 13 grams fat, 65 grams carbohydrate, and 10 grams protein per serving.
</aside>

© Marypat Zitzer

Chapter 2

Lunch and Snacks

Five days on the trail and your mind is dancing with visions of the all-you-can-eat buffet at your local pizza place. You tear into the lunch sack and find gorp dregs, a few energy bars, a tube of peanut butter, and a slightly green bagel. Not again! As your taste buds run for cover, you realize that you've hiked into the dreaded Lunch Zone, a culinary black hole that sucks in even experienced outdoorspeople.

But take heart. Whether you're headed out for a weekend or two weeks, there are many good-tasting, on-the-go options to lift lunch out of the doldrums. The lunch quandary is usually born out of the simple fact that most of us don't like to cook at midday. There are places to see, miles to cover, and who wants to deal with the stove? Lunch fare has to be low fuss and filling.

The best strategy is to think of lunch as a process, not an occasion. View it as a series of snacks and mini-meals spanning the period between breakfast and dinner, not as a single meal eaten when the sun is at its zenith. Nutritionists agree with this many-small-meals approach. A carbohydrate snack every hour or hour and a half helps replenish glycogen levels and can head off those debilitating energy crashes.

It's not enough to ingest calories. Follow your stomach's whims in deciding what to eat during your breaks, but try to get 40 percent of your calories each day from lunch and snacks and get those calories from all three calorie sources (see Hot Topic 13). Carbos are concentrated in bready and sweet foods, anything with flour, sugar, and fruit. Look for proteins in cheese, nuts and seeds and their butters, sardines, jerky, tuna, and salami. Some fatty foods overlap with proteins; you'll find fats in cheese and nuts, salami, chocolate, and trail mix, among others.

Variety is the only way to fend off monotony when you're snacking frequently. After all, how many fig bars can one human consume in a day? Think of lunch ingredients in several broad categories, with a wide selection in each from which you can pick and choose without getting bored.

- **Energy bars.** Originally designed for athletes, energy bars are filled with lots of carbos, vitamins, and minerals in a handy package. Some outdoor folk rely on them exclusively for lunches and snacks. Bars are expensive, though, and to get the requisite number of calories you have to eat four or five a day, a prospect that may faze even those with tough stomachs and simple tastes. And at $1.00 to $1.50 per bar, the tab goes up quickly.

- **Fruit-based foods.** Dried fruit, fruit leather, fruit-filled cookies, and jam contain simple carbohydrates, which get burned fastest. Eating only simple carbos will leave you buzzing from one hit to the next.

- **Bready foods.** Bagels, crackers, tortillas, pita, pretzels, and trail-baked breads are major sources of complex carbohydrates, which are burned more slowly than simple carbos. The bread of choice is often the bagel—that sturdy, calorie-laden, carbohydrate-rich, glycogen-producing staff of trail life. The problem is, bagels tend to become stiff and moldy after too long in your pack. Plus, how many can you eat before hitting the "bagel barrier"? You need to explore other options.

  —Crackers. Crackers last surprisingly well when carefully packaged. Use the cylinders in which some chips are packaged, plastic food storage boxes, or clean milk cartons to provide protection.

  —Tortillas. Depending on where you are, store-bought tortillas can keep for about a week in your pack. Or, you can easily make them on trail. Served with cream cheese and fruit roll-ups, they provide a sweet snack. Served with hummus or bean spread and salsa, they come out savory.

  —Trail-baked bread. You'll need one of the specialized trail bakers and some patience, but the prospect of fresh bread for lunch can make anyone step lively. Bake the night before, allow the bread to cool, place it in a plastic bag, and tuck it into a protected area of your pack.

Snacking on a Maine coast island

Fuel up often on long days. © Alan Kesselheim

—Fry/bake breads. If you can't deal with baking but can handle a pancake flipper, try whipping up Bannock (page 54) while you're downing breakfast. Use homemade Biscuit Mix (page 31) or one from the supermarket. You can also take off-the-shelf cornbread mix, add water so the batter is a little thicker than the consistency of pancakes, and make biscuit-sized cornbreads.

—Other flour-based carbos. Pretzels, bread sticks, fish crackers—cruise the supermarket aisles and see what appeals.

- **Trail salads.** There's more to lunch than bread alone. Make Tabouli Salad, Packer's Coleslaw, Carrot-Pineapple Crunch, or other packable salads to add zest to a long day (see both Lunch and Dinner salads).

- **Spreads.** Store-bought hummus and bean spread have become backcountry staples. Liven up the hummus with something crunchy (a crisp pickling cucumber, a few sticks of carrot) and the bean spread with salsa and cheese.

- **Dehydrated vegetables.** Dry your own snack veggies, such as tomatoes or zucchini with mixed herbs, garlic, and a dash of salt. Or, go to the health food store and buy freeze-dried peas seasoned with wasabi, a spicy-hot Japanese condiment similar to horseradish. Dried veggies are low in calories but can provide welcome variety in taste, texture, and eye appeal.

- **Miscellaneous snacks.** Trail mix, corn nuts, sesame sticks, and other snackables are generally high in fat and therefore in calories. Chocolate offers primarily fats and simple carbos. Hard candy gives you a shot of quickly-burned simple carbohydrates.

Nutritional Information for Lunch and Snacks

	AMOUNT	CALORIES	FAT	CARBOHYDRATE	PROTEIN
Almond butter	1 tablespoon	101	10	3	2
Apple	1	70	0	18	0
Apple, dried	5 rings	78	0	21	0
Apricots, dried	5 halves	70	0	18	1
Bagel	1	336	3	65	12
Bannock	3 pieces	288	8	47	9
Black bean spread*	½ cup	136	1	23	8
Bread, 9-grain	1 slice				
Candy, hard	1 ounce	110	0	28	0
Cashews	¼ cup	196	16	10	6
Cashew butter	1 tablespoon	95	8	5	3
Cheese, cheddar	1 ounce	115	9	1	7
Cheese, Parmesan	1 ounce	110	7	1	11
Cheese, string	1 ounce	80	6	0	7
Chocolate, milk	1 ounce	145	9	16	2
Couscous salad*	½ cup	103	5	13	2
Crackers, fish	55 fish	150	6	20	3
Crackers, rye	1 slice	30	1	7	1
Crackers, pilot	1 cracker	70	2	13	2
Crackers, pilot, homemade	1 cracker	101	3	16	3
Energy bar, from store**	2 bars	230	3	45	10
Fig bars	2 bars	110	3	22	1
Granola bars	2 bars	180	6	29	4

Nutritional Information for Lunch and Snacks

	AMOUNT	CALORIES	FAT	CARBOHYDRATE	PROTEIN
Hummus*	½ cup	111	7	10	4
Jam	1 tablespoon	55	0	14	0
Nuts, mixed	½ cup	390	34	15	14
Orange	1	65	0	16	1
Peaches, dried	5 halves	156	0	40	3
Peanuts, dry roasted	½ cup	354	29	12	21
Peanut butter	1 tablespoon	95	8	4	4
Pears, dried	5 halves	230	0	61	2
Pita bread	1	106	1	21	4
Pretzels, plain	20 mini	110	0	25	3
Pretzels, yogurt	7 pieces	190	8	29	1
Prunes	4	70	0	18	1
Raisins	½ cup	240	0	64	2
Refried bean spread*	½ cup	136	1	23	8
Salami	1 ounce	130	11	0	7
Sardines	3 ounces	175	9	0	20
Sesame sticks	1 ounce	160	11	13	3
Soy nuts	⅓ cup	140	7	9	11
Tabouli*	½ cup	161	10	17	2
Tahini (sesame butter)	1 tablespoon	89	8	3	3
Tortillas, flour	1 7-inch	150	4	25	3
Trail mix, from store	¼ cup	160	11	9	5

*Made from store-bought mix
**Values for one popular bar; values vary per brand
Trace amounts and no amount have both been recorded as "0"

›› *Fruit Bars*

Use your imagination in pairing fruit and nuts. Apricots and almonds are a natural duo, as are dates and walnuts. With all the different dried fruit and nuts available, there are bound to be some winners. The batter here is fairly thick, so if you make half a batch of two different types, you can bake them in one pan.

At home, chop in a food processor:

1 cup dried fruit

1½ cups nuts

Mix fruit and nuts with:

½ cup honey

⅔ cup flour

½ cup wheat germ

2 tablespoons oil

Add:

4 tablespoons juice or water

to form thick batter. Mix well. Press into an 8 x 8-inch square greased pan. Bake at 350 degrees for 30 minutes or until firm. Cool. Cut into 12 bars and package in convenient numbers. Store in a refrigerator or freezer.

> **Servings:** Six servings of 2 bars each.
>
> **Nutritional information:** 220 calories, 20 grams fat, 44 grams carbohydrate, and 20 grams protein per serving.

Ready for a snack, Tetons National Park, Wyoming © Marypat Zitzer

›› Golden Bricks of the North

Servings: Nine servings of 2 squares each.

Nutritional information: 468 calories, 28 grams fat, 54 grams carbohydrate, and 6 grams protein per serving.

When I was a student and then instructor at the Outward Bound School in Minnesota in the early 1970s, these oat-based "flapjacks" anchored lunch. They provide lots of calories by themselves and even more when slathered with peanut butter and jelly. I made the bars at another outdoor program, where my students dubbed them Golden Bricks of the North. We carried 3 1/2 x 3 1/2-inch squares, which fit nicely into a cardboard milk container for protection. Nutritional information here is for 3 x 3-inch bars made in cake pans.

At home, combine:

4¼ cups rolled oats	½ cup peanuts or almonds
1 cup sugar	1 cup margarine
2½ tablespoons honey	2½ tablespoons corn syrup

Divide dough and place in two 9 x 9-inch, well-greased cake pans (or comparably sized cookie sheets with raised edges), pressing dough into a compact layer. Bake at 350 degrees for 20 minutes or until golden brown. Remove from the oven and cut into squares. Let squares cool before removing them from the pans.

›› Daniel Bars

Here's a fruity bar that you can whip together quickly.

At home, combine:

2 cups rolled oats	½ cup melted margarine
½ cup brown sugar	¼ cup honey
½ cup raisins	½ cup dried cranberries
½ cup chopped nuts	

Servings: Nine servings of 1 bar each.

Nutritional information: 292 calories, 16 grams fat, 40 grams carbohydrate, and 3 grams protein per serving.

Mix well. Press into an 8 x 8-inch microwaveable pan. Microwave on high for 5 to 7 minutes, or until the mixture starts to turn brown. It should be soft to the touch when you take it out of the oven. Cool, cut into squares, and wrap in plastic.

Recipe from: *Daniel Rossi, Backpacker*

›› Chocolate-Fruit Bars

Have these at breakfast if you can handle chocolate that early, or as a midmorning snack. Use your favorite dried fruit—blueberries, chopped apricots, cranberries, and strawberries are all tasty.

At home, combine and boil for 1 minute:

1½ cups honey   ¼ cup butter

2 ounces white chocolate

Remove from heat and add:

1 tablespoon vanilla

Stir into chocolate mixture:

1 cup nuts or sunflower seeds   1 cup diced dried fruit

⅔ cup crunchy peanut butter   5 cups quick-cooking oats

½ cup wheat germ or shredded coconut

Pour dough onto a cookie sheet and flatten into one large rectangle about 1 inch thick. Cool, then cut into bars.

Recipe from: *Patty Minami, Backpacker*

Servings: Twenty-four servings of 1 bar each.

Nutritional information: 254 calories, 10 grams fat, 39 grams carbohydrate, and 7 grams protein per bar.

›› Logan Bread

Because this bread is so rich (read: high-fat), it doesn't freeze hard as other breads do, so it is excellent for winter outings.

At home, combine:

1½ cups whole wheat flour   1½ cups unbleached white flour

1¼ cups rolled oats   ¾ cup brown sugar

½ cup honey   ¼ cup molasses

¼ cup powdered milk   3 eggs

¾ cup chopped nuts   1 cup raisins

½ tablespoon baking powder   1 teaspoon salt

1 cup margarine   ½ cup oil

Stir well. Pour into two 9 x 9-inch greased pans and bake at 350 degrees for 45 minutes or until done. After bread has cooled, slice it and store it in the refrigerator or freezer.

Serves: Makes eighteen 3 x 3-inch pieces.

Nutritional information: 389 calories, 22 grams fat, 47 grams carbohydrate, and 6 grams protein per piece.

Jerky is a flavorful, chewy snack during the day and a tasty addition to evening soups or stews. It's also a concentrated source of protein. You can buy jerky at the store, but if you make it, you can tailor it to your taste buds and skip the preservatives. Plus, you can choose from a variety of base foods, from game to beef, poultry, fish, or tofu.

If you are using an oven instead of a dehydrator, buy an oven thermometer so you can better monitor the temperature. Open the door of the oven an inch or two to allow air to circulate. Turn the meat over from time to time and switch trays from one position to another so that meat dries more evenly.

›› *Beef Jerky*

This simple recipe provides jerky for two for a weekend trip.

Servings: Four servings of 1 ounce each.

Nutritional information: 243 calories, 1 gram fat, 0 grams carbohydrate, and 8 grams protein per serving.

At home, slice into ¼-inch strips:

1 pound lean flank or round steak

Make the marinade by combining:

2 tablespoons tamari or soy sauce   1 tablespoon Worcestershire sauce

1 clove garlic, crushed   ¼ teaspoon salt

Place strips in marinade, cover, and refrigerate for 12 to 24 hours. Stir the mixture periodically. Drain liquid and pat strips dry. Dry at 145 degrees until it is somewhere between pliable and brittle.

Jerky provides a quick hit of flavor and protein.
© Ben Townsend

›› Big Batch of Beef or Game Jerky

If you enjoy jerky in a big way, make a lot and use it liberally.

At home, slice into ¼-inch strips:

8 pounds raw, lean meat

Make a marinade by combining:

1 tablespoon salt

1 teaspoon black pepper

⅔ cup brown sugar

1 cup soy sauce or tamari

1½ tablespoons garlic powder

1 teaspoon minced fresh ginger

1 cup teriyaki sauce

Place strips in marinade, cover, stir periodically, and refrigerate 12 hours. Dry at 145 degrees until done.

Recipe from: Alan Kesselheim, Backpacker

Servings: Twenty-four servings of 1 ounce each.

Nutritional information: 260 calories, 1 gram fat, 4 grams carbohydrate, and 8 grams protein per ounce.

›› Pineapple Fish Jerky

When you mention fish in a backcountry context, most folks think of the frying pan, but this tangy jerky can quickly become a favorite.

At home, slice into strips ¼ to ½ inch thick:

1 pound fish fillets

Make the marinade by combining:

1 cup pineapple juice

2 teaspoons fresh lemon juice

2 teaspoons soy sauce or tamari

2 cloves minced fresh garlic

Place strips in marinade, cover, refrigerate and marinate at least 3 hours, turning the slices several times. Dry at 145 degrees until done. Dried fish is fairly brittle and somewhat flaky.

Recipe from: Alan Kesselheim, Backpacker

Servings: Four servings.

Nutritional information: 158 calories, 3 grams fat, 11 grams carbohydrate, and 24 grams protein per serving.

How to Make Jerky (Use a glass or ceramic bowl.)

Beef and game:
- With beef, buy lean meat (such as round steak, rump roast, or sirloin tip) and trim away all fat.
- Partially freeze meat (making it easier to handle) and cut into slices ¼ inch thick.
- Marinate at least several hours to add flavor and, with some marinades, to help preserve the meat.
- Pat dry and lay on trays.
- Dry at 145 degrees for 10 to 12 hours, or less if you have cut the meat extra thin. (The U.S. Department of Agriculture recommends that medium-rare beef be cooked at an internal temperature of 145 degrees to destroy possible pathogens, so it's important to keep the oven at this temperature while drying.)
- If you dry at too high a temperature, the heat will seal the outside of the meat, leaving moisture inside. "Case hardened" meat will spoil quickly.
- Moreover, certain harmful anaerobic bacteria can grow in moist food stored in an airtight container. Always make sure that jerky (and any food) has been properly dried.
- Remove a sample from the dryer and let cool 5 minutes before testing for dryness. Some people like jerky leathery and others like it brittle. The more moisture, the shorter the shelf life.
- When jerky is dry, cool and package in convenient amounts. For the long term, store in the refrigerator or in the freezer.

Poultry and pork:
- Always cook poultry and pork before drying. Then, slice ¼ inch or thinner. Follow instructions for drying beef; drying time will be considerably shorter.

Fish:
- Choose lean fish such as halibut, whitefish, flounder, or perch.
- Clean and fillet into slices ¼ to ½ inch thick. If slices are too thick, make extra cuts so that the fish will dry evenly.
- If oil appears while you are drying, remove it with a paper towel.
- Follow instructions for drying beef.

›› Spicy Teriyaki Turkey Jerky

At home, cut into ¼-inch slices:
  2½ pounds skinless, cooked turkey

Mix in a bowl:
  ½ cup teriyaki sauce
  ½ cup soy sauce or tamari
  ¼ teaspoon fresh-ground black pepper
  ½ teaspoon dried basil
  Pinch cayenne pepper, or to taste

Add turkey to bowl, stir, refrigerate, and marinate overnight. Dry at 145 degrees until done; turkey jerky will feel leathery and somewhat brittle.

Recipe from: Alan Kesselheim, Backpacker

Servings: Twenty.

Nutritional information: 194 calories, 5 grams fat, 0 grams carbohydrate, and 33 grams protein per serving.

›› Ginger Tofu Jerky

Not into meat or fish? Try this nontraditional recipe.

At home, slice into ¼-inch strips:
  1 pound firm tofu

Make the marinade by combining:

  ¼ teaspoon salt   ¼ teaspoon pepper
  1 tablespoon minced fresh ginger   1 clove fresh garlic, minced
  ¼ cup soy sauce or tamari   2 tablespoons brown sugar

Place strips in marinade, cover, refrigerate and marinate for 2 to 3 hours, turning the slices several times. Dry at 130 degrees until done. Tofu strips will be fairly stiff and only slightly bendable.

Recipe from: Alan Kesselheim, Backpacker

Servings: Five servings of 4 slices each.

Nutritional information: 95 calories, 4 grams fat, 6 grams carbohydrate, and 7 grams protein per serving.

›› *Tabouli*

Servings: Two servings of 1¼ cups each.

Nutritional information: 266 calories, 14 grams fat, 70 grams carbohydrate, and 5 grams protein per serving.

You can make Tabouli without heating water, but the rehydration time will increase. The actual time varies according to the coarseness of the bulgur. Fine grains rehydrate promptly, while coarse grains may need to soak several hours.

At home, combine:

½ cup bulgur

10 to 15 slices or pieces of dehydrated tomato

3 tablespoons dried onion or scallions

2 tablespoons parsley flakes

½ tablespoon mint flakes

Pack separately:

2 tablespoons lemon juice

2 tablespoons olive oil

On trail, place dry ingredients in a pot and add:

1½ cups boiling water

Cover and let stand 20 minutes or until bulgur is fully rehydrated. If there is any excess liquid, drain it and then add lemon juice and oil. Season with salt and pepper. Mix well and carry in leakproof container until lunch.

Hiking the slot, Zion National Park, Utah
© Marypat Zitzer

›› Curried Apple-Cashew Couscous

Make this dish at breakfast and you'll have a lunch that's full of flavor.

At home, combine in the corner of a zipper-lock bag:

½ teaspoon coriander   ½ teaspoon turmeric

¼ teaspoon cumin   ⅛ teaspoon cardamom

Pinch cayenne pepper

Tie off the corner. Toast, cool, and then place in the bag:

⅓ cup cashews

Pack individually:

⅓ cup raisins

1 piece fresh ginger (to produce 1 teaspoon grated)

½ cup couscous

1 teaspoon vegetable oil

Also pack:

1 small onion

1 small carrot

1 apple

On trail, place couscous in a bowl and add:

¾ cup boiling water

Dice the onion, carrot, and apple. Sauté the onion until soft and slightly browned. Mix in carrot, apple, and raisins. Add grated ginger and bagged spices. Add couscous and cook for a few more minutes until heated through. Salt to taste. At lunch, add cashews.

Servings: Two servings of 1½+ cups each.

Nutritional information: 369 calories, 6 grams fat, 75 grams carbohydrates, and 8 grams protein per serving.

When *Backpacker* magazine held the Great Gorp Contest, the staff solicited entries from far and wide. Here are the top picks in four categories (there's another in Breakfast), as presented by Kristin Hostetter and Susan Newquist.

›› *Chocoholic's Dream Gorp*

Servings: Six servings of 2.6 ounces each, or about ½ cup.

Nutritional information: 347 calories, 18 grams fat, 43 grams carbohydrate, and 8 grams protein per serving.

By our reckoning, at least one out of every three backpackers is a self-professed chocoholic, which is why this gorp quickly became a staff favorite. Says the chef, Brett Claxton, "What makes it unique is the slight smoky perfume from the smoked almonds and how, if the gorp gets warm, the chocolates melt together. Keep in a zipper-lock bag and dip in a cool trout stream to firm up the chocolate."

At home, combine:

1 ounce dried mangoes

2 ounces dried tart cherries

2 ounces beer nuts

3 ounces dark chocolate coins

2 ounces dried blueberries

2 ounces smoked almonds

3 ounces white chocolate coins

A handful of 39 flavors: Blueberry, bubble gum, buttered popcorn, cantaloupe, cappuccino, champagne punch, chocolate pudding, cinnamon, and many others.

›› Healthiest Gorp

"Calories are seldom a problem for the hiker, but fat and cholesterol can be, especially for us aging boomers," says gorp creator Wayne Limberg. "This recipe is designed to keep those bad numbers down and save wear and tear on aging arteries. The secret is the corn nuts: They're low in fat but salty enough to keep you drinking water."

At home, combine:

½ cup almonds

½ cup corn nuts

½ cup dried bananas, chopped if they come in long pieces

½ cup other dried fruit (small fruits or chopped)

½ cup Wheat Chex cereal or fish cracker pretzels

Servings: Five servings of ½ cup each.

Nutritional information: 202 calories, 11 grams fat, 28 grams carbohydrate, and 4 grams protein per serving.

›› Best Twist on the Original

"Tastes standard at first chomp, but then the cinnamon kicks in for a nice surprise," reported one tester after subsisting on little more than this gorp and water on a round-trip climb of Washington's Mount Saint Helens. Another likened it to "cinnamon toast with chocolate." Creator Bevan Quinn took it winter camping and found that the mice like it, too.

At home, combine:

15 ounces dry-roasted peanuts

14 ounces Crispy M&Ms

9 ounces cinnamon raisins

With a wide variety of dried fruit available, there's no reason to rely solely on raisins.

Moving carefully in Yellowstone National Park, Wyoming
© Marypat Zitzer

Servings: Fourteen servings of ½ cup each.

Nutritional information: 361 calories, 19 grams fat, 41 grams carbohydrate, and 10 grams protein.

›› Hottest Gorp

Servings: Eleven servings of ½ cup each.

Nutritional information: 172 calories, 9 grams fat, 23 grams carbohydrate, and 3 grams protein per serving.

At first, only a few of the diehard "heat" lovers among the editors appreciated this spicy gorp from Barbara Burke. But after five days of taste-bud-numbing dehydrated food, our crew finally saw the light: Sprinkle a handful of this crispy heat over pasta to add a kick. We quickly dubbed it a backpacker's hot sauce!

At home, combine:

2 cups Rice Krispies cereal	2 cups raisin bran cereal
½ cup raisins	1 cup cashew halves
¼ cup sliced, dried jalapeño peppers	2 tablespoons vegetable oil
½ teaspoon salt	2 tablespoons sugar

Stir until ingredients (especially the oil and sugar) are well distributed.

Letting the rays soak in, Tetons National Park, Wyoming
© Marypat Zitzer

›› Zippy Trail Nuts

Servings: Five servings of ½ cup each.

Nutritional information: Varies with type of nuts used; with peanuts, 379 calories, 34 grams fat, 14 grams carbohydrate, and 14 grams protein per serving.

This recipe comes from a Backpacker writer, though it wasn't an entry in the contest. Use peanuts, slivered almonds, walnuts, or pecans—or a combination of your favorites.

At home, add to a large skillet over medium heat:
1 tablespoon peanut oil

Then add:
2 teaspoons Chili Powder Plus (recipe follows)
2 teaspoons sugar
½ teaspoon ground cumin
½ teaspoon garlic powder
½ teaspoon cayenne

Stir until aromatic, about 30 seconds. Add:
2½ cups unsalted nuts

Stir until well coated, about 1 ½ to 2 minutes. Transfer nuts to large cookie sheet. Bake them, stirring occasionally, for about 10 minutes at 350 degrees. If desired, add salt to taste. Drain on paper towels. When cool, store in an airtight container in the refrigerator.

Recipe from: *Terry Krautwurst,* Backpacker

›› Chili Powder Plus

A small amount of this home brew can add Southwestern fire and flavor to any dish of your choice.

At home, combine:

2 tablespoons chili powder

2 tablespoons paprika

1 tablespoon ground coriander

1 tablespoon garlic powder

2 teaspoons ground cumin

1 teaspoon crushed dried hot chili or red pepper flakes

1 teaspoon ground oregano

½ teaspoon ground cayenne

½ teaspoon ground black pepper

½ teaspoon ground allspice

To retain freshness, store in a small glass container in a cool, dark place.

Recipe from: *Terry Krautwurst,* Backpacker

Servings: Makes almost ½ cup seasoning.

Nutritional information: These seasonings have only tiny amounts of nutrients.

›› Corny Gorp

The creator of this gorp claims that it weighs about half as much as regular gorp. Try it and see for yourself.

At home, combine:

¼ cup toasted sunflower seeds

¼ cup toasted pumpkin seeds

¼ cup soy nuts

½ cup roasted corn or freeze-dried corn

Salt to taste

Recipe from: *Rick Guthrie,* Backpacker

Servings: Four servings of a little less than ⅓ cup each.

Nutritional information: 109 calories, 10 grams fat, 13 grams carbohydrate, and 7 grams protein per serving.

›› Vegetable Leather

This recipe has few calories but lots of taste. Eat as a snack or reconstitute into a sauce or soup base.

Servings: Four large pieces.

Nutritional information: 50 calories, 1 gram fat, 11 grams carbohydrate, and 2 grams protein per piece.

At home, combine:

4 cups diced tomatoes

1 cup sliced carrots

½ cup chopped onion

½ cup chopped celery

½ cup chopped red bell pepper

2 cloves garlic, minced

1 teaspoon dried basil or a handful of fresh basil leaves

½ teaspoon salt, or to taste

Add enough water to cover ingredients and cook, stirring occasionally, until vegetables are tender. Drain, then purée in blender or food processor. If you have a dehydrator, with a special plastic liner for moist food, use it, but first cover it with freezer paper, wax paper, parchment paper, or plastic wrap or the leather will stick to the tray. If you're drying with an oven, use nonstick cookie sheets.

Spread the purée about ¼ inch thick and dry at 120 degrees until the leather easily pulls away from the liner or tray. Start checking for doneness after about 8 hours. Depending on humidity level, leather thickness, and a host of other factors, drying could take up to 16 hours. (See Hot Topic 8 for more information about making leather.)

Recipe from: *Diane Bailey,* Backpacker

›› *Fruit Leather*

If you're looking for a lightweight snack that vibrates with flavor, check out fruit leathers. Eat them plain, spread them with cream cheese and roll them up for a spellbinding treat, or soak them in water for a dazzling sauce.

Use fresh fruit (which tastes best, of course), canned fruit, or a combination of the two. Try these combos: apricots and raspberries; bananas and blackberries; apples and bananas; and pears and rhubarb. Add sugar to taste when using tart fruit. You can tinker with the flavor by adding a wedge of lemon (puréed, peel included), orange juice concentrate, cinnamon, ginger, allspice, coriander, or honey. Taste what you make. If you like it fresh, you'll like it dried.

> **Servings:** Five large pieces of fruit leather.
>
> **Nutritional information:** 61 calories, 4 grams fat, 15 grams carbohydrate, and 1 gram protein per serving.

Strawberry-Apple Fruit Leather

You might want to start with something known, then branch out. At home, clean, hull, and purée in a blender:

16 ounces strawberries

Add:

14 ounces applesauce

Blend until you have an even consistency; add water as needed. If using your oven, spread mixture $1/8$ to $1/4$ inch thick on a nonstick cookie sheet. If using a dehydrator, cover trays with a layer of plastic wrap, then spread.

Dry at 130 to 135 degrees until the purée is leathery and there are no small pockets of moisture. Drying time varies, but averages 8 to 10 hours for thin leather and up to 48 hours for thick leather. (Tip: Before the purée is done, but when it is leathery enough to peel from the tray, lift it and then set it down again. You'll have an easier time removing it later.) Roll in wax paper or plastic wrap.

›› Biscuits

After the first few days of a trip, the yearning for something with moist crumb and gentle fragrance can only be met by baking. Make a double batch of these biscuits the night before and save half for the next day's lunch.

On trail, combine:
1 cup Biscuit Mix (page 31)
⅓ cup water

Servings: Two servings of 3 biscuits each.

Nutritional information: 288 calories, 8 grams fat, 47 grams carbohydrate, and 9 grams protein per serving.

Knead the dough in the bag until it's well blended and forms a ball. Pinch off 6 portions and pat them into biscuits.

For the Standard BakePacker (7 ½ inches in diameter): Lay biscuits in a clean baking bag in a single layer on the BakePacker grid. Boil/bake for 12 to 15 minutes.

For the Ultra-light BakePacker (5 ½ inches in diameter): Use ½ cup mix and 3 tablespoons water, or use the entire recipe and bake in two shifts. Boil/bake for 8 to 10 minutes.

For the Alpine Banks Fry-Bake Pan: Bake in greased pan for 10 to 12 minutes or until golden.

For the Outback Oven: Heat to "bake" range, then bake for 10 to 12 minutes.

›› Variation: Bannock

Bannock is a flat pan bread, usually made with baking powder as the leavening. The dough should be thinner than for biscuits and thicker than for pancakes. Start with ⅓ cup water per cup Biscuit Mix and increase as needed. Fry or pan bake (use a minimal amount of oil and let the skillet bake one side at a time).

One recipe makes 1 large piece or several smaller ones.

Preparing the day's bread in the Northwest Territories.

›› *Variation: Tortillas*

Tortillas are easy to make and cook quickly; they also let you play with your food! Add ⅓ cup water per 1 cup Biscuit Mix. Knead the dough until it is smooth. Pinch off a ball of dough and flatten until it is paper thin. Use as little oil in the pan as possible—tortillas should pan bake rather than fry.

One cup Biscuit Mix makes 6 tortillas.

A smooth rock is a good working surface.

Hot Shots

Next time you're headed out when it's nippy, pack a steaming something of tea, cocoa, or soup (see Soup and Chowders: Instant Soup). A hot, satisfying drink midday can rekindle your furnace and recharge your spirits. The key is finding an insulated container that holds heat when the chill is on. Stainless steel vacuum bottles out-perform foam jackets, last practically forever, and are far lighter than models made twenty years ago.

COMPARISON OF INSULATED BOTTLES

	Weight	Thermal efficiency*
Vacuum bottle, steel lined	1 lb, 7 oz	170 degrees
Vacuum bottle, glass lined	1 lb, 7 oz	165 degrees
Plastic bottle with commercial foam jacket	9 oz	135 degrees
Plastic bottle with homemade foam jacket**	7 oz	110 degrees

*Each container was filled with boiling water and placed in a 0-degree freezer for 3 hours.
**Made from closed-cell foam and duct tape
Note: All containers except the glass-lined bottle easily survived being dropped from a height of 3 feet.

›› Pilot Crackers

Servings: Four servings of 3 squares each.

Nutritional information: 303 calories, 8 grams fat, 48 grams carbohydrate, and 8 grams protein per serving.

Pilot biscuits, pilot crackers, ship bread, hardtack, hardbread—all refer to a dense, unleavened "bread" that lasts a long time without spoiling and can handle the rigors of the pack. Most pilot breads are thin wafers, but some are thicker. They don't have much taste by themselves, but they carry PB&J, honey, or other spreads nicely. New Englanders may have better luck finding them on the supermarket shelf (check the cracker aisle) than people in other parts of the country. If you can't buy them, you can still enjoy their finer qualities.

At home, combine:

2 cups flour

2 tablespoons butter

¾ teaspoons salt

¾ cup milk

1½ teaspoons brown sugar

Mix the ingredients into a dough and roll out to a thickness of about ¹/₂ inch. Cut into 2 x 2-inch squares. Prick the squares with a fork or knife. Place them on a lightly greased baking pan and bake at 400 degrees for 20 to 30 minutes, until golden brown.

Recipe from: *Susan Newquist,* Backpacker

Chapter 3

Soups and Chowders

The wind has whipped your face all day and you pull into camp dreaming of a cup of hot soup before you get on with camp chores. Something tasty, quick, and easy is high on the list. How about Tomato–Black Bean, Cashew–Carrot, or Oatmeal? When you make your own soup, you get exactly what you want and nothing more. While many instant soup makers appear to be sensitive to the need to limit sodium in the diet, one off-the-shelf brand contains—in one serving—a whopping two-thirds of the day's recommended amount of salt in a 2,000-calorie-a-day diet. For comparison, one cube of bouillon may contain 40 percent of a day's worth of salt, and low-salt alternatives ring in at 1 percent.

For people with a sensitivity to monosodium glutamate (MSG), prepared soups can be a mine field. Check the label for MSG or ingredients such as autolyzed yeast and yeast extract that contains MSG.

The author enjoying a mug of soup on the trail. © Ben Townsend

›› *Instant Tomato–Black Bean Soup*

A dollop of dehydrated salsa makes a great addition to this soup.

Servings: One serving of 1 cup.

Nutritional information: 62 calories, 0 grams fat, 12 grams carbohydrate, and 4 grams protein per serving.

At home, combine:

1 tablespoon plus 1 teaspoon tomato powder

1 tablespoon plus 1 teaspoon black bean powder

Generous dash salt, or to taste

Generous dash garlic powder

Generous dash chili powder

On trail, pour soup mix into an insulated mug and add:

1 cup boiling water

Cover and let stand 5 minutes.

Six Servings: Instant Tomato–Black Bean Soup

½ cup tomato powder   ½ cup black bean powder

½ teaspoon salt, or to taste   ⅛ teaspoon garlic powder

¼ teaspoon chili powder, or to taste

Use ¼ cup mix per 1 cup boiling water.

Cold hands, warm heart en route to South Branch Pond, Maine
© Ben Townsend

›› Instant Minestrone Soup

Use stellini pasta or any other small pasta product that cooks in 5 minutes or less. Choose dried vegetables such as grated carrots and thin slices of mushrooms, green pepper, tomato, and scallions, which rehydrate quickly. It's fine to include flakes of dried onion, although with only 10 minutes to rehydrate, the flakes will still be a little tough.

At home, combine:

¼ cup mixed dried vegetables

⅙ teaspoon oregano

⅙ teaspoon thyme

1 tablespoon pasta

⅙ teaspoon basil

1 cube bouillon, crushed

On trail, pour mix into an insulated mug and add:

1 cup boiling water

Stir, cover, and let stand 10 minutes.

Six Servings: Instant Minestrone Soup

1½ cups mixed dried vegetables

¼ cup plus 2 tablespoons pasta

1 teaspoon oregano

1 teaspoon basil

1 teaspoon thyme

6 cubes bouillon, crushed

Use ¼ cup plus 1½ tablespoons mix per 1 cup boiling water.

Servings: One serving of 1 cup.

Nutritional information: 80 calories, 0 grams fat, 12 grams carbohydrate, and 4 grams protein per serving.

›› *Instant Almond Soup*

Servings: One serving of 1 cup.

Nutritional information: 74 calories, 5 grams fat, 4 grams carbohydrate, and 5 grams protein.

The almond grains tend to settle, so give your mug a swish before drinking.

At home, combine:

1 cube bouillon, crushed

1 tablespoon powdered milk

1 tablespoon ground almonds

Salt and pepper to taste

On trail, pour mix into an insulated cup and add:

1 cup boiling water

Stir, cover, and let stand 3 minutes.

Six Servings: Instant Almond Soup

6 cubes bouillon, crushed

¼ cup plus 2 tablespoons ground almonds

¼ cup plus 2 tablespoons powdered milk

Salt and pepper to taste

Use ¹/₄ cup plus scant 1 tablespoon mix in 1 cup water.

Negotiating muck in the Everglades

›› Instant Cashew–Carrot Soup

At home, combine:

1 tablespoon dried onion

2 tablespoons dried chopped apple

2 teaspoons tomato powder

1 tablespoon chopped cashews

Dash garlic powder

1 tablespoon dried shredded carrot

1 tablespoon instant rice

1 tablespoon raisins

Generous dash curry powder

⅛ teaspoon salt, or to taste

On trail, pour mix into insulated mug and add:

1 cup boiling water

Stir, cover, and let stand 10 minutes.

Six Servings: Instant Cashew-Carrot Soup

¼ cup plus 2 tablespoons dried onion

¼ cup plus 2 tablespoons dried shredded carrot

¾ cup dried chopped apple

¼ cup plus 2 tablespoons instant rice

¼ cup tomato powder

¼ cup plus 2 tablespoons raisins

¼ cup plus 2 tablespoons cashews, chopped

½ teaspoon curry powder

¼ teaspoon garlic powder

¾ teaspoon salt, or to taste

Use ¹/₂ cup mix per 1 cup boiling water.

Hot Tips: Making Your Own Instant Soup Recipes

It's easy to make your own lightweight soups that cost substantially less than you would pay for commercial counterparts, which may run to as much as $1.50 or more per cup for fancier concoctions. You can save packaging, too, as most instant soups sold in supermarkets come in one-cup cardboard/plastic containers, some of which are further shrink-wrapped with cardboard jackets. When you think in terms of a cup each night for six nights—or a cup each for a group of six—the savings in cost and packaging add up. You can also adapt the recipes to your taste or experiment with entirely new combinations.

The instant soups here are designed to be made in a covered, insulated mug; the insulation allows you to use boiling water only and not actually cook the ingredients. If you want to make recipes like these, the ingredients you choose must be thin enough that they will cook/rehydrate in boiled water. Angel hair pasta, stellini, alphabets, pasta for babies, couscous, instant potatoes, instant black beans, and instant hummus will work; macaroni, spaghetti, and large-grained bulgur will not.

If you are dehydrating vegetables for use in instant soups, choose ones like mushrooms, scallions, green peppers, and tomatoes that can be sliced very thin or grated. If you are shopping for dehydrated vegetables, read the directions to see if the vegetables will rehydrate by soaking for 5 to 10 minutes in hot water. Sun-dried tomatoes, for example, are generally too thick, but would work in an instant soup if you sliced them into thin strips. Dehydrated onions will have good flavor but will still be a bit chewy. Be careful with dehydrated veggie mixes sold as a soup starter because they usually contain peas, corn, and other vegetables that are quite dense when dried and won't rehydrate adequately in an instant soup.

As you would taste soup for flavor at home, you should test soup for doneness on trail. If the rice is a little crunchy, give it a few more minutes. At high altitude, where water boils at a lower temperature, some soup ingredients may not rehydrate on their own, so the soup should be simmered.

›› *Oatmeal Soup*

This soup tastes a lot better than it sounds.

At home, place a skillet over medium heat. Without oil, brown (but do not burn):

¼ cup quick-cooking oats

Cool oats, then combine with:

3 tablespoons dehydrated onion

Generous dash garlic

½ cube bouillon, crushed

1 tablespoon tomato powder

On trail, pour mix in an insulated mug and add:

1 cup boiling water

Stir, cover, and let stand 10 minutes.

Six Servings: Oatmeal Soup

1 ½ cups quick-cooking oats

½ cup dried onion

¾ teaspoon powdered garlic

3 cubes bouillon, crushed

¼ cup plus 2 tablespoons tomato powder

Use ¹/₂ cup mix with 1 cup boiling water.

> **Servings:** One serving of 1 cup.
>
> **Nutritional information:** 113 calories, 2 grams fat, 24 grams carbohydrate, and 6 grams protein.

›› *Backpack Sukiyaki Soup*

Servings: Two.

Nutritional information: 455 calories, 4 grams fat, 78 grams carbohydrate, and 24 grams protein.

For extra flavor, add ten small, dried shrimp to the jerky and carry ½ teaspoon nori flakes (nori is a roasted seaweed) for seasoning.

At home, combine:
  ¼ cup Spicy Teriyaki Turkey Jerky, chopped (page 45)
  ¼ cup Ginger Tofu Jerky (page 45)

In another zipper-lock bag, place:
  ¼ cup dried bean sprouts
  ½ cup dried onions, carrots, celery, and mushrooms
  Pinch garlic powder

Also pack:
  1 package ramen or Chinese noodles
  1 packet soy sauce or tamari

At midday, place the vegetables in a leakproof container and add enough water to cover. Let soak. At dinnertime, put the vegetables and soaking water into a pot, adding enough water to make 3 cups. Add the contents of the jerky bag and bring to a boil. Simmer for 4 minutes or until the jerky is soft enough to eat; no matter how long you cook it, the jerky will remain chewy.

Add the noodles with seasoning packet and cook until noodles are done, about 3 minutes. Serve with soy sauce and nori.

Recipe from: *Ilo Gassoway,* Backpacker

›› Onion Soup

At home, cut into rings:

2 large onions

Sauté until onions are browned but not scorched (about 10 minutes) in:

2 tablespoons oil

Place on paper towel to absorb excess oil. Then, toast:

4 pieces French bread

Cube bread. Dry both onion and bread at 130 degrees in dehydrator or oven. When bread is dry, let cool and place in zipper-lock bag. When onions are dry, let cool and place in another zipper-lock bag; store in refrigerator.

Pack individually:

4 cubes bouillon or equivalent soup base

⅔ cup Parmesan cheese

On trail, cover onions with:

1½ cups boiling water

Allow to rehydrate. Then, add crushed bouillon and:

2½ cups water

Bring to a boil and stir until bouillon is completely dissolved. Remove from heat, add the croutons, and sprinkle the cheese on top. Cover and let stand 3 minutes to allow the cheese to warm. Add black pepper to taste.

Servings: Four servings of 1 cup each.

Nutritional information: 213 calories, 14 grams fat, 18 grams carbohydrate, and 6 grams protein per serving.

›› Chicken Vegetable Soup

Servings: Four servings of 2+ cups each.

Nutritional information: 213 calories, 2 grams fat, 32 grams carbohydrate, and 19 grams protein per serving.

Veggies such as carrots, green beans, corn, and peas are welcome in this long-cooking soup.

At home, combine:

¼ cup dried celery

1 tablespoon dried parsley

¾ cup dried chicken pieces or cubes

1 cup dried mixed vegetables

¼ cup dried onion

Pack separately:

2 chicken bouillon cubes

On trail, boil:

7 cups water

Add the dry mix, cover, remove from heat, and let stand 30 minutes. Return to the heat, crush the bouillon cubes and add them to the pot, and simmer until the ingredients are tender; times may vary according to the vegetables used. Add salt and pepper to taste.

Recipe from: *Diane Bailey,* Backpacker

A well-deserved break near Markham Lake, Northwest Territories, Canada

›› *Hearty Miso Soup with Shrimp*

Arame is a sea vegetable. Look for arame, miso, bonito, mung bean threads, Japanese pepper, and shiitake mushrooms at an Asian food store. Some large supermarkets carry these ingredients.

Servings: Five 1-cup servings.

Nutritional information: Not available.

At home, combine:

½ cup miso paste

⅓ cup freeze-dried shrimp

¼ cup dried carrots

1 teaspoon onion flakes

4 dried shiitake mushrooms, torn up

¼ cup loosely packed, thin bonito shavings

½ cup loosely packed arame

¼ cup dried cabbage

¼ cup dried celery

1 teaspoon dried chives

Pack separately:

1 ounce mung bean threads (1 winding)

Also pack:

Small amount of hot Japanese pepper

2 tablespoons sesame seeds

On trail, add veggie mix to:

6 cups water

Bring to a boil, then reduce heat and simmer for 5 to 10 minutes, until vegetables and shrimp rehydrate. Add bean threads and simmer 5 minutes longer. Serve with a sprinkling of hot Japanese pepper and sesame seeds.

Recipe from: Carol Steinberg, Backpacker

›› Side Dish: Chickpea Fritters

Servings: Two servings of 3½ fritters each.

Nutritional information: 296 calories, 16 grams fat, 20 grams carbohydrate, and 8 grams protein per serving.

These fritters go well with Miso Soup.

At home, pack in a zipper-lock bag:

¾ cup garbanzo bean (chickpea) flour

¼ teaspoon baking soda

½ teaspoon salt, or to taste

¼ teaspoon ground cumin

Also pack:

2 tablespoons oil

On trail, add to dry mix:

⅓ cup water (more for moister fritters)

Pour half the oil into frying pan and heat over medium flame. Drop batter by spoonfuls into pan and press into 2-inch rounds. Cook slowly and turn when fritters begin to brown. Add more oil as needed for the next batch.

Recipe from: *Carol Steinberg,* Backpacker

›› Curried Potato Soup

Make this soup at home and dehydrate, or dry the ingredients separately and bring them together on trail. Masala (or garam masala) is a hot spice mixture that contains black pepper, cloves, cardamom, cinnamon, and other ingredients; it is similar to but not as spicy as curry. To increase the protein content, cut the potatoes by half and substitute an equal portion of red beans or chickpeas.

At home, wash and dice:

1 pound potatoes

Set aside. To a large pot, add:

1½ tablespoons oil

Over medium heat, sauté for about 10 minutes:

2 chopped onions

Add and sauté for 2 minutes:

4 cloves garlic, sliced

Add and sauté until oil turns brown:

½ tablespoon masala

Add and cook for 5 more minutes:

2 chopped tomatoes

Add potatoes, then add enough water to cover everything. Bring to a boil, then simmer for 20 to 30 minutes, stirring occasionally. Cool, then spread onto dehydrator trays. Dehydrate for 5½ hours, or until food is dry and crumbly. Let cool. Package in doubled zipper-lock bags and store in a cool, dark, dry place.

On trail, place dry ingredients in a large pot and cover ingredients with water. Bring to a boil and simmer 15 to 20 minutes, or until ingredients are thoroughly rehydrated. Add more water as necessary to maintain soup consistency.

Recipe from: Kyle McCarthy, Backpacker

Servings: Four.

Nutritional information: 192 calories, 5 grams fat, 67 grams carbohydrate, and 7 grams protein per serving.

›› *Daal*

Servings: Three.

Nutritional information:
370 calories, 9 grams fat, 80 grams carbohydrate, and 21 grams protein per serving.

To prepare Daal, a lentil stew, use the Curried Potato Soup recipe (page 69), and substitute lentils for potatoes.

Follow the Curried Potato Soup recipe, using:

1 pound (2⅔ cups) rinsed lentils

Instead of potatoes use 2 parts water to 1 part lentils for thick stew and 3 parts water for a thinner stew. Cook 12 to 20 minutes, until lentils are tender. Serve as is or over rice.

Recipe from: Kyle McCarthy, Backpacker

Photographing the photographer, Glacier National Park, Montana © Marypat Zitzer

›› *Cheddar Cheese Chowder*

Dehydrate your own potatoes or buy dehydrated hash browns at the supermarket for this delicious soup. Serve with a firm bread that holds up well in the pack.

At home, combine and pack:

1 cup dehydrated potatoes
⅓ cup dehydrated onion (1 medium onion)

Pack individually:

¼ cup margarine or clarified butter
½ pound grated Cheddar cheese

Combine and pack:

3 tablespoons flour	2 tablespoons parsley
¼ teaspoon sage	1 bay leaf
¼ teaspoon cumin	¼ teaspoon nutmeg

On trail, add potatoes and onion to:

3⅔ cups water

Bring to a boil and simmer 10 minutes or until vegetables are rehydrated and tender. Stir in margarine. Add flour mixture a tablespoon at a time, stirring well. Add cheese. Simmer until soup thickens, stirring all the while.

Servings: Four servings of 1¼ cups each.

Nutritional information: 468 calories, 33 grams fat, 22 grams carbohydrate, and 23 grams protein per serving.

›› Fish Chowder

Linda Frederick Yaffee wrote High Trail Cookery: All-Natural, Home-Dried, Palate-Pleasing Meals for the Backpacker. *She recommends using haddock, halibut, or sole in this chowder.*

Servings: Four servings of 2+ cups each.

Nutritional information: 503 calories, 4 grams fat, 83 grams carbohydrate, and 43 grams protein per serving.

At home, bring to a boil in a large saucepan:

1 cup clam juice
1 pound boneless fish fillets

3 cups water

Cook, covered, for 5 minutes, or just until fish flakes easily. Remove the fish with a slotted spoon, crumble it, and set it aside.

Add to the stock:

8 small russet potatoes, diced
½ teaspoon minced dried thyme

Cook, covered, for 10 minutes, or until the potatoes are tender.

Heat in a skillet over medium heat:

2 teaspoons canola oil

Sauté until light brown:

1 onion, diced

Add cooked fish and onion to the potatoes. Also add:

10 saltines, crushed
2 cups skim milk
½ teaspoon salt, or to taste
½ teaspoon freshly ground black pepper
⅛ teaspoon cayenne pepper

Stir and cook for 5 minutes. Spread on dehydrator trays. Dehydrate at 145 degrees for 5 ½ hours, or until food is dry and crumbly. Let cool. Package in doubled zipper-lock bags and store in a cool, dark, dry place.

On trail, pour the dried meal into a pot and add enough water to cover. Bring to a boil, stir, and serve.

Recipe from: *Linda Frederick Yaffe*, Backpacker

Chapter 4

Dinner

We made it to camp just after it had gotten dark enough to need a headlamp. My feet screamed for sandals. We broke out one of the quick-cooking dinners and ate by the light of a half moon. The bright stars Sirius, Procyon, Pollux, Castor, Capella, and Aldebaran circled Orion the hunter. We contemplated Baboquivari, the mountain of the Tohono O'odham, which soared on the horizon. We had been there, on its summit.

Different camp, different trip. We pulled into a riverside site and unloaded the boats. It was my night to cook. I measured water into a big pot and stirred in the ingredients. Then I took a towel and camp clothes and went around the bend for a swim. Exquisitely cold water snatched my breath and made my blood pump. When I returned to the hubbub, I heated the chili, set out tortillas and cheese, and called for dinner. The little bag of dehydrated ingredients made enough for everyone to have seconds and then some. We were content.

Backcountry dinners aren't just about food. They are about a place, companions, and activity. At home, the food may be the main event, but in the backcountry, dinners have added dimensions—the difficulties of the day, the sharpness of your appetite, and the eloquence of the view all combine with the quality of the food to produce a memorable meal.

As you cruise through these recipes, look for ones that suit your style and your intended trip. If you want fast food, choose quick-prep. If you enjoy the process of cooking, choose recipes that direct you to sauté the onions. If you plan a long, slow meal, provide snacks for the hunger-impaired. Keep in mind that while breakfast and lunch fire you forward, dinner is the culmination of the day. If you've been anticipating dinner as an antidote to adverse weather and steep trails, then the meal had better be good.

In the following recipes, "instant rice" refers to precooked, dried rice to which you add boiling water and then let stand.

Top row from left: Bulgur, rice mix, wild rice, brown rice; Bottom row from left: Couscous, basmati rice, quinoa, instant rice.

Cooking Times and Yields for 1 Cup (Dry) Grains and Lentils			
	WATER	**COOKING TIME**	**YIELD**
Barley, quick	3 cups	10 to 12 minutes	3 cups
Bulgur, large-grained	2 cups	20 minutes	2½ cups
Bulgur, small-grained	2 cups	Add boiling water, let stand 20 minutes	2½ cups
Couscous	2 cups	Add boiling water, let stand 5 minutes	3 to 3½ cups
Kasha	2 cups	10 to 15 minutes	3 cups
Lentils, green	3 cups	45 minutes	2¼ to 3 cups
Lentils, green	3 cups	Soak 5 hours, 10 to 15 minutes	2¼ to 3 cups
Lentils, red	2 cups	15 minutes	3 cups
Millet	2 cups	25 to 30 minutes	3½ cups
Peas, split	3 cups	45 to 60 minutes	2¼ cups
Quinoa	1½ cups	15 minutes	2½ cups
Rice, basmati	2 cups	15 minutes, let stand 5 minutes	3 cups
Rice, brown	2 cups	40 minutes	3 cups
Rice, brown or white, instant	2 cups	Add boiling water, let stand 10 minutes	2 cups
Rice, parboiled	2 cups	25 to 30 minutes	3 cups
Rice, wild	4½ cups	60 or more minutes	3 to 3¾ cups
Rice, wild, precooked	2 cups	7 to 15 minutes	2½ cups

›› *Cashew-Ginger Chicken and Rice*

This is my all-time favorite meal. Sometimes I use almonds instead of cashews and home-dried savoy cabbage and carrots instead of corn. A packet of Thai Coconut Ginger Soup Mix, which contains ginger, lemon grass, and other ingredients, supplies the flavor; look for it or a similar product in the supermarket aisle with international foods. If you are not fond of ginger, substitute 1 tablespoon lemon-pepper seasoning or 1 packet lemon-chicken seasoning. The nuts, freeze-dried corn, and chicken make this entrée more expensive than, say, chili, but it's still inexpensive compared to eating at a restaurant. Remember, you're on vacation.

Servings: Two servings of 1⅞ cups each.

Nutritional information: 451 calories, 24 grams fat, 66 grams carbohydrate, and 47 grams protein per serving.

At home, toast:

½ cup cashews

Let cool and pack in a zipper-lock bag. In another bag, pack:

1 cup instant brown rice

⅔ cups freeze-dried corn

½ cup thinly sliced dry shiitake mushrooms

¼ cup onion flakes

Also pack:

1 (10-ounce) can of chicken, mixed white and dark meat

2 (1-ounce) packets Thai Coconut Ginger Soup Mix paste

On trail, place dry mix, chicken, and 1 packet seasoning in pot and cover with water; mix well. Bring to a boil; simmer 5 minutes; taste; add some of second seasoning packet if needed. Simmer 5 minutes (adding more water as needed) or until done.

›› Red Hot Rice

Make sure all your fellow campers like hot stuff before serving this spicy side dish.

At home, combine:

2½ cups instant white rice

½ package (total 1.2 ounces) tomato soup mix

1½ ounces (about 1 cup) dried vegetables or vegetable flakes

⅔ teaspoon red pepper

¾ teaspoon black pepper

On trail, pour bagged ingredients into a pot with:

3 cups water

Bring to a boil. Stir once or twice. Lower heat to simmer; cover and cook 5 minutes. Let stand 5 minutes. Fluff with a fork.

Recipe from: *Liz Rusch,* Backpacker

Servings: Four.

Nutritional information: 272 calories, 1 gram fat, 59 grams carbohydrate, and 6 grams protein.

›› Nutty Rice

For extra flavor, toast the seeds and nuts before packing.

At home, combine:

2½ cups instant brown rice

¾ cup slivered almonds

2 tablespoons chicken bouillon granules

¾ cup sunflower seeds

2 tablespoons parsley

On trail, pour bagged ingredients into a pot with:

3 cups water

Bring to a boil. Stir once or twice. Lower heat to simmer, cover, and cook 5 minutes. Let stand 5 minutes. Fluff with a fork.

Recipe from: *Liz Rusch,* Backpacker

Servings: Four.

Nutritional information: 517 calories, 27 grams fat, 54 grams carbohydrate, and 16 grams protein per serving.

›› *Greek Spinach Pilaf*

Use spinach that is fresh and unblemished, with no wilt or brown edges. If it is unwashed, wash it before packing. Plan this recipe for the first night out, to catch the spinach at full flavor. See Hot Topic 2 for a shortcut to making tomato powder.

Servings: Two servings of about 2½ cups each.

Nutritional information: 520 calories, 15 grams fat, 89 grams carbohydrate, and 11 grams protein per serving.

At home, combine:

2 cups instant rice, white or brown	2 tablespoons dried mint
2 tablespoons dried oregano	1 tablespoon dried thyme

Pack these ingredients individually:

2 tablespoons onion flakes	2 tablespoons olive oil
2 tablespoons tomato powder	4 ounces feta cheese
1 (6-ounce) package fresh baby spinach	

On trail, sauté onion in olive oil for 2 minutes. Mix tomato powder with:

½ cup water

Add to pot. Stir in spinach and simmer, covered, for 2 to 3 minutes, until spinach is wilted. Stir in the rice mixture and add:

1½ cups water

Bring to a boil, stir, cover, and simmer 5 minutes. Let stand 5 minutes. Sprinkle crumbled feta cheese over the rice before serving.

Recipe from: *Liz Rusch,* Backpacker

Servings: Three.

Nutritional information:
753 calories, 32 grams fat, 87 grams carbohydrate, and 24 grams protein per serving.

›› *Pesto Walnut Risotto*

Try this trail version of creamy risotto.

At home, combine:

½ cup walnuts, chopped

1 (½-ounce) package dried pesto mix

Pack individually:

1½ cups short-grain white rice (not instant)

4 cubes chicken bouillon

1 small onion

2 tablespoons olive oil

1 cup grated Parmesan cheese

On trail, chop the onion and sauté it in hot oil over a low flame until it's soft, about 3 minutes. Add the rice and cook another 3 minutes while stirring. Add one crushed bouillon cube and:

1 cup water

Simmer about 5 minutes, stirring constantly. Add another crushed bouillon cube and:

1 cup water

Stir constantly for another 5 minutes. Add the remaining crushed bouillon cubes and:

2 cups water

Simmer and stir for another 10 to 15 minutes, or until the liquid is almost completely absorbed. Add the remaining ingredients and stir until smooth and creamy. Serve immediately.

Recipe from: *Liz Rusch,* Backpacker

›› *Chicken Curry over Brown Rice*

Serve this curry with a piece of pita bread and a garnish of sliced cucumber covered with ranch dressing made from powdered mix and a sprinkle of dill weed. If you can't find the Golden Curry Sauce called for here, use half a package of cream of mushroom soup mix and 1 or 2 teaspoons curry.

At home, pack together:
  ¼ cup plus 2 tablespoons (about ½ ounce) freeze-dried chicken
  ¼ cup sliced dried mushrooms
  1 tablespoon onion flakes
  ¼ cup freeze-dried peas

Pack in another zipper-lock bag:
  1 cube chicken bouillon, crushed
  ½ tablespoon chopped crystallized ginger

Pack individually:
  1 cup instant brown rice
  ½ tablespoon clarified butter or margarine
  ¼ package Golden Curry Sauce
  1 cup tropical fruit trail mix

On trail, place chicken mix in a bowl and cover with hot water. Let stand to rehydrate (10 to 30 minutes, depending on the size of the vegetable pieces). Add bouillon and ginger and stir well.

Meanwhile, add rice to:
  2 cups water

Bring to a boil, cover, remove from heat, and let stand 5 minutes. In another pot, combine Golden Curry Sauce and margarine. Add:
  3 cups water

Heat and stir until thickened. Combine sauce and chicken mixture, adding more water if needed for desired thickness. Serve over rice.

Recipe from: *Maggie Stafsnes*, Backpacker

> **Servings:** Two servings of about 2 cups each.
>
> **Nutritional information:** 386 calories, 5 grams fat, 73 grams carbohydrate, and 14 grams protein per serving.

›› *Lake Conway Chicken*

Servings: Three servings of about 1¾ cups each.

Nutritional information: 476 calories, 13 grams fat, 33 grams carbohydrate, and 57 grams protein per serving.

The Scouts of Troop 283 give this recipe a thumbs-up; they've eaten it while backpacking through Ocala National Forest and the Smoky Mountains.

At home, combine in a zipper-lock bag:

1 cup instant brown rice
¼ cup slivered almonds
¼ cup dried mushrooms
2 tablespoons onion flakes
1 tablespoon green or red bell pepper flakes
½ teaspoon salt, or to taste

Pack separately:

2 cans (a total of 20 ounces) chicken
2 packages instant cream of chicken soup mix

On trail, stir the rice mixture into:

2½ cups water

Simmer for 15 minutes. Open chicken but do not drain; stir both chicken and soup mix into the rice. Simmer for an additional 3 to 5 minutes, adding water if necessary to achieve desired consistency.

Recipe from: *Steve Diedrich,* Backpacker

Small Grain, Many Options

To tailor rice to your taste, add a pinch of this or that:

- Your favorite instant soup cooked with rice makes a nice side dish, although the flavor is a little thin because the soup spices have to perk up a larger quantify.
- For an easy, cheesy rice, add butter powder and grated Parmesan cheese to hot, cooked rice.
- Try rehydrated peas and chopped mint for a green rice.
- The juice or zest of a lemon or orange, along with a dash of olive oil, makes for a tangy, fruity rice.

—Liz Rusch, *Backpacker*

›› Hobo Dinner

To lighten the load, use dried carrots, chives, and pineapple. Instant rice cuts the cooking time substantially.

At home, pack:

  1 cup long-grained rice
  1 (15-ounce) can salmon
  1 (8-ounce) can pineapple chunks
  ½ cup pine nuts, toasted
  ¼ cup fresh chives
  ½ cup fresh Jerusalem artichokes, water chestnuts, or fresh jicama
  3 medium carrots

On trail, cook the rice according to package directions. Cut the artichokes and carrots into thin slices and place in a second pot. Add the salmon and pineapple with its juice. When the rice is done, heat the contents of the second pot. Chop the chives if using fresh. Serve rice with salmon mix spooned on top. Sprinkle on pine nuts and chives. Add salt and pepper to taste.

Recipe from: Steve Dixon, Backpacker

Servings: Four servings of about 2 cups each.

Nutritional information: 373 calories, 13 grams fat, 37 grams carbohydrate, and 27 grams protein per serving.

Waiting for dinner, Tetons National Park, Wyoming
© Marypat Zitzer

Hot Tips: Textured Vegetable Protein

This food with an unappetizing name is actually a healthy, all-natural meat substitute that can bolster breakfast, lunch, and dinner alike. If you're wondering why you should consider textured vegetable protein, here are some stellar stats: It has almost no fat and no cholesterol; it's packed with potassium, protein, and all eight essential amino acids; and it's low in calories. Plus, it is extremely lightweight, will not spoil, needs only hot water to rehydrate, is very filling, and can add a completely new dimension to trail cuisine because it takes on any flavor you add to it. One cup dry rehydrates into two full cups. It's also inexpensive.

I've used soy protein with great success in the Mojave Desert, the Amazon jungle, and parts in between. It's the perfect staple item for "beefing" up soups, stews, rice, pasta, or virtually any recipe. It can accommodate any cooking style, from the simplest of meals to the most complex.

A creative cook can use it as a topping for pan pizza, a hearty addition to bean burritos, a complement to stir fry, or—when combined with other ingredients and spices—as the basis for ersatz meatballs with spaghetti and tomato sauce.

Soy protein is available in most health food stores and through mail-order companies. It comes in various forms, including granules, short strips, and chunks, and is even available in a light-colored "poultry" version. Chunks are perfect for kebabs, soups, or stews. Strips are ideal for burritos or rice. The granules make superb veggie burgers and can be rolled into "meatballs." As a rule, wherever you would normally add meat, you can replace it with soy protein. Just remember that this protein is tasteless, so it's up to you to give it an identity.

Textured vegetable protein is made by combining soybeans, which are nearly 40 percent protein, and wheat gluten (the protein substance that gives dough its cohesiveness) to produce soy flour. Next the oil is extracted, leaving mostly protein and carbohydrate. The remaining dry product is mixed with water and cooked under pressure, then forced through small holes of various sizes and cut into pieces. The final product, which looks like small chunks of volcanic rock, merely needs to be cooked. Backpackers usually use soy protein that has also been dried, so it must be rehydrated before cooking.

—Josh Coen, *Backpacker*
(Check out Josh's Heavenly Hash Browns, made with TVP.)

›› *Stuffed Peppers*

Here's an easy supper you can make without a stove. The original recipe calls for green peppers, but red bells are a luscious alternative.

At home, cook:

½ cup brown rice

Cool and store in zipper-lock bag in refrigerator. Pack these items individually:

8 dried shiitake mushrooms, chopped

1 (12-ounce) can or 2 foil packets (total 14 ounces) tuna

1 teaspoon dill

2 green bell peppers

On trail, cover mushrooms with water and soak until plump (about 15 minutes). Combine cooked rice, mushrooms, and tuna. Cut tops off peppers and clean out seeds. Spoon half of the stuffing in each. Sprinkle with dill and black pepper.

Recipe from: *Marjorie McCloy,* Backpacker

Servings: Two.

Nutritional information: 369 calories, 3 grams fat, 43 grams carbohydrate, and 44 grams protein per serving.

A river flows through it—
Northwest Territories, Canada

>> Banana-Pecan-Tofu Curry

Servings: Two servings of 2+ cups each.

Nutritional information: 526 calories, 31 grams fat, 58 grams carbohydrate, and 26 grams protein per serving.

If you don't have all the spices needed for this recipe, substitute 2³/₄ teaspoons curry powder. Fresh ginger and garlic are light for their value, but if you wish to carry powdered, add ¹/₈ teaspoon each ginger and garlic powder to the spice bag.

At home, combine in a zipper-lock bag:

2 tablespoons chopped banana chips

2 tablespoons chopped pecans

2 tablespoons raisins

2 tablespoons unsweetened coconut flakes

2 teaspoons powdered milk

In another bag, combine:

½ teaspoon turmeric   ½ teaspoon coriander

¼ teaspoon nutmeg   ¼ teaspoon cinnamon

¼ teaspoon cardamom   Dash cayenne pepper

Also pack individually:

1 (12- to 16-ounce) package tofu

1 chunk ginger (to yield ½ tablespoon finely chopped)

2 cloves garlic (to yield ½ tablespoon finely chopped)

½ tablespoon honey

1 tablespoon oil

Pinch salt, or to taste

1 cup instant rice

On trail, boil:

2¾ cups water

Place banana chip mixture in a bowl and add:

¾ cup boiling water

Cover and set aside. Add rice to remaining water. Stir, cover, and remove from heat. Let stand 10 minutes. In a pan, heat the oil and brown the tofu, then add the dry spice mixture, ginger, and garlic. Cook for a few more minutes, then add the banana chip mixture and honey. Mix well and cook until the curry is hot. Add salt to taste, and serve over rice.

Recipe from: *Allison Carroll*, Backpacker

›› *Wheat Pilaf with Bacon*

Bacon and cheese are a surefire combo in this super-easy recipe.

At home, combine:

2 cups bulgur

⅔ cup dried veggies, sliced thin for quick rehydration, or 1 cup freeze-dried corn

¼ cup plus 2 tablespoons bacon bits

Pack separately:

2 ounces Cheddar cheese

On trail, place dry mix in pot and add:

5⅓ cup water

Bring to a boil and simmer until done, about 10 minutes (depending on the type of bulgur and the thickness of the dried veggies). Serve and sprinkle with grated cheese.

Servings: Two servings of 2½ cups each or three servings of 1⅔ cups each.

Nutritional information: For three servings, 483 calories, 9 grams fat, 69 grams carbohydrate, and 35 grams protein per serving.

Bacon in the Backcountry

Bacon strips are real food—tangy, chewy pieces of bacon that make you think that someone just beamed them down from home. Cooked bacon strips in an oxygen-free plastic pouch will last without refrigeration until you open the package; then, the bacon should be used within "a short time," that elastic description that means anywhere from 24 hours (when it's freshest) to several days—but these estimates depend entirely on the ambient temperature.

Bacon also comes precooked and crumbled; 1 tablespoon equals 1 strip of bacon. These crumbles are available in glass jars, cans, and plastic pouches; go for the pouches. A 3-ounce pouch contains about 12 tablespoons. This kind of bacon is great for flavor. You can use it in breakfast eggs, hash browns, or even hot cereal, or most any soup or stew. As with bacon strips, once the container is open, the contents should be used promptly.

Bacon substitutes, which contain some sort of bacon-flavored soy product, are low in fat and don't require refrigeration after the jar has been opened. These imitation bacon morsels are crunchy rather than chewy and don't provide the "mouth-feel" (in other words, the fat) that real bacon does. Still, they are a flavorful substitute for those who don't want to eat or can't eat bacon.

›› Simple Ginger-Curry Couscous

This recipe originally called for 3 cups couscous—which would rehydrate into 6 cups couscous—plus the veggies and cashews, producing about 8 cups food. Although that's the right amount for Drew Ross and his hiking partner on a long trip, it may be a bit much for other folks. I've reduced the amount of couscous but kept everything else the same. Still, the servings are generous.

At home, combine in a zipper-lock bag:

2 cups couscous

3 tablespoons powdered shortening (or 6 tablespoons oil separately packed)

1 teaspoon curry powder

1 teaspoon ground ginger

Pack these items individually:

¾ cup cashews

1½ cups dried vegetables

On trail, in the morning, place vegetables in a large-mouth quart water bottle and cover with water to rehydrate.

At dinnertime, bring to a boil:

4 cups water

Add everything except nuts, including rehydrated veggies with their water. Bring to a boil. Cover, remove from heat, and let stand 10 minutes, or continue cooking—and stirring—for a few minutes until couscous is rehydrated. Sprinkle cashews on top.

Recipe from: *Drew Ross,* Backpacker

Firing up the next meal, Tetons National Park, Wyoming
© Marypat Zitzer

›› Curried Chicken and Barley

Barley is an overlooked grain that offers a nice change of pace from rice.

At home, combine in a zipper-lock bag:

1 cup quick-cooking barley

1 ounce (⅔ cup) freeze-dried chicken

1.5 ounces (about 1 cup) freeze-dried vegetable mix

½ cup dried apple pieces

3 chicken bouillon cubes, crushed

1 tablespoon mild curry powder

Pack individually:

½ cup unsweetened coconut flakes

½ cup raisins

½ cup toasted cashews

On trail, bring to a boil

3 cups water

Add all ingredients except coconut, raisins, and cashews. Simmer at least 10 minutes or until barley is cooked and vegetables are rehydrated. Serve with toppings.

Recipe from: Carol Steinberg, Backpacker

Servings: Two servings of 1¾ cups each.

Nutritional information: 851 calories, 32 grams fat, 140 grams carbohydrate, and 32 grams protein per serving.

Powdered Shortening

Powdered shortening turns to oil as soon as it is heated, so you can use it for frying, baking, and boosting calories. Powdered shortening is handy if you aren't using regular oil or shortening in any other recipes and aren't planning on carrying a container. Powder disperses more easily in a baking mix. Powder is, however, more expensive than oil or shortening, so you have to evaluate whether the ease is worth the cost. To substitute oil or regular shortening, double the amount of powdered shortening. (Note: Unlike powdered shortening, powdered butter does not revert to oil so you cannot use it for frying.)

›› *Kasha Burgers*

Servings: Three.

Nutritional information: 317 calories, 7 grams fat, 56 grams carbohydrate, and 11 grams protein per serving.

Serve these delicious burgers with hearty all-wheat bread or plan to have them as a side dish. Kasha is buckwheat groats; groats are hulled grain that has been cracked into pieces. Nutritional yeast (see Hot Topic 15) is available in health food stores and some supermarkets.

At home, combine in the corner of a zipper-lock bag:

2 tablespoons nutritional yeast

1 teaspoon oregano

½ teaspoon salt, or to taste

1 teaspoon basil

¼ teaspoon black pepper

Tie off the corner with a twist-tie. Add to the bag:

¼ cup finely chopped dried mushrooms

¼ cup black bean flakes

Pack these ingredients individually:

⅓ cup kasha

1 clove garlic

1 small onion

1 tablespoon tomato paste or 2 tablespoons tomato powder

1 teaspoon oil, or more as needed

On trail, rinse kasha. Boil:

1 cup water

Take ⅓ cup of that water and add it to a bowl containing the mushrooms and black beans; stir often to ensure even rehydration. Add kasha to the remaining ⅔ cup water in pot and simmer, covered, for 10 to 15 minutes, or until all the water is absorbed. Dice garlic and onion. Add kasha, garlic, onion, tomato paste, and spice mix to the mushrooms and stir well. Using clean hands, shape into 3 patties. Fry kasha burgers in vegetable oil on medium-high heat until well browned.

Recipe from: *Allison Carroll,* Backpacker

›› Quinoa–Sweet Potato Salad

Quinoa is a grain of the Andes. It has a natural coating that must be rinsed off or it will taste bitter. To rinse, place the grain in a pot and swish with water. Then, pour everything through a bandanna or piece of cheesecloth. (Yes, you have to like quinoa to go to this trouble on trail.) Discard the water.

Servings: Two.

Nutritional information: 561 calories, 26 grams fat, 80 grams carbohydrate, and 9 grams protein per serving.

At home, mix in a leakproof, screw-top container:

2 tablespoons olive oil

½ teaspoon salt, or to taste

1 tablespoon apple cider vinegar

¼ teaspoon nutmeg

Place in a zipper-lock bag:

½ cup raisins

¼ cup coarsely chopped pecans

Pack individually:

½ cup quinoa

1 medium sweet potato

½ onion

1 piece fresh ginger (to yield 2 teaspoons grated)

On trail, rinse the quinoa well, then combine with:

¾ cup water

Simmer, covered, for 12 to 15 minutes. Peel and cube sweet potato and place in a separate pot. Cover potato with water and bring to a boil. Slightly reduce heat and cook for 5 minutes or until somewhat tender. Discard the water and combine the sweet potato and the cooked quinoa. Dice the onion and grate the ginger, then add both. Stir in the oil and vinegar mixture, raisins, and pecans. Mix well and cool in a creek or snowbank, or eat warm.

Recipe from: *Allison Carroll*, Backpacker

›› Chili

Look for chili mix in the natural foods section of the supermarket; some health food stores sell it in bulk. Corn chips add some crunch and a contrast in texture.

At home, combine:
  1 (6.4-ounce) box dry chili mix
  2 ounces sun-dried tomatoes, cut into small pieces
  Dehydrated kidney beans from 2 cans (total 30 ounces) beans

Pack individually:
  40 corn chips
  Hot sauce as desired
  3 ounces Cheddar cheese

On trail, place dry mix in pot and add:
  7½ cups water (more as needed)

Stir well. Bring to a boil and simmer 15 minutes or until done. Stir throughout. Serve in bowls; stir 1 ounce cheese in each bowl and sprinkle with ⅓ of the corn chips.

›› Chili with Bulgur

For a beanless (and perhaps less gas-producing) chili, substitute for the beans:
  1 cup bulgur

On trail, use:
  6½ cups water (more as needed)

Simmer for 15 to 20 minutes, or until bulgur is cooked.

Dehydrated ingredients weigh less than 12 ½ ounces and make 8 cups chili.

›› *Tenaya Beans and Rice*

This make-ahead dinner calls for many of the ingredients in chili, but it looks and tastes quite different. The recipe has great eye appeal, with its palate of black beans, red tomatoes, yellow corn, red pepper, and green pepper, cilantro, and parsley. Because of the low fat content—only 6 percent of the calories are from fat—you can happily pair this with a gooey, decadent dessert.

Servings: Four servings of 2+ cups each.

Nutritional information: 435 calories, 3 grams fat, 85 grams carbohydrate, and 16 grams protein per serving.

At home, combine:

2 cups brown rice

4 cups water

Bring to a boil, let boil uncovered for 30 seconds, then cover and reduce the heat. Simmer for 40 minutes. Meanwhile, heat a heavy skillet and add:

2 teaspoons oil   1 onion, chopped

Sauté until clear, about 10 minutes.

Add and sauté:

2 cloves garlic, sliced

Add:

1½ teaspoons cumin

1 teaspoon chili powder, or to taste

4 low-fat pork and turkey sausages, cut into ⅛-inch slices

1 cup frozen corn

1 (15-ounce) can black beans, drained and rinsed

1 (14-ounce) can crushed tomatoes with juice

Simmer the bean mixture, covered, for about 15 minutes. Then add:

¼ cup chopped fresh cilantro   ¼ cup chopped fresh parsley

½ cup diced red bell pepper   ½ cup diced green bell pepper

Simmer for 5 minutes and remove from the heat. When rice is done, combine rice and beans. Spread on dehydrator trays in a very thin layer and dry at 130 degrees for 8 to 10 hours, or until dry.

On trail, generously cover with water and let stand until ingredients are rehydrated, about 1 hour. Bring to a boil and stir for a minute or 2 until dish is thoroughly heated. Or, add water, bring to a boil, and simmer until done.

When dehydrated, one cup Tenaya Beans and Rice weighs 1½ ounces.

Hot Tips: Minimizing Gas

Here's a typical scene: You and your buddy ate a big pot of chili, crawled into your backpacking tent, and battened down the hatches. The fumes are awful—especially as they're yours. What can you do?

Backpacking foods are notorious natural gas producers. Staples such as whole-grain products (bagels, oat bran, granola, pasta, and whole-grain breads), peas and beans (lentils, chili, and soy products), onions, apples, and grapes are all rich in the sugars that feed normal gas-producing bacteria in your gut.

In addition, the complex sugar lactose, found in most creamy, cheesy sauces, can elevate your gas level, even if you aren't lactose intolerant.

What can you do to de-gas? Here are a couple of suggestions:

- Experiment with different trail foods to figure out which cause the most fumes. Once you've identified the worst offenders, gradually introduce them into your home diet by adding them to several meals over the course of a week or two. That should give your intestinal tract plenty of time to adapt, if it can. But if the foods still produce fumes at home, you can bet they will in the field as well.
- Swap smartly. Substitute dehydrated cherries or blueberries for the raisins in your trail mix. Instead of oatmeal with dehydrated apples and powdered milk, try cooked rice with honey and pecans.
- Try over-the-counter remedies available at grocery stores and pharmacies. Some food supplements contains alpha-galactosidase, an enzyme that helps break down the complex carbohydrates in beans and certain other vegetables so they're easier to digest. Other products contain the enzyme lactase that digests the sugar in dairy products.

—Stern Dixon, *Backpacker*
See Stern's recipes for Pecan Rice Cereal, Hobo Dinner, and Oyster Casserole.

›› Black Beans and Rice

If you use home-dried corn in this recipe, dehydrate $^2/_3$ cup corn. On trail, cover with hot water and let soak 20 to 30 minutes, or until it has completely rehydrated.

Servings: Two servings of 2+ cups each.

Nutritional information: 601 calories, 14 grams fat, 30 grams carbohydrate, and 16 grams protein per serving.

At home, pack in a zipper-lock bag:

1⅔ cups instant black beans

⅔ cup instant rice

2 teaspoons chili powder, or more to taste

¼ teaspoon dry mustard, or more to taste

¼ teaspoon ground cumin, or more to taste

¼ cup onion flakes

⅔ cup freeze-dried corn

Pack individually:

2⅔ ounces Cheddar cheese (⅔ cup grated)

⅔ cup broken corn chips

On trail, add rice mixture to:

4 cups boiling water

Stir while the water regains a boil. Simmer 10 minutes or until done. Add salt and pepper to taste. Grate cheese. Spoon dinnner into bowls and sprinkle cheese and chips on top.

›› Mexican Corn Pie

Make a double batch, eat a fine dinner, and dehydrate the remainder for an easy-prep meal later.

Servings: Four servings of 2+ cups each.

Nutritional information: 440 calories, 17 grams fat, 60 grams carbohydrate, and 18 grams protein per serving.

At home, preheat oven to 350 degrees. Grease a 9 x 13-inch glass casserole dish. Beat all of these ingredients together in a large bowl:

4 whole eggs or 6 egg whites

2 tablespoons corn oil

2 (15-ounce) cans creamed corn

1 (4-ounce) can mild green chilies, diced

1 large onion, minced

⅓ cup whole wheat flour

⅓ cup coarse cornmeal

½ teaspoon baking soda

½ teaspoon salt

⅛ teaspoon cayenne pepper

½ cup finely grated Parmesan cheese

Pour the mixture into the casserole dish and bake for 45 minutes, or until a toothpick inserted in the pie's center comes out clean. Spread in a thin layer on dehydrator trays and dehydrate at 145 degrees for 5 hours.

On trail, pour the mixture into a pot and add enough water to cover. Bring to a boil and cook until rehydrated, stirring occasionally.

Recipe from: *Linda Frederick Yaffe,* Backpacker

›› *Oyster Casserole*

This recipe originally called for ¹/₄ cup each butter and mayonnaise. I have halved both ingredients. If you want to cut further, leave out one or the other entirely. Plan to serve something fruity that's high in carbos but low in fat for dessert.

Servings: Two.

Nutritional information: 824 calories, 39 grams fat, 94 grams carbohydrate, and 24 grams protein per serving.

At home, fry:

 4 slices bacon

Crumble the bacon and place in a zipper-lock bag.

Pack these items individually:

 2 tablespoons butter

 Mayonnaise packets to equal 2 tablespoons

 8 ounces cornbread stuffing mix

 1 (8-ounce) can whole oysters

 1 lemon

In camp, heat the butter in a medium-sized pan and add the cornbread stuffing mix and mayonnaise. Mix thoroughly. Add the oysters, including the liquid, and the bacon. Squeeze the lemon, then add half of the juice to the pan. Add enough water to rehydrate the cornbread crumbs if the mixture is too dry. Stir well, cover, and simmer until heated through, about 3 minutes.

Recipe from: Stern Dixon, Backpacker

›› Mediterranean Polenta

Servings: Three.

Nutritional information: With cheese, 327 calories, 11 grams fat, 48 grams carbohydrate, and 12 grams protein per serving.

At home, dehydrate at 130 degrees for 10 to 12 hours or until dry:

3 artichoke hearts, sliced into ⅛-inch pieces

2 tablespoons black olives, halved

Cool and crumble artichokes and olives, then place in a zipper-lock bag with:

¼ cup sun-dried tomatoes, chopped

½ teaspoon basil

⅛ teaspoon thyme

¼ teaspoon marjoram

¼ teaspoon oregano

Pack these items individually:

1 clove garlic

2 teaspoons olive oil

1 cup cornmeal

¾ cup grated Cheddar or Jack cheese (optional)

On trail, place dried veggies in a bowl and cover with:

2 cups boiling water

Cover and allow veggies to soak. When they have rehydrated, drain the remaining water and set both aside. Sauté the veggies with sliced garlic in half the oil. Add 1½ cups of the reserved water. Slowly stir in cornmeal. Cook for 5 minutes, until cornmeal is a thick, sticky mass of polenta. Add salt to taste. Remove from heat and allow to cool slightly. Using clean hands, shape the polenta into a log. Cool thoroughly in a zipper-lock bag by placing it in a pot of cold water or snow. Then, slice the log into ¾-inch thick rounds. Sauté each round in the remaining oil, flipping as necessary, until each is thoroughly heated and well browned on both sides. If desired, sprinkle each slice with grated cheese just before serving.

Recipe from: *Allison Carroll,* Backpacker

Many pasta recipes call for cheese. If you don't eat milk products, consider substituting toasted pine nuts, which provide both flavor and calories.

Top row: Instant macaroni, instant rotini

Second row: Pesto-flavored linguini

Third row: Rotini, orzo, tortellini, shells, penne, gemelli

Bottom row: Capellini (angel hair)

Cooking Time and Yield for 4 Ounces Pasta			
PASTA	**DRY AMOUNT**	**COOK TIME**	**YIELD COOKED**
Angel hair	Clump ⅞ inch diameter*	2 to 4 minutes	2 cups
Gemelli	1⅓ cup	8 to 9 minutes	1¾+ cups
Macaroni	1 cup	7 to 8 minutes	2 to 2¼ cups
Macaroni, no-boil	2 cups	Add boiling water; let stand 10 minutes	4 cups
Orzo	⅔ cup	7 to 8 minutes	1 cup
Shells, small	1⅓ cups	7 to 8 minutes	1+ cup
Spaghetti	1 cup broken pieces; clump ⅞ inch diameter*	8 to 10 minutes	1½ cups
Tortellini	1 cup	15 minutes	2 cups
*To make a circle ⅞ inch diameter, draw a circle around a nickel.			

›› Shell Pasta with Pesto and Dried Tomato

Servings: Two servings of 2+ cups each.

Nutritional information: 658 calories, 16 grams fat, 80 grams carbohydrate, and 23 grams protein per serving.

Pine nuts make a nice garnish because they offer a bit of crunch, a contrast to chewy veggies and firm shells.

At home, combine in a zipper-lock bag:
1 cup thinly sliced dried tomatoes
½ cup thinly sliced dried mushrooms

Pack these items individually:
1½ cups small shells   ⅓ cup pesto (recipe provided)
¼ cup toasted pine nuts (optional)

On trail, place the veggies in a bowl. Boil a pot of water and use some to cover the veggies. Let them stand until they have rehydrated, about 10 or more minutes. Meanwhile, add more water to the pot, bring to a boil, and add shells. Cook for 7 to 8 minutes or until al dente. Drain pasta and veggies, then combine. Mix pesto into the pot or serve individually. Garnish with pine nuts.

›› Pesto

Use frozen pesto within 24 hours. Or, buy preserved pesto—look for a metal tube, which is lighter than glass. The envelopes of pesto sauce to which you add oil simply don't compare in flavor and texture.

Servings: Nine servings of 2½+ tablespoons each.

Nutritional information: 145 calories, 5 grams fat, 1 gram carbohydrate, and 3 grams protein per serving.

At home, place these ingredients in a food processor and blend for 10 seconds or until ingredients are well chopped and mixed:
4 cups packed fresh basil leaves   ½ cup olive oil
2 cloves garlic, sliced and mashed   6 sprigs parsley
¼ cup pine nuts or walnuts   ½ cup grated Parmesan cheese
Salt and pepper to taste

Divide into convenient amounts (say, ⅓ cup for two people), double bag in zipper-lock bags, and store in the freezer.

›› *Spaghetti with Marinara Sauce*

Use your favorite brand of ready-to-use spaghetti sauce and this recipe is a snap to make. As long as you are drying, make an extra batch and save it for future use. Angel hair spaghetti cooks quickly, but it is easy to over-cook, so monitor it carefully. Substitute other pasta to taste.

Servings: Two servings of 2½+ cups each.

Nutritional information: 625 calories, 10 grams fat, 102 grams carbohydrate, and 31 grams protein per serving.

At home, combine

⅓ cup textured vegetable protein

⅔ cup hot water

Let stand until TVP has rehydrated. Drain water. Add TVP to:

1½ cups (or more to taste) spaghetti sauce

Dehydrate sauce (see Hot Topic 8 for instructions) and pack sauce leather in a zipper-lock bag.

Pack individually:

6 ounces angel hair spaghetti, or more to taste

¼ cup grated Parmesan cheese

On trail, boil:

1½ cups water

Remove from heat, add the sauce leather, stir and cover. Let stand until rehydrated. Then, fill to ¾ full your largest pot and bring water to a boil. Add pasta and stir so it doesn't clump or stick to the bottom of the pot. Cook for 2 to 4 minutes or until al dente. Serve pasta and sauce separately or stir them together first. Top with Parmesan.

›› *Tortellini Stew*

Servings: Two servings of 2½ cups each.

Nutritional information: 513 calories, 16 grams fat, 69 grams carbohydrate, and 22 grams protein.

I made this dish on a winter trip when we arrived at our cabin just as dark fell. The recipe was so popular that night that I've used it again and again, adding whatever dried vegetables I have on hand. The cooking water becomes a tasty broth that can help you rehydrate after a long day. Tortellini is a small prepared pasta filled with cheese. Look for dried tortellini in the dried pasta aisle at your local grocery.

At home, place these ingredients in a zipper-lock bag:

2 cups dried tortellini

1 cup thinly sliced dried tomatoes

3 tablespoons dried, chopped green pepper

⅓ cup onion flakes or dried scallions

1 teaspoon basil

1 teaspoon oregano

1 teaspoon thyme

¼ teaspoon powdered garlic

Also pack:

⅓ cup grated Parmesan cheese or toasted pine nuts

On trail, add tortellini mixture to:

2 quarts boiling water

Stir until water returns to a boil. Cook uncovered for 20 to 25 minutes, stirring occasionally. Spoon into bowls and sprinkle with cheese or nuts.

›› *Linguini with Clams*

A big bowl of pasta garnished with clams tastes good, fills your stomach, and replenishes your store of glycogen in preparation of the next day's events.

At home, pack individually:

8 ounces linguini

2 (6.5-ounce) cans minced clams

⅓ cup grated Parmesan or toasted pine nuts

1 clove garlic

1 teaspoon olive oil

On trail, slice garlic and sauté in oil. Drain clams and reserve broth. Add clams to garlic and sauté. Add broth, bring to a boil, remove from heat, and cover. Bring a large pot of water to boil and cook linguini for 9 to 11 minutes, or until al dente. Serve linguini, clam sauce, and cheese or nuts.

Servings: Two servings of almost 2 cups each.

Nutritional information: 630 calories, 11 grams fat, 96 grams carbohydrate, and 36 grams protein per serving.

Hot Tips: Choosing and Cooking Pasta

Pasta comes in many shapes and sizes that can add variety to your backcountry cuisine. Also look for pasta enriched with lemon pepper, chili pepper, roasted bell pepper and garlic, basil, and tomato or other flavors, any of which can enhance a meal.

Pasta should be cooked *al dente*, or "firm to the tooth." Pasta is undercooked when it is hard to chew and overcooked when it is entirely soft. It has cooked the proper time when the outside layer is soft and the inner layer offers slight resistance, thus providing texture.

In the home kitchen, pasta should be cooked in a big pot of water, allowing about 1 quart water for every 4 ounces. If this ratio is not possible on trail, use the biggest pot you have but try not to overload too much. It is important that the water boil continuously. Cooking times may vary slightly from brand to brand, so check package directions. Taste about a minute before the pasta should be done so you can catch it at just the right moment.

Four ounces is considered a serving, but use this number only as a guide. Figure out how much pasta will satisfy you after a full day of vigorous activity and plan accordingly. Next time you have pasta at home, measure the amount you eat—how much more would you want on the trail?

›› Pasta with Tofu and Spicy Peanut Sauce

Servings: Two servings of about 2½ cups each.

Nutritional information: 1061 calories, 35 grams fat, 147 grams carbohydrate, and 42 grams protein per serving.

If you are going the light and dry route, combine 1 teaspoon garlic powder, 2 teaspoons powdered ginger, and a dash cayenne pepper; also combine ¹/₄ cup dried peppers and 3 tablespoons onion flakes.

At home, combine in a bowl, stir well, and place in a leakproof container:

2 tablespoons balsamic vinegar   ¼ cup peanut butter

⅓ cup honey

Also pack individually:

8 ounces pasta of your choice

1 bell pepper

½ onion

1 tablespoon oil

1 (12- to 16-ounce) package tofu

2 cloves garlic

1 piece ginger (to yield 2 tablespoons finely chopped)

3 tablespoons soy sauce or tamari

Cayenne pepper (in spice kit)

On trail, chop onion and pepper or, if using dehydrated versions, place in a bowl and cover with hot water; cover and let stand until rehydrated. Heat a pan over medium flame and add the oil. Crumble the tofu and brown. Add the pepper, onion, and spices; sauté for a few minutes. Add the peanut butter sauce and mix well. Set aside while you cook the pasta according to package directions. Drain pasta and add the tofu mixture. Stir well and heat briefly until hot.

Recipe from: *Allison Carroll,* Backpacker

›› Southwestern Pasta

This recipe combines the culinary traditions of Italy and the Americas.

At home, cook according to directions on package (until tender):

12 ounces linguini, vermicelli, or other thin pasta

Drain pasta and return to pot. Add:

3½ cups spaghetti sauce

4 ounces Italian dry salami, minced, or tofu, crumbled

1 (15-ounce) can ranch-style baked beans

1 (4-ounce) can mild green chilies, diced

Place pot on low for 5 minutes until all ingredients are hot. Spread in a thin layer on dehydrator trays and dry at 145 degrees for 5½ hours.

On trail, pour the dried meal into a pot and add enough water to cover. Bring to a boil and cook until rehydrated, stirring constantly.

Recipe from: Linda Frederick Yaffe, Backpacker

> **Servings:** Two.
>
> **Nutritional information:** 685 calories, 19 grams fat, 110 grams carbohydrate, and 26 grams protein per serving.

›› Shell Surprise

At home, combine in a zipper-lock bag:

3 cups small shell pasta

2 cups thinly sliced dried tomatoes

2 tablespoons powdered shortening

3 teaspoons basil

1 package onion soup mix

1 package cream of mushroom soup mix

On trail, bring to a boil:

6 cups water

Add ingredients and simmer for 10 minutes, stirring occasionally. Remove from stove, cover, and wait 5 minutes. Retain the water and eat Shell Surprise as you would soup.

Recipe from: Drew Ross, Backpacker

> **Servings:** Two servings of about 3 cups each.
>
> **Nutritional information:** 893 calories, 14 grams fat, 154 grams carbohydrate, and 15 grams protein per serving.

›› *Quick Seafood Capellini*

Servings: Four servings of 2+ cups each.

Nutritional information: Using tuna, 492 calories, 17 grams fat, 36 grams carbohydrate, and 30 grams protein per serving.

At home, cook according to package directions:

8 ounces capellini (angel hair) pasta

Drain and set aside. Heat a heavy skillet over low heat and add:

¼ cup olive oil

When the oil is hot, add:

6 cloves garlic, minced

½ cup whole wheat flour

Sauté until very lightly browned. Slowly add, stirring constantly:

2 cups water, milk, or stock (vegetable, beef, or chicken)

Stir in:

2 packages (total 14 ounces) tuna or 1 (12-ounce) can crab or minced chopped clams

¼ cup minced fresh basil or 1 tablespoon plus 1 teaspoon dried basil

¾ teaspoon salt, or to taste

¼ teaspoon cayenne pepper, or to taste

Cook for 5 minutes. Blend pasta with sauce. Spread in a thin layer on dehydrator trays and dehydrate at 145 degrees for 5 hours.

On trail, pour the mixture into a pot and add enough water to cover. Bring to a boil and cook until rehydrated, stirring occasionally.

Recipe from: *Linda Frederick Yaffe,* Backpacker

›› Pasta Alfredo with Salmon, Corn, and Basil

If you prefer not to use a commercial sauce mix because of the additives, don't add it. The major flavors—smoked salmon, Parmesan, basil, and corn—will hold up well by themselves.

At home, combine in a zipper-lock bag:

½ packet (a total of 0.6 to 0.8 ounces) Alfredo sauce mix

2½ tablespoons powdered milk

1 teaspoon butter powder

2 tablespoons grated Parmesan cheese

1 pinch black pepper

Pack these ingredients individually:

8 ounces pasta

1.2 ounces (about 1 cup) freeze-dried corn

½ bunch fresh basil or 1 tablespoon dried basil

4 ounces smoked salmon, crumbled

On trail, mince the basil, if using fresh. Cook pasta 1 minute less than the recommended time. Add corn to pasta and set aside, covered but undrained. In a separate pot, add to the dried sauce mix:

¾ cup water

Simmer 5 minutes, stirring frequently. Drain pasta and corn mixture. Add sauce and toss well. Add basil and salmon. Toss gently.

Recipe from: Liz Rusch, Backpacker

Servings: Two servings of 2+ cups each.

Nutritional information: 611 calories, 9 grams fat, 104 grams carbohydrate, and 33 grams protein per serving.

›› *Mussels Marinara*

Servings: Two servings of almost 2 cups each.

Nutritional information: 625 calories, 14 grams fat, 94 grams carbohydrate, and 25 grams protein per person.

The recipe originally called for a 4-ounce tin of smoked mussels to be shared among three or four people. I like smoked mussels, so I've taken the liberty of increasing the amount. For more information on tomato sauce leather, see Hot Topic 8.

At home, pack these ingredients individually:

1 clove garlic

1 small onion

6 ounces pasta

1 tablespoon olive oil

Tomato sauce leather (to yield ⅓ cup sauce)

1 (4-ounce) tin smoked mussels

On trail, mince garlic and chop onion. Cook pasta 1 minute less than the recommended time. Set aside, covered but undrained. In a separate pot, sauté onions until almost translucent, then add garlic and sauté until golden. Add:

⅓ cup water

Tear tomato sauce leather into small pieces and add to the water, stirring until leather has rehydrated; add more water if necessary. Drain pasta. Add sauce and toss gently.

Recipe from: *Liz Rusch,* Backpacker

Home on the range, Wind Rivers, Wyoming
© Marypat Zitzer

With a cell phone, you can order takeout almost anywhere.
© Ben Townsend

Hot Tips: Pasta Prep in the Field

Thin pasta cooks faster, but skinny spaghetti and delicate angel hair often look like the flour they're made of after a few days in a pack. I recommend sticking with the thicker, bite-size kinds that'll hold up to the bumps and bruises of the trail and are easier to handle when you have to make a separate sauce.

When you are packing, dried spices with similar flavors can commingle. You can, for example, premix dried or hard, grated cheeses with the spices. I always keep a concoction of grated Parmesan cheese, dried basil, oregano, and pepper on hand to liven up dinner. Garlic travels best in clove form; chop it in camp.

How to cook pasta in one pot and sauce in another over one burner? First, cook the noodles—but not all the way. Boil them 1 minute less than the recommended time. If the directions suggest 6 to 8 minutes, boil the pasta for 5 minutes. Then set it aside, covered but not drained. The just-boiled water continues to cook the noodles while you whip up the sauce. For best results, use the thicker pasta shapes.

Delicate pastas, such as angel hair, will turn to mush if left immersed in water, so use them with no-cook sauces. You can drain most of the water, then dump a store-bought sauce packet in with the pasta and stir. While it won't taste like your mom's home-made sauce, it does the trick when you're hungry. Many of the packet sauces available at the grocery store can be treated this way, even if the directions tell you to cook them.

Remember to treat the water you drain off the pasta like you'd treat dirty dishwater: Scatter it in the bushes at least 100 feet from camp.

—Liz Rusch, *Backpacker*

›› One-Step Lasagna

Concentrate on the taste, not the form, when enjoying this backcountry treat.

Servings: Four servings of 2+ cups each.

Nutritional information: 721 calories, 36 grams fat, 58 grams carbohydrate, and 43 grams protein per serving.

At home, preheat oven to 375 degrees. Grease a 9 x 13-inch glass casserole dish. Assemble these ingredients:

4 cups spaghetti sauce

9 no-cook lasagna noodles

15 ounces ricotta cheese

3 tablespoons fresh basil, minced, or 1 tablespoon dried

1 pound firm tofu, drained and crumbled

8 ounces mozzarella cheese, grated

Layer the ingredients in the dish in this order: 1 cup sauce, 3 noodles, and a third of each of the remaining ingredients. Repeat until all ingredients have been used, topping the casserole with the last cup of sauce. Cover the casserole and bake for 30 minutes. Uncover and bake for another 10 minutes, then remove from the oven and let stand for 10 minutes. Using a spatula, break up the noodles and spread the lasagna in a thin layer on dehydrator trays. Dehydrate at 145 degrees for 5 hours.

On trail, pour the dried meal into a pot and add enough water to cover. Bring to a boil, stir until rehydrated, and serve.

Recipe from: *Linda Frederick Yaffe,* Backpacker

›› Quick Hoppin' John

The Joy of Cooking *says that this dish brings good luck when eaten on the first day of the new year—but it's tasty any time.*

At home, rinse:

1 cup dried black-eyed peas

Put them in a large saucepan with:

6 cups water

4 cloves garlic, minced

1 onion, finely chopped

1 bay leaf

3 tablespoons salsa

½ teaspoon liquid smoke

Bring to a boil, then simmer for 50 minutes. Remove the bay leaf. Cook according to package directions:

1½ cups orzo

Drain. Add orzo and the following ingredients to the beans:

3 cups spaghetti sauce

1 teaspoon salt, or to taste

Stir and simmer for 5 minutes. Spread in a thin layer on dehydrator trays and dry at 145 degrees for 5 hours.

On trail, pour the dried meal into a pot and add enough water to cover. Bring to a boil, stir until rehydrated, and serve.

Recipe from: *Linda Frederick Yaffe,* Backpacker

Servings: Four servings of 2+ cups each.

Nutritional information: 503 calories, 5 grams fat, 95 grams carbohydrate, and 21 grams protein per serving.

›› Tofu Vermicelli

Servings: Four servings of 2+ cups each.

Nutritional information: 733 calories, 29 grams fat, 87 grams carbohydrate, and 33 grams protein per serving.

Because tofu is neutral, the dominant flavors here are garlic, spinach, Parmesan, and tomatoes.

At home, heat in a large, heavy skillet or Dutch oven over low heat:

2 tablespoons olive oil

When the oil is hot, add:

1 pound firm tofu, drained and crumbled

6 cloves garlic, minced

⅔ cup cashews, finely chopped

Sauté for 5 minutes. Cook separately according to package directions:

12 ounces vermicelli

Add pasta and these ingredients to the skillet:

1 pound spinach, washed, stems removed and finely chopped

4 tablespoons soy sauce or tamari

3 tablespoons dry sherry

½ cup finely grated Parmesan cheese

2 cups tomato sauce or crushed tomatoes

1 teaspoon salt, or to taste

Stir for 5 minutes to blend well. Spread in a thin layer on dehydrator trays and dehydrate at 145 degrees for 5 hours.

On trail, pour the dried meal into a pot and add enough water to cover. Bring to a boil, stir until rehydrated, and serve.

Recipe from: *Linda Frederick Yaffe*, Backpacker

›› Black Bean Chili Mac

This recipe has lots of carbohydrates and protein—and, of course, it tastes good.

At home, cook in a large pot according to package directions:

10 ounces (2½ cups) small shell pasta or small elbow macaroni

Drain. Pour the pasta back into the pot and add:

1 (15-ounce) can black beans, drained and rinsed

3 cups spaghetti sauce

½ cup salsa

3 cloves garlic, minced

½ teaspoon salt, or to taste

3 tablespoons finely grated fresh Parmesan cheese

Heat briefly. Spread in a thin layer on dehydrator trays. Dehydrate at 145 degrees for 5½ hours.

On trail, pour the dried meal into a pot and add enough water to cover. Bring to a boil, stir until rehydrated, and serve.

Recipe from: *Linda Frederick Yaffe,* Backpacker

Servings: Four servings of 2+ cups each.

Nutritional information: 483 calories, 10 grams fat, 87 grams carbohydrate, and 19 grams protein per serving.

Reaching the summit is only half the trip, Baxter Peak, Maine

›› Hot or Cold Rotini

Servings: Three servings of 2⅓ cups each.

Nutritional information: 412 calories, 34 grams fat, 38 grams carbohydrate, and 14 grams protein per serving.

This colorful dish is especially nice when made with fresh vegetables. For cold rotini salad, allow the pasta to cool before folding in the other ingredients.

At home, bag these ingredients individually:

3 cups (8 ounces) multi-color rotini

1 cup grated Cheddar cheese

⅓ cup Italian salad dressing

Pack together:

1 cup thinly sliced dried tomatoes

3 tablespoons dried green pepper or 1 fresh pepper

⅓ cup dried scallions or 2 fresh scallions

On trail, add rotini and dried vegetables to:

2 quarts boiling water

Stir until water returns to a boil and cook 10 to 12 minutes. Drain liquid. If using fresh vegetables, chop them and fold into drained pasta. Add cheese and salad dressing and stir well. Add salt and pepper to taste.

›› Alpine Mac 'n' Cheese

Use the best Swiss cheese you can afford for this elegant version of an old standby.

At home, combine in a zipper-lock bag:

3 tablespoons flour

2 teaspoons mustard powder

½ teaspoon salt, or to taste

½ cup powdered milk

1 tablespoon parsley

½ teaspoon black pepper

In another bag, combine:

⅓ cup chopped dried tomatoes

8 ounces (2 cups) small shell pasta

Pack individually:

5 ounces Swiss cheese

¼ cup dry white wine (optional)

In camp, cut the cheese into very small chunks.

Bring to a boil:

3½ cups water

If you are using wine, add it to the pot, then add the pasta and tomato pieces. Boil until the pasta is slightly tender, stirring occasionally. Stir in the dry ingredients, then stir in the cheese. Turn off the heat and stir until the cheese melts.

Recipe from: *Cheryl Manning,* Backpacker

Servings: Two servings of about 2¼ cups each.

Nutritional information: 712 calories, 16 grams fat, 103 grams carbohydrate, and 35 grams protein per serving.

›› *Ramen Supreme*

Servings: Two servings of 2+ cups each.

Nutritional information: 439 calories, 17 grams fat, 48 grams carbohydrate, and 21 grams protein per person.

If you are sensitive to MSG, throw away the flavor pouch that comes with the noodles and pack 1 tablespoon mixed herbs (basil, oregano, thyme, dill, and a pinch of tarragon if you have some).

At home, combine in a zipper-lock bag:

⅓ cup freeze-dried peas or ⅓ cup snow peas

⅓ cup thinly sliced dried mushrooms or ½ cup fresh

1½ tablespoons onion flakes or 2 whole scallions

½ cup freeze-dried chicken or 1 (12.5 ounce) can chicken

Pack individually:

¼ cup slivered almonds

1½ packages low-salt, chicken-flavored ramen noodles

On trail, place dry veggie mix in a pot and cover with hot water. Set aside for 10 minutes or until ingredients have rehydrated. If using fresh ingredients, chop and set aside.

Meanwhile, bring to a boil:

6 cups water

Break up the noodles and add them to the pot along with the flavor packets. Cook for 3 minutes, stirring occasionally. Drain most of the water. Add rehydrated items (or, fresh veggies and canned chicken), stir, cover, and remove from heat. Let stand a few minutes. Add almonds just before serving. Add salt and pepper to taste.

Recipe from: *Maggie Stafsnes*, Backpacker

›› *Sweet and Sour Pan-Fried Noodles*

Home drying allows you to take complex dishes into the backcountry.

Servings: Four servings of 2+ cups each.

Nutritional information: 508 calories, 7 grams fat, 114 grams carbohydrate, and 3 grams protein per serving.

At home, cook for 5 minutes and drain:

16 ounces Chinese rice stick noodles

Heat a large wok or deep frying pan over medium-low heat and add:

2 teaspoons sesame oil

1 tablespoon canola oil

When oil is hot, add:

1 onion, minced

4 cloves garlic, minced

Sauté for 3 minutes. Add the noodles and:

12 ounces mushrooms, finely chopped

1 carrot, grated

Sauté, stirring occasionally, until browned. Add:

1½ cups crushed tomatoes

3 tablespoons finely grated fresh ginger

¼ cup rice vinegar

3 tablespoons soy sauce or tamari

1 tablespoon honey

½ teaspoon salt, or to taste

¼ teaspoon cayenne pepper

Stir over low heat for 5 minutes. Spread in a thin layer on dehydrator trays and dehydrate at 145 degrees for 5 hours.

On trail, pour the dried meal into a pot, add enough water to cover, bring to a boil, stir until rehydrated, and serve.

Recipe from: *Linda Frederick Yaffe,* Backpacker

›› *Beef Stroganoff*

Servings: Two servings of about 2½+ cups each.

Nutritional information: 623 calories, 15 grams fat, 96 grams carbohydrate, and 17 grams protein per serving.

Backpacker's editors changed a fresh-food venison stroganoff recipe by Carol Donaldson into this trail recipe.

At home, combine in a zipper-lock bag:

¼ pound jerky, chopped into tiny pieces

2 teaspoons onion flakes

½ tablespoon paprika

1 ounce (2 tablespoons) dried mushrooms

¾ teaspoon tomato powder (optional)

1 (1-cup) serving package instant cream of mushroom soup

¼ cup instant potatoes

In a separate bag, combine:

¼ cup plus 2 tablespoons sour cream powder

¾ teaspoon parsley

Also pack:

8 ounces egg noodles

On trail, pour the contents of the jerky bag into a pot and add:

1¾ cups water

Bring to a boil, then simmer 15 minutes, stirring occasionally. Add more water if needed. Remove from heat and let stand. Then, fill the largest pot with water, bring the water to a boil, and add the egg noodles. Follow package directions for cooking time. Drain. Put the stroganoff pan on the heat, add the sour cream mix and heat but do not boil. Serve over noodles immediately.

›› *Spud Surprise*

Simplicity, ease of preparation, and great flavor make this recipe a favorite.

At home, pack:

2 large baking potatoes, baked   3 scallions, washed

2 tins (total 8 ounces) smoked oysters

On trail, chop scallions and drain oysters. Cut open potatoes and smother with oysters and scallions.

Recipe from: *Marjorie McCloy,* Backpacker

Servings: Two.

Nutritional information: 445 calories, 9 grams fat, 75 grams carbohydrate, and 18 grams protein per serving.

›› *Vegetable Frittata*

Servings: Four servings of 2+ cups each.

Nutritional information: 756 calories, 27 grams fat, 95 grams carbohydrates, and 39 grams protein per serving.

A frittata is an Italian omelette; the eggs and vegetables are mixed together before being cooked.

At home, clean and dice:

10 small (4½ pounds) russet potatoes

Place potatoes in a sauce pan. Cover with water, bring to a boil, then cook for 10 minutes or until tender. Drain and set aside.

Wash, remove the stems, and chop into small pieces:

1 pound (1 bunch) spinach or Swiss chard

Place spinach or chard in a large saucepan and add:

½ cup water

Cover and cook for 8 minutes or until tender; drain.

Whisk together:

8 whole eggs or 10 egg whites⅔ cup milk

5 cloves garlic, minced

1 teaspoon salt, or to taste

¾ teaspoon freshly ground black pepper

2 teaspoons thyme

Stir in the cooked potatoes and spinach or chard. Preheat a large oven-proof skillet on the stove top (over medium heat), then add:

2 tablespoons canola oil

When oil is hot, stir in the potato mixture. Cover, reduce heat to very low, and cook for 12 minutes. Sprinkle with:

2 cups finely grated Parmesan cheese

Place the uncovered skillet beneath a preheated broiler. Broil for 4 minutes or until light brown. Spread in a thin layer on dehydrator trays and dry at 145 degrees for 5 hours.

On trail, pour the dried meal into a pot and add enough water to cover. Bring to a boil, stir until rehydrated, and serve.

Recipe from: *Linda Frederick Yaffe,* Backpacker

›› *Mashed Potato Pancakes*

Serve this for dinner or a spicy breakfast. Applesauce makes a fine accompaniment.

At home, combine in a zipper-lock bag:

  1½ ounces instant mashed potatoes

  1½ tablespoons whole wheat flour

  ¼ teaspoon cayenne powder

  ½ teaspoon onion powder

  1¼ teaspoons garlic powder

  ¼ teaspoon salt, or to taste

  ¼ teaspoon black pepper

Pack these items individually:

  2½ ounces instant hash browns

  2 ounces Cheddar cheese, grated

On trail, cover hash browns with boiling water and let stand 10 minutes. Whisk into mashed potato mixture:

  1 cup boiling water

Gently fold in hash browns and cheese. Spoon onto greased skillet and flatten. Cook like a pancake.

Recipe from: *Terry Krautwurst,* Backpacker

> **Servings:** Two.
>
> **Nutritional information:** 335 calories, 7 grams fat, 53 grams carbohydrate, and 15 grams protein per serving.

›› *Shepherd's Pie*

One-pot meals are easy, but sometimes it's nice to have two distinct foods, one served over the other.

Servings: Two servings of 2+ cups each.

Nutritional information: 653 calories, 34 grams fat, 28 grams carbohydrate, and 32 grams protein per serving.

At home, bag individually:

1½ cups instant mashed potatoes

½ cup dried or 1 cup freeze-dried vegetables

Prepare the sauce by combining in a zipper-lock bag:

2 tablespoons flour, white or whole wheat

⅓ cup powdered milk

½ teaspoon Worcestershire sauce powder

Also pack:

2 tablespoons margarine, clarified butter, or oil

1 (3-ounce) can chicken

On trail, rehydrate vegetables by covering with boiling water. If you are using dried veggies, let them stand until rehydrated; freeze-dried veggies will rehydrate in 10 minutes. Meanwhile, add to a pot:

1¼ cups water

Bring to a boil, add instant potatoes, and stir quickly for 5 to 10 seconds. Add rehydrated vegetables and stir well. Set aside. Add margarine to a frying pan or small pot, melt, and gradually add flour mixture, stirring to form a smooth paste. Stir briskly and slowly add:

1 cup water

Then add chicken. Add salt and pepper to taste. Serve chicken over vegetable-potato mixture.

›› *Mexi-Bean Salad*

You can also use this salad, with a few slices of cheese, as filling for a vegetable burrito.

At home, combine in a large bowl:

1 tablespoon minced cilantro

½ teaspoon salt, or to taste

1 tablespoon vinegar

⅓ cup salsa

Stir well and add:

1 (15-ounce) can kidney beans, rinsed and drained

1 cup frozen corn

½ bell pepper, sliced into strips

2 scallions, chopped

Stir well, cover the bowl, and marinate for at least 24 hours before drying. Place in a thin layer on dehydrator trays and dry for 15 hours at 130 degrees. The salad is dry when the beans are crunchy and the corn is still a bit leathery. Place a single serving (¼ cup) of the dried mix in each zipper-lock bag.

On trail, add an equal amount of water to each portion of salad (¼ cup water to ¼ cup salad) and allow it to reconstitute for at least 1 hour.

Recipe from: *J. Lynn Cutts,* Backpacker

> **Servings:** Three servings of ½ to ¾ cup each.
>
> **Nutritional information:** 178 calories, 0 grams fat, 34 grams carbohydrate, and 10 grams protein per serving.

›› Bulgur-Chickpea Salad

Serve this side dish warm or cold.

Servings: Two servings of almost 1 cup each.

Nutritional information: 287 calories, 9 grams fat, 47 grams carbohydrate, and 10 grams protein per serving.

At home, buy a small can of chickpeas and dehydrate:
¼ cup

Pack in a zipper-lock bag:
½ teaspoon basil
¼ teaspoon oregano
¼ cup bulgur

Pack dehydrated chickpeas in another zipper-lock bag and add:
¼ cup chopped dried tomatoes

Place in a leakproof container:
1½ tablespoons lemon juice
1 tablespoon olive oil

Pack individually:
1 small cucumber
½ small onion
1 clove garlic

On trail, add bulgur mixture to:
½ cup boiling water

Remove from heat and let stand until water is absorbed. In a separate pot, cover chickpeas and tomatoes with boiling water and soak 15 minutes or until rehydrated. Discard water and add bulgur. Peel the cucumber, then dice all the vegetables. Add them to the pot. Add the lemon juice and oil, then salt and pepper to taste.

Recipe from: *Allison Carroll*, Backpacker

›› Carrot, Raisin, and Nut Salad

Crunchy carrots in the backcountry give you real-food taste and texture. If it's available, buy a packet or two of salad dressing from the salad bar of your supermarket instead of carrying a separate container.

At home, combine:
  1⅔ cups shredded carrot (2 large carrots), dehydrated
  3 tablespoons raisins

Pack individually:
  3 tablespoons toasted cashews
  3 tablespoons salad dressing

On trail, place carrots and raisins in a pot and add:
  2¾ cups hot water

Cover and let stand until rehydrated, about 15 minutes. Let cool and drain liquid. Just before eating, add cashews and salad dressing.

> **Servings:** Two servings of 1 cup each.
>
> **Nutritional information:** 234 calories, 9 grams fat, 29 grams carbohydrate, and 3 grams protein per serving.

›› Carrot–Pineapple Crunch

This recipe takes longer to make, but the dressing is built in so you don't have to carry a separate container.

At home, pack in a zipper-lock bag:
  1 tablespoon toasted almonds

Then, combine in a pan:
  Grated rind from ½ large lemon   ½ cup sugar, or less to taste
  ¼ cup lemon juice

Simmer gently until the sugar has dissolved. Place in a bowl:
  2 large carrots, peeled and shredded
  4 ounces crushed pineapple, drained

Pour juice mixture over carrots and pineapple, cover the bowl, and marinate for at least 24 hours. Stir occasionally. Dehydrate mixture for about 15 hours or until done, then package in a zipper-lock bag.

On trail, cover dry ingredients with water and reconstitute for at least half an hour. When ready to serve, add almonds.

Recipe from: J. Lynn Cutts, Backpacker

> **Servings:** Two servings of ¾ to 1 cup each.
>
> **Nutritional information:** 252 calories, 2 grams fat, 64 grams carbohydrate, and 2 grams protein per serving.

›› *Packer's Coleslaw*

Servings: Four servings of about ¾ cup each.

Nutritional information: 90 calories, 0 grams fat, 27 grams carbohydrate, and 1 gram protein per serving.

Try this crisp coleslaw, and energy bars will never taste the same.

At home, combine in a large bowl:
½ tablespoon noniodized or canning salt
½ cup water

Allow salt to dissolve, then add:
¼ cabbage, washed and finely shredded

Let soak for 1 hour. Add:
½ stalk celery, shredded   ½ carrot, shredded
¼ green pepper, shredded

Let soak for 20 minutes. Drain and rinse thoroughly. Meanwhile, combine in a pan:
¼ cup and 2 tablespoons vinegar   ½ teaspoon mustard seed
¼ teaspoon celery seed   ½ cup sugar

Bring to a boil; boil and stir until sugar has dissolved. Pour the dressing over the rinsed vegetable mix in the bowl and marinate, covered, for at least 24 hours. Stir occasionally. Dehydrate slaw for about 15 hours or until done, then package in a zipper-lock bag.

On trail, cover dry mix with water and allow mix to reconstitute for at least half an hour.

Recipe from: *J. Lynn Cutts,* Backpacker

›› Zucchini–Apple Salad

Put shredded apples in the lemon juice mixture right away to keep them from turning brown.

At home, combine in a bowl:

¼ cup lemon juice

2 tablespoons sugar

1 tablespoon minced fresh ginger

Stir until the sugar dissolves. Add:

1 large apple, cored and shredded

1 large (but not jumbo) zucchini, shredded

Mix well, cover, and marinate for at least 24 hours, stirring occasionally. Dehydrate for about 15 hours or until done, then package in a zipper-lock bag.

On trail, cover dry mix with water and allow mix to reconstitute for at least half an hour.

Recipe from: *J. Lynn Cutts,* Backpacker

Servings: Three.

Nutritional information: 80 calories, 0 grams fat, 21 grams carbohydrate, and 1 gram protein per serving.

Everyone likes to eat, Downeast, Maine

›› *Chinese Cabbage Salad*

Servings: Eight.

Nutritional information: 118 calories, 7 grams fat, 13 grams carbohydrate, and 1 gram protein per serving.

This recipe is as good on trail as it is at home.

At home, pack the topping:

1 teaspoon toasted sesame seeds
½ tablespoon toasted slivered almonds

Then, combine in a bowl:

2 tablespoons vinegar
¼ teaspoon salt
2 tablespoons soy sauce or tamari

½ cup sugar
¼ cup oil

Stir until the sugar has dissolved. Place in a large bowl:

½ large Chinese cabbage, shredded (about 8 cups loosely packed)
½ bunch scallions, chopped (white bulb discarded)

Pour the marinade over the vegetables and stir well. Marinate for 24 to 36 hours. Dehydrate for about 15 hours or until done, then package in a zipper-lock bag.

On trail, cover dry mix with water and allow mix to reconstitute for at least half an hour. Sprinkle with seeds and nuts just before serving.

Recipe from: *J. Lynn Cutts,* Backpacker

Hot Tips: Packable Salads

Salads are great at dinner and they also add punch to a trailside lunch. In the morning, I divide the dried ingredients into individual servings in zipper-lock bags, add water, and by noon, I have a crispy, refreshing salad to augment crackers, cheese, and beef jerky. Eat it out of the bag and there are no dishes to wash.

- Shredded vegetables dry more thoroughly and rehydrate faster than sliced, and are less likely to crumble into powder inside a pack. A food processor fitted with a medium grating disk is ideal for shredding firm veggies. For tomatoes and other soft fruits and veggies, stick to slices or chunks.
- Marinate your vegetables in spices for at least 24 hours before drying and you won't need to pack dressing ingredients. To get the full flavor blast, my marinade contains double the amounts of spices I'd normally use in camp.
- Cabbage in all its forms dries exceptionally well, even pickled red cabbage and sauerkraut straight from the jar. Every version of coleslaw—unless it has a creamy dressing—makes the transformation from fresh to dry salad successfully.
- Other trailworthy candidates for shredding include carrots, zucchini, yellow squash, and apples.
- If you double the recipe, you'll have salad for the upcoming trip and the one after that.
- Dried salads last for up to 6 months in the freezer without spoilage or loss of flavor and texture.

It may seem frivolous to spend time on salads. How many calories can you get from carrots, after all? But rehydratable salads add taste, texture, and variety to the usual suspects in the backcountry food sack. If you return from a trip not craving fresh veggies, then you know that salads have truly made a difference in your trail cuisine.

—J. Lynn Cutts, *Backpacker*

›› Snow Pea and Red Pepper Salad with Ginger–Soy Dressing

Servings: Four servings of about ½ cup each.

Nutritional information: 107 calories, 9 grams fat, 5 grams carbohydrates, and 1 gram protein.

This colorful salad adds flavor and crunch to any meal.

At home, pack

1 cup snow peas

2 tablespoons toasted sesame seeds

1 red bell pepper

Combine in a leakproof container:

1 tablespoon soy sauce or tamari

1 tablespoon seasoned rice wine vinegar

2 tablespoons safflower oil

½ tablespoon finely chopped crystallized ginger

On trail, dice the snow peas and pepper and place in a bowl. Sprinkle on the sesame seeds. Pour on the dressing and mix well.

Recipe from: Maggie Stafsnes, Backpacker

Hot Tips: Going Stoveless, #1

Going stoveless has lots of advantages.

- You can eat sooner. With less prep time and no endless waits for water to boil, you can feed your tummy when it starts growling, not 45 minutes later.

- You can stay flexible. Dark clouds forming over the ridge? A no-cook meal gets you fed and back in the tent before the rain begins.

- You can put an end to mechanical failures. There's no fixing clogged jets or going hungry because you forgot the fuel pump.

- With no camp kitchen, you carry a more compact load.

- You can travel easier. You no longer have to worry about airline officials confiscating your expensive stove, buying fuel at your destination, or figuring out what to do with leftover fuel.

Going stoveless won't necessarily lighten your load (see p. 133). Ready-to-eat foods contain more water than dehydrated meals do, so your normal load of 2 to 2½ pounds of food per person may jump to 3 pounds or more, especially if you pack canned goods. Not carrying a stove, fuel, or cookset saves you about 5 pounds, but in the end, soloists gain the most by going stoveless.

—Steve Howe, *Backpacker*

›› *Pesto Tuna Wrap*

Sealed, pasteurized yogurt will remain edible for at least 48 hours in virtually any weather, says Backpacker field editor Steve Howe. You can also freeze it, which extends its trail life by 12 hours. Pesto is available in small glass jars and in metal tubes.

At home, place in the corner of a zipper-lock bag:

1 tablespoon toasted pine nuts

Tie off and place in the other corner:

¼ teaspoon dried basil

Tie off. In the remaining part of the bag, place:

2 teaspoons grated Parmesan cheese

Pack these items individually:

1 (6- to 7-ounce) package tuna

2 (12-inch) spinach tortillas

1 (6-ounce) container plain yogurt (you'll need ¼ cup)

1 small container pesto (you'll need 2 tablespoons)

On trail, mix ¹/₄ cup yogurt, 4 teaspoons pesto, and the other filling ingredients. Spread on tortillas and wrap.

> **Servings:** Two servings of 1 wrap each.
>
> **Nutritional information:** 294 calories, 12 grams fat, 20 grams carbohydrate, and 29 grams protein per wrap.

›› *Avocado–Salmon Sandwich*

If you wish, substitute bagels or pitas for the tortillas.

At home, pack individually:

1 fresh avocado

4 ounces Swiss cheese

Juice of one lemon

1 (6-ounce) can salmon

4 tortillas

On trail, slice cheese. Peel and slice the avocado, sprinkle with half the lemon juice, and place on the tortillas. Drain the salmon, break into chunks, and layer over the avocado slices. Sprinkle with the remaining juice. Top with cheese slices.

Recipes from: Steve Howe, Backpacker

> **Servings:** Two servings of 2 tortillas each.
>
> **Nutritional information:** 773 calories, 43 grams fat, 57 grams carbohydrate, and 41 grams protein per serving.

›› Pita Pockets with Quinoa

Servings: Two servings of 1 pita (2 halves) each.

Nutritional information: 591 calories, 20 grams fat, 70 grams carbohydrate, and 31 grams protein per serving.

These pockets offer more calories than you might think, as well as real-food texture. It is important to rinse the quinoa, as it has a bitter coating called saponin; this coating washes off easily.

At home, rinse:

½ cup quinoa

Drain. Add:

1 cup water

Dash salt

Bring to a boil and simmer 10 to 15 minutes or until grain is translucent. Cool and store in a zipper-lock bag. Meanwhile, cut into ¹/₄-inch slices:

1 (15- to 16-ounce) package extra-firm tofu

Sauté tofu in:

Butter, as needed

Soy sauce or tamari, to taste

Cook over low heat for 20 minutes, turning as needed, until the tofu loses most of its moisture. Cool and store in a zipper-lock bag. Pack these ingredients individually:

2 handfuls bean sprouts

2 handfuls shredded red cabbage

2 pita pockets

8 dried shiitake mushrooms, sliced thin

Store all ingredients in the refrigerator until you leave on your trip. On trail, cover mushrooms with water and let soak 5 to 10 minutes or until plump. Stuff all ingredients into pita pockets.

Recipe from: *Marjorie McCloy,* Backpacker

›› Crab-Stuffed Pita Pockets

This dinner is good with assorted cheeses and crackers.

At home, pack:

2 tablespoons diced red onion

1 medium tomato

1 single-serving packet (2 tablespoons) ranch salad dressing

2 whole pitas

1 medium avocado

1 (6-ounce) can crabmeat

On trail, dice the avocado and tomato and drain the crabmeat. Combine all filling ingredients. Cut pitas in half and fill the pockets with the mixture.

Recipe from: *Steve Howe*, Backpacker

> **Servings:** Two servings of 1 pita (2 halves) each.
>
> **Nutritional information:** 430 calories, 17 grams fat, 36 grams carbohydrate, and 30 grams protein per serving.

›› Falafel Pita Pockets

Falafel is a Middle Eastern dish made with garbanzo beans and spices. A dry mix of these ingredients is widely available in health food stores and supermarkets (check the natural food section).

At home, combine and stir well:

¾ cups water

1 cup falafel mix

Let stand 15 minutes to absorb water. Heat frying pan and add:

1 tablespoon oil

Drop chunks of falafel into the pan, and as soon as they start to cook, break them into small pieces. Stir pieces until they are evenly browned. Cool and place in a zipper-lock bag. Store in the refrigerator.

Pack individually:

¼ cup tahini (sesame paste)

½ cup dried corn

2 pitas

On trail, at breakfast add to corn:

1 cup water

Seal container and let rehydrate during the day. In the evening, drain water and add falafel. Mix well. Spoon into pita halves and drizzle the tahini on top.

> **Servings:** Two servings of 1 pita (2 halves) each.
>
> **Nutritional information:** 743 calories, 34 grams fat, 67 grams carbohydrate, and 21 grams protein per serving.

Hot Tips: Going Stoveless #2

On trips of three days or fewer, with warm temps, low altitude, and unthreatening weather, think bold: Forget the stove, fuel bottle, pots, pans, lids, pot handle, and dish detergent. The alternative? Healthy, fresh, precooked foods.

No-stove foods have a lot of texture, color, and flavor—an unbeatable combination when you're ravenous at day's end. They also satisfy a backpacker's weight concerns because with each meal you're carrying less, so pack weight drops dramatically. Because your total kitchen—consisting of a plate, cup, knife, spoon, and scrubby—weighs in at a whopping few ounces, you'll feel like you're carrying a day pack toward the end of your trip.

No-stove food has other advantages as well. You don't have to fiddle with a stove that's not there, and you're not stuck eating crunchy pasta if your mechanical source of fire decides to act up. Nothing gooey gets baked onto the bottom of your pans. Cleanup is almost nonexistent, so you spend less time cooking and cleaning up and have more time to enjoy the sunset.

No-stove meals need little or no water. That means you can camp in airy abandon, carrying only the water you need for drinking. Ditto for the middle of a desert, the edge of a hanging valley, or anywhere else you feel like plopping down for the night.

The key is to make sure these carefree meals are tasty and filling. Three of my favorites are Stuffed Peppers, Spud Surprise, and Pita Pockets with Quinoa. You probably have meals you eat at home that could easily be adapted to trail use as well. A two-day menu might look something like this:

Day One

Breakfast: Bagels with cream cheese and nectarines

Lunch: Pita pockets stuffed with bean sprouts, quinoa, and shiitake mushrooms (mushrooms need water)

Dinner: Baked potato (precooked) with canned smoked oysters and scallions

Day Two

Breakfast: Brown rice (precooked) with cinnamon, nuts, and raisins

Lunch: Baked potato (precooked) with cream cheese and Tofu Jerky

Dinner: Bell pepper stuffed with rice (precooked) and tuna (in foil package)

Snacks

Energy bars, dried or fresh fruit, crackers with instant hummus (needs water) or make fresh at home

Even if you go stoveless, remember to take matches or a lighter. You may not need to light your stove, but in an emergency you may need to light a fire.

—Marjorie McCloy, *Backpacker*

›› Quesadillas

Quesadillas are the Mexican version of a wrap. Take a tortilla, fold it over, stuff it with cheese, or cheese and something, and grill to melt. A 6-ounce can of crabmeat transforms quesadillas from ordinary to outrageous. If you like heat, pack along chili pepper flakes.

At home, bag these ingredients individually:

8 small (7- to 8-inch) tortillas

6 ounces grated or sliced Cheddar cheese

½ cup each, thinly sliced dried onion, green pepper, tomato and/or mushrooms

2 tablespoons oil

On trail, place veggies in a pot, add water to cover, and bring to a boil. Remove from heat, cover, and let stand until veggies are rehydrated, about 10 minutes, then drain. Sprinkle half of each tortilla with ⅛ of the cheese and ⅛ of the vegetables; fold over. Coat the bottom of the frying pan with oil. Fry the quesadillas, one or two at a time, over medium heat. Turn so that both sides are browned. Quesadillas are done when the cheese has melted. Add a little more oil to the pan for each batch.

Servings: Two servings of 4 quesadillas each.

Nutritional information: 787 calories, 36 grams fat, 84 grams carbohydrate, and 31 grams protein per serving; with crab instead of veggies, 848 calories, 37 grams fat, 77 grams carbohydrate, and 47 grams protein per serving.

With Stove and Without		
	WITH STOVE	**WITHOUT STOVE**
1 person/2 days	9 pounds	6 pounds
1 person/5 days	15 pounds	15 pounds
2 people/2 days	13 pounds	12 pounds
2 people/5 days	25 pounds	30 pounds
4 people/2 days	21 pounds	24 pounds
The middle column represents the weight of dehydrated meals plus 5 pounds of cooking equipment. The column on the right includes only the weight of the food.		

» *Aunt Dorothy's Battered Trout Almandine*

Servings: Four servings of ½ pound fish each.

Nutritional information: 427 calories, 17 grams fat, 17 grams carbohydrate, and 49 grams protein.

Jonathan Dorn, Executive Editor of Backpacker, *is a devout catch-and-releaser, but there are places—remote streams and lakes thick with fish—than can handle the occasional harvest. If you plan to fish, contact the appropriate agency to inquire about state regulations and the condition of the fishery in the area you will be visiting.*

For this recipe, use a non-stick skillet and spatula; a heat diffuser comes in handy when you have a big fish and a small skillet. This recipe will coat two 1-pound fish.

At home, combine in a gallon-size zipper-lock bag:

⅓ cup flour

⅓ cup cornmeal

½ teaspoon salt, or to taste

½ teaspoon pepper

Pinch cinnamon

3 tablespoons slivered almonds, broken into pieces

Also pack:

2 tablespoons oil

On trail, toss your cleaned catch into the bag and shake. Heat the oil over a medium-hot stove, then lay the fish flesh-side down in the pan. Fry until deeply browned, about 5 to 8 minutes for a 1-pound trout, then turn and fry just long enough to brown the skin side.

Recipe from: *Jonathan Dorn,* Backpacker

›› Side Dish: Salmonberry Compote

Serve this fruit compote with fresh fish and wild rice, and you're in for a treat. You'll need the sugar only if the freshly picked berries are tart.

At home, combine in a zipper-lock bag:

¼ cup raisins

¼ cup onion flakes

¼ cup dried apples

¼ cup dried pineapple (optional)

Pack individually:

¼ cup walnut or cashew pieces

2 sprigs fresh cilantro

1 tablespoon sugar

On trail, place raisin mixture in a pot and add:

1 cup water

Bring to a gentle boil, reduce heat, and simmer for 10 minutes.

Drain excess water, add:

1 cup fresh salmonberries or any other edible berries

If berries are tart, add the sugar. Simmer for 1 more minute to heat berries. Remove from heat and keep warm until dinner. Add nuts just before serving.

Recipe from: Nancy Pritchard, Backpacker

> **Servings:** Two servings of about 1 cup each.
>
> **Nutritional information:** 317 calories, 9 grams fat, 57 grams carbohydrate, and 5 grams protein per serving.

›› Lemon-Butter Sauce for Fish

If you prefer your fish (practically) unadorned, take some clarified butter and lemon juice and whip up this simple but delicious sauce.

At home, pack individually:

⅓ cup clarified butter

3 tablespoons lemon juice

Carry in your spice kit:

Garlic powder

On trail, combine ingredients in a small pan and add a pinch garlic and salt and pepper to taste. Simmer until the ingredients are well blended. Dribble over fish.

> **Servings:** Four servings of 2 tablespoons each.
>
> **Nutritional information:** 136 calories, 16 grams fat, 1 gram carbohydrate, and 0 grams protein per serving.

›› Beef and Berry Stew with Dumplings

If berries are in season, add 1 cup just before you add the cornstarch.

At home, combine in a zipper-lock bag:

2 tablespoons dried chopped onions

2 tablespoons dried chopped bell peppers

¼ cup dried chopped tomatoes

2 tablespoons dried chopped carrots

2 tablespoons dried chopped celery

Pinch dried basil

Pinch dried thyme

Pinch dried parsley

Pack these ingredients individually:

2 tablespoons cornstarch

6 ounces dried beef

1 cup Biscuit Mix (page 31)

On trail, rinse excess salt off dried beef. Discard salty water. Cut or tear beef slices into small pieces. To a large pot, add:

2 cups water

Add all ingredients except cornstarch. Cover and bring to a boil; reduce heat and simmer for 15 minutes. Add water as needed to cover ingredients. Mix cornstarch with a few tablespoons water and slowly add to pot.

To make dumplings, add to the Biscuit Mix bag:

⅓ cup water

Knead mixture to form dough. Cut one corner off the bag and squeeze dough in large drops onto the surface of the boiling stew. Serve when dumplings have cooked (they will be bready inside).

Recipe from: *Nancy Pritchard*, Backpacker

Servings: Two servings of about 2 cups each.

Nutritional information: 561 calories, 12 grams fat, 78 grams carbohydrate, and 37 grams protein per servings.

›› Cornbread

This recipe makes a sweet cornbread; if you wish, cut the sugar in half. If you are using the Ultralight BakePacker, make half the recipe or plan on cooking two batches.

Nutritional information: For ⅓ of recipe, 365 calories, 12 grams fat, 70 grams carbohydrate, and 11 grams protein.

At home, combine in a zipper-lock bag:

1 cup flour

⅓ cup sugar

¾ teaspoon salt, or to taste

2 teaspoons baking powder

¾ cup cornmeal

⅓ cup powdered milk

2 tablespoons powdered eggs

Also pack:

2 tablespoons oil or margarine

On trail, add oil and water to the zipper-lock bag or combine all ingredients in a bowl. Mix well.

For the Ultralight BakePacker (5½ inches in diameter): Use half the recipe and a little less than ½ cup water. Bake/boil 12 to 14 minutes; let stand several minutes. Makes one or two servings.

For the Standard BakePacker (7½ inches in diameter): Use ¾ cup water and bake/boil 20 to 25 minutes; let stand several minutes. Makes three servings.

For the Outback Oven (9 inches in diameter): Use 1 cup plus 2 tablespoons water and bake 25 minutes. Makes three servings.

›› Cornbread for the Alpine Banks Fry-Bake Pan

Servings: Two.

Nutritional information: 443 calories, 13 grams fat, 73 grams carbohydrates, and 11 grams protein per serving.

The cornbread recipe on page 137 is too much for the Banks Fry-Bake Pan, which should not be filled more than half full. Use this recipe instead.

Pack together:

⅔ cup flour

¼ cup sugar

½ teaspoon salt, or to taste

1⅓ teaspoons baking powder

½ cup cornmeal

¼ cup powdered milk

4 teaspoons powdered eggs

Pack separately:

2 teaspoons oil or margarine

On trail, combine dry mix, oil, and:

¾ cup water

Bake in greased pan for 15 to 20 minutes.

Base camp, Talkeetna Mountains, Alaska

Chapter 5

Dessert

I usually flinch at the quippy philosophies espoused on car bumper stickers, but when I spotted one that said, "Life is short, eat dessert first," I knew a great mind was at work somewhere. On the trail, dessert is what I live for.

There are good reasons, other than simply satisfying a sweet tooth, for having dessert. Desserts top off scanty dinners, filling the gastrointestinal crannies and pumping up essential calorie intake after an arduous day. Beyond that, something sweet and scrumptious is always a morale booster. With a dessert going down, bad weather doesn't seem so terrible, and your muscles aren't as sore. Desserts are also a great way to celebrate—a birthday, an anniversary, reaching the top of a peak, a change in the weather, anything.

So why do so many backcountry travelers include sweet treats only as an afterthought? And even then why is it only a handful of gorp or a candy bar? It probably can be traced back to one too many experiences with crumbly oatmeal cookies, pudding that never does pud, or no-bake creations that leave a processed taste in the mouth.

What follows is some sweet inspiration on the backcountry confections frontier. Some of the recipes are dead easy, others a tad elaborate, and there are a few you prepare at home and carry along. A full day of backpacking gives you license to eat dessert without the slightest twinge of guilt, so indulge.

—Alan Kesselheim, *Backpacker*

›› *Cheesecake Pudding*

Make this dessert the first night out to ensure your cream cheese is fresh.

At home, pack individually:

4 graham crackers, regular or chocolate, crumbled

8 ounces cream cheese

¼ cup seedless raspberry jam

⅓ cup instant lemon pudding mix

On trail, combine the cream cheese and pudding mix, then add:

1 cup water

Mix well. Spoon into individual bowls. Top each with graham cracker crumbs and 1 tablespoon raspberry jam.

Recipe from: Cheryl Manning, Backpacker

Servings: Four.

Nutritional information: 303 calories, 20 grams fat, 33 grams carbohydrate, and 4 grams protein per serving.

›› *Decadent Pudding*

Ilo Gassoway says that chocolate pudding can't be beat in this serenely splendid dish.

At home, combine in a zipper-lock bag:

1 package instant pudding

¾ cup powdered milk

Pack individually:

¼ cup crushed peanuts

⅓ cup chocolate cookies

Pack in leakproof containers:

3 ounces chocolate syrup

3 ounces Kahlua or Rumplemintz

On trail, combine the pudding mix and liqueur, then add:

2 cups water

Stir or shake well. Put crumbled cookies into individual cups, spoon on pudding, and allow pudding to set—about 15 minutes. Warm chocolate syrup, then drizzle over dessert. Sprinkle with nuts.

Recipe from: Ilo Gassoway, Backpacker

Servings: Four.

Nutritional information: 417 calories, 6 grams fat, 71 grams carbohydrate, and 10 grams protein per serving.

›› Tapioca Pudding

Tapioca is an old-fashioned dessert, one that's easy to make in the backcountry. You can go with just sugar, tapioca, and milk powder, but the vanilla adds an at-home taste.

At home, combine in a zipper-lock bag:

⅓ cup sugar

3 tablespoons quick-cooking tapioca

1 cup powdered milk

Pour into a small leakproof plastic container:

1 teaspoon vanilla or other flavoring

On trail, add tapioca mixture to:

2¾ cups water

Stir to dissolve milk. Let stand 5 minutes. Place over heat and stir for about 5 minutes, until mixture comes to a full boil. Remove from heat, stir in vanilla or other flavoring, and let cool 20 minutes.

Servings: Four servings of ¾ cup each.

Nutritional information: 150 calories, 0 fat, 31 grams carbohydrate, and 8 grams protein per serving.

›› Rice Pudding

There is a reason why Rice Pudding has long been a trail favorite: It's simple and it tastes good.

At home, combine in a zipper-lock bag:

⅔ cup instant rice

⅓ cup raisins

½ teaspoon cinnamon

3 tablespoons powdered milk

⅓ cup brown sugar, or less to taste

⅓ teaspoon dried grated lemon rind (optional)

On trail, slowly add dry mix to:

1⅓ cups boiling water

Simmer for 5 minutes or until rice is done.

Servings: Two servings of ⅔ cup each.

Nutritional information: 286 calories, 1 gram fat, 55 grams carbohydrate, and 4 grams protein per serving.

Spiced Rice Pudding

Servings: Two servings of 1 cup each.

Nutritional information: 518 calories, 1 gram fat, 126 grams carbohydrate, and 11 grams protein per serving.

To the dry mix for Rice Pudding (previous page) add:

¼ teaspoon nutmeg

¼ teaspoon ginger

Pack separately:

½ cup chopped apricots

Make pudding as on page 141, adding apricots after the dry mix. Add more water if needed.

›› *Creamy Date Pudding*

Make this recipe with dates, or experiment with other fruit, such as apricots, prunes, or crushed dried bananas. You can buy crushed graham crackers or crush your own (three graham crackers equal 1 cup). On trail, whip the topping until it forms soft peaks; use a small kitchen whisk or a backpacking whisk available from an outdoor store. If you increase the recipe, pour the ingredients into a small water bottle and shake until sufficient air has been introduced. (If you cannot eat dairy products, simply omit the powdered milk.) If 1¼ cups per person seems like too much, simply cut the whipped topping to 3 teaspoons and the powdered milk to 2 tablespoons.

Servings: Two servings of 1¼ cup each.

Nutritional information: 268 calories, 9 grams fat, 33 gram carbohydrate, and 1 grams protein per serving.

At home, combine and pack:

1 cup crushed graham crackers   ⅓ cup chopped dates

3 tablespoons chopped pecans

Combine in a separate container:

½ envelope (5 teaspoons) whipped dessert topping

3 tablespoons powdered milk

On trail, empty bag of dessert topping and powdered milk into a small water bottle and add:

¼ cup cold water

Whip with a small whisk until contents reach the consistency of whipped cream. Fold into the graham cracker mix and serve.

To dress up Creamy Date Pudding, take along one-person graham cracker pie crusts (and pack them carefully).

›› *No-Bake Berry Pie*

Strawberries, huckleberries, raspberries, blackberries, blueberries, bilberries—pick whatever is in season. If you want to impress, skip the crust ingredients and pack along two small, serving-size graham cracker crusts (look for them in the baking aisle of your supermarket) and spoon in the berries.

At home, combine in a zipper-lock bag:

½ cup sugar

2 tablespoons flour

½ teaspoon cinnamon

1½ teaspoons finely ground lemon zest, dried

1 tablespoon butter powder (optional)

Pack separately:

6 graham crackers, crumbled

On trail, pick:

2 cups berries

Combine half the berries and the sugar mixture in a medium pot and add:

2 tablespoons water

Bring to a slow boil and simmer for 10 minutes. Stir in remaining berries and remove from heat. Let cool and set up for at least 30 minutes. To serve, put graham crumbles in the bottom of each bowl and spoon the filling on top.

Recipe from: *Nancy Pritchard*, Backpacker

Hot Tips: Berrying

While gathering berries conjures images of summer idylls, there are a few precautions worth mentioning. Bears are as fond of ripe berries as you are, so keep a watchful eye out for the four-legged competition. Some varieties of nonpoisonous snakes fancy berries, as well, so watch your step. Learn to identify poison oak, sumac and ivy because they tend to enjoy the same growing conditions as the brambly berries. And beware of the stickers on wild blackberries and raspberries. Anything that good has to come with a catch.

—Nancy Prichard, *Backpacker*

›› Backcountry Fruit Tart

Using fresh fruit, of course, makes this recipe even better.

At home, combine and pack:
 ½ cup freeze-dried blueberries
 ½ cup freeze-dried strawberries

Combine and pack:
 1 package lemon pudding mix
 ¾ cup powdered milk

Pack individually:
 4 single-serving sponge cakes
 ½ cup slivered almonds

On trail, hydrate the berries by covering with hot water; set aside for 30 minutes. To pudding mix, add:
 2 cups water

Stir well and let stand 15 minutes. Top the sponge cakes first with pudding, then berries, and then a sprinkling of almonds.

Recipe from: *Maggie Stafsnes*, Backpacker

Servings: Four.

Nutritional information: 262 calories, 6 grams fat, 46 grams carbohydrate, and 8 grams protein per serving.

›› *Elegant Backcountry Layer Cake*

Servings: Eight servings of 1 piece each.

Nutritional information: 290 calories, 14 grams fat, 39 grams carbohydrates, and 3 grams protein per serving.

Canoe guide Shawn Taudvin of Into the Wild Expeditions in Portland, Maine, serves this delicious, crowd-pleasing, and delightfully easy dessert. Pound cake is relatively heavy for backpacking, but this recipe is perfect for travel by canoe. Pack it in the cooler if you're carrying one; otherwise place it in a plastic container that will keep it from getting crushed. If you are baking your own cake on trail, split it into two layers and use the same filling and topping. As for the chocolate, use chips or bar, milk or dark, according to your preference.

At home, pack individually:
  1 (11-ounce) pound cake
  4 or 5 ounces of chocolate
  ½ cup raspberry jam

On trail, slice the pound cake into four layers. Use the jam as filling between each layer. Heat the chocolate, being careful not to let it boil (it can burn), then drizzle over the cake.

›› *Sweet Torts*

These torts are barely a bake. They taste best pan fried in butter, but butter burns easily, so be careful. Margarine and oil are safer, though not quite as flavorful.

At home, combine:

3 tablespoons brown sugar   ⅓ teaspoon cinnamon

dash nutmeg

Pack individually:

2 corn or flour tortillas

1 tablespoon oil, butter, or margarine

On trail, heat oil in a frying pan at medium heat. Brown one side of a tortilla, then flip it over. Sprinkle half the sugar and spice mixture onto the tortilla, cover the pan, and heat until the tortilla is crisp and the sugar melts. Bake the other tortilla in the same way.

Recipe from: *Alan Kesselheim,* Backpacker

Servings: Two servings.
Nutritional information: 194 calories, 7 grams fat, 33 grams carbohydrate, and 2 grams protein per serving.

Not thinking about dessert when leaving Carey Lake, Ontario, Canada

›› Fresh Berry Pie

This recipe is sized for an 8- or 9-inch baking pan. If your pan is smaller, bake a few extra minutes; if it is larger, bake a few minutes less.

Servings: Four servings of ¼ pie each.

Nutritional information: 458 calories, 18 grams fat, 75 grams carbohydrate, and 8 grams protein per serving.

At home, combine:

1 cup Biscuit Mix (page 31)

¼ cup shortening

Cut shortening into the mix and store in a zipper-lock bag. Combine in another zipper-lock bag:

½ cup sugar   3 tablespoons cornstarch or flour

1 teaspoon cinnamon

Also pack:

1 tablespoon margarine

On trail, collect

3 to 4 cups berries

Add to Biscuit Mix:

2 tablespoons water (more if needed)

Stir mix until it is moist and pat into greased baking pan. Make filling by combining berries and remaining ingredients. Spread into crust. If you did not use all of the margarine to grease the pan, dot the pie with the remainder. Bake the pie hot (you're aiming for 425°) for 40 minutes. Cool somewhat and cut into quarters.

›› *Ginger Crisp*

This recipe is sized for a 7- or 8-inch pan (Alpine model Banks Fry-Bake Pan, Standard BakePacker, and Outback Oven).

At home, combine in a zipper-lock bag:

¾ cup crushed gingersnap cookies

¼ cup brown sugar

Dash salt (optional)

Pack individually:

1¼ cups dried fruit

2½ tablespoons margarine

On trail, combine fruit with:

2 cups water

Bring to boil and simmer 5 minutes or until most of the water has been absorbed. Drain. Combine cookie mixture and margarine, then spread over rehydrated fruit. Bake 15 to 20 minutes; if using the BakePacker, let stand an additional 5 minutes.

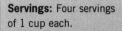

Servings: Four servings of 1 cup each.

Nutritional information: 397 calories, 11 grams fat, 106 grams carbohydrate, and 2 grams protein per serving.

Working up an appetite

›› *Apple Cobbler*

Servings: Three.

Nutritional information: 397 calories, 9 grams fat, 73 grams carbohydrate, and 6 grams protein.

Store-bought dried apples are fairly moist. You can substitute any fruit, but if you use something tart such as cherries, you may want to increase the sugar. This recipe is sized for an Outback Oven, a Standard BakePacker, and the Alpine model Banks Fry-Bake Pan.

At home, combine in a zipper-lock bag:

½ cup plus 1 tablespoon flour

¼ teaspoon salt

1 teaspoon baking powder

2 tablespoons shortening or margarine

2 teaspoons sugar

2 tablespoons powdered milk

At home, combine in another bag:

1 cup (7 ounces) dried apple ¼ cup sugar, or more to taste

½ tablespoon flour ¼ teaspoon cinnamon

On trail, combine fruit mixture with:

1¾ cups water (1⅓ cups for BakePacker)

Pour into greased pan. Place flour mixture in a bowl and add:

¼ cup water

Stir thoroughly; make into a large, thin biscuit the size of the pan; place on top of the apples. Bake for 15 to 20 minutes; with the BakePacker, allow to stand an additional 5 minutes.

›› *Apple Cobbler for Six*

This recipe is sized for an Expedition-size Banks Fry-Bake Pan and a traditional Dutch oven. Follow the instructions for Apple Cobbler, using instead:

Flour mixture:

1¾ cups flour

1 tablespoon baking powder

2 tablespoons sugar

½ teaspoon salt

⅓ cup shortening or margarine

½ cup powdered milk

Fruit mixture:

2⅔ cups (1 pound) dried apples

1½ tablespoons flour

¾ cup sugar

1 teaspoon cinnamon

On trail, add:

5⅓ cups water

Bake for 30 minutes.

Servings: Six to eight.

Nutritional information: For six, 555 calories, 12 grams fat, 79 grams carbohydrate, and 9 grams protein. For eight, 414 calories, 9 grams fat, 52 grams carbohydrate, and 7 grams protein.

Burning calories on Grand Funk Railway, Stone Mountain, N.C.

Hot Tips: Baking a Cake from a Commercial Mix

To make a cake from a supermarket mix, use one of the baking devices discussed in Hot Topic 11 and follow these directions. If you add fruit or nuts to BakePacker recipes bake 3 to 5 minutes longer, even longer on other devices. For a no-fuss "frosting," sprinkle a handful of chocolate chips on top when the cake is done; let the chips melt.

Banks Fry-Bake Alpine Pan (7 inches)

1 cup cake mix

1 tablespoon powdered eggs

$\frac{1}{2}$ cup minus 1 tablespoon water

Bake in greased pan 15 minutes or until done.

Makes three or four servings.

Banks Fry-Bake Expedition Pan (9 inches)

3 cups cake mix

3 tablespoons powdered eggs

1¼ cups plus 1 tablespoon water

Bake in greased pan 30 to 35 minutes or until done.

Makes six servings.

BakePacker Ultra-light (5½ inches)

1 cup cake mix

1 tablespoon powdered eggs

½ cup water

Bake/boil 12 minutes and let stand 3 minutes. Makes two servings.

- If you use ¾ cup cake mix, adjust the eggs and water, boil/bake 8 to 10 minutes, and let stand 3 minutes. Makes one to two servings.
- If you use 1½ cups cake mix, adjust the other ingredients, boil/bake 15 to 18 minutes, and let stand 5 minutes. Makes two to three servings.

BakePacker Standard (7½ inches)

2 cups cake mix

2 tablespoons powdered eggs

1 cup water

Boil/bake 20 minutes and let stand 5 minutes.

Makes three or four servings.

- With ¾ cup cake mix, adjust the other ingredients, boil/bake 8 to 10 minutes, and let stand 3 minutes. Makes one to two servings.
- With 1½ cups cake mix, adjust the other ingredients, boil/bake 15 to 18 minutes, and let stand 5 minutes. Makes two to three servings.
- With 3 cups cake mix, adjust the other ingredients, boil/bake 22 to 26 minutes, and let stand 5 minutes. Makes four to six servings.

Outback Oven with your own pot: Use a quick-release sheet (available as accessory) or grease pan well.

- For a 6-inch pot use:

  ¾ cup cake mix

  2 teaspoons powdered eggs

  ¼ cup plus 1 tablespoon water

  Bake for 15 minutes.

  Makes one to two servings.

- For a 7-inch pot use:

  1 cup cake mix

  1 tablespoon powdered eggs

  ½ cup minus 1 tablespoon water

  Bake 15 minutes.

  Makes two servings.

- For an 8-inch pot use:

  1½ cups cake mix

  1 tablespoon plus 1 teaspoon powdered eggs

  ½ cup plus 2 tablespoons water

Bake 15 minutes or until done.

  Makes three or four servings.

Outback Oven pan: (8 inches)

2 cups cake mix

2 tablespoons powdered eggs

¾ cup plus 1 tablespoon water

Bake 15 to 20 minutes or until done.

Makes four servings.

›› *Stuffed Dates*

These little goodies are fun to make and to eat. You can buy small packets of cream cheese at bagel-to-go shops; also check your supermarket for 3- or 4-ounce packets.

At home, pack individually:

10 to 12 pitted dates

4 (1-ounce) packages cream cheese

10 to 12 pecan halves

On trail, split open each date, squeeze a generous dollop of cream cheese into the cavity, and settle a pecan firmly atop the cream cheese.

Recipe by: *Alan Kesselheim,* BACKPACKER

> **Servings:** Two.
>
> **Nutritional information:** 297 calories, 17 grams fat, 35 grams carbohydrate, and 4 grams protein per serving.

›› *Stuffed Figs*

This recipe is adapted from one used at I Trulli, a swanky restaurant in New York City. The piquant lemon and fennel balance the sweet figs, and the almond provides a savory crunch. (You might warn diners about the nut, as they might think that it's a pit.)

At home, toast in a 350-degree oven 6 to 8 minutes:

8 almonds

Let the almonds cool. Make a hole in each of:

8 figs

Stuff each fig with an almond and pack figs in a zipper-lock bag.

Add to the bag:

1 teaspoon grated lemon rind, dried

½ teaspoon fennel seeds

On trail, place ingredients in a small pot. Add water so that figs are barely covered. Bring to a boil, then simmer for 5 minutes. Serve with broth.

> **Servings:** Two servings of 4 figs each.
>
> **Nutritional information:** 142 calories, 2 grams fat, 31 grams carbohydrates, and 1 gram protein per serving.

›› Fruit Fondue

Servings: Four servings of 5 or 6 pieces each.

Nutritional information: 367 calories, 15 grams fat, 52 grams carbohydrate, and 5 grams protein per serving.

Use dried pineapple, apricots, pears, peaches, bananas, or whatever suits your taste buds. Toothpicks (or forks, if you carry them) work well for retrieving chocolate-coated goodies from the pan. Recipes for chocolate fondue sauce call for using evaporated milk, which is double-strength milk that has not been sweetened. It does, however, have double the amount of fat, which definitely adds to the "mouth-feel" of the sauce. If you are traveling at a time when you cannot carry a can, pack ¹/₂ cup powdered milk with the chocolate and add ¹/₂ cup water on trail. If you have clarified butter or margarine on hand, add a dollop to the sauce.

At home, pack individually:

1 cup semisweet chocolate pieces

½ cup evaporated milk

20 to 24 pieces of dried fruit

On trail, place milk and chocolate in your smallest pot. Pour a few inches of water into a larger pot and settle the smaller pot inside. Place over the flame; bring the water to a boil and stir the fondue as the chocolate melts. (If you melt the fondue directly over a flame, you may scorch the chocolate, making it inedible.) Fondue is a leisurely affair, so enjoy the process.

›› Stewed Fruit

Serve Stewed Fruit over pancakes in the morning or as dessert at night. It's particularly good with a sprinkle of crumbled cookies, graham cracker crumbs, or toasted chopped nuts.

Servings: Two servings of ⅔ cup each.

Nutritional information: 116 calories, 1 gram fat, 30 grams carbohydrate, and 1 gram protein per serving.

At home, combine:

⅔ cup chopped mixed dried fruit

½ teaspoon cinnamon

2 teaspoons honey or brown sugar (optional)

On trail, add ingredients to:

1⅓ cups water

Cook 5 to 10 minutes over low heat until fruit is tender.

›› *Fruit Soup*

While canoeing across the tundra one year, we met some adventurers from Scandinavia. We traded some extra sugar and shortening for Fruit Soup, one of their staples. They ate it before dinner, as the Germans do, instead of as a dessert.

Servings: Two servings of 1 cup each.

Nutritional information: 254 calories, 2 grams fat, 66 grams carbohydrate, and 2 grams protein per serving.

At home, combine and pack:

⅔ cups chopped dried fruit

1¼ teaspoons tapioca

2 tablespoons brown sugar or honey powder

Dash cloves

¼ teaspoon cinnamon

1¼ teaspoons grated lemon rind, dried

On trail, add ingredients to:

2 cups boiling water

Simmer about 10 minutes, until fruit is tender.

Blueberries ripe for the picking

›› Apricot Soup

When trekking in the Himalayans, Kyle McCarthy watched Nazarulla Baig make this super-easy soup. Chef Baig used apricots with pits—the soup apparently has more flavor that way—but apricots are generally pitted by the time they make it into Western supermarkets.

At home, pack individually:

½ pound dried apricots

4 chapatis

On trail, combine apricots with:

4 cups water

Bring to a slow boil. Meanwhile, slice chapatis into long, thin strips. As soon as the soup acquires a strong fruity flavor (about 5 minutes or to taste), remove apricots to a large platter. Add the chapati noodles and simmer for 10 to 15 minutes. Remove the pits from the apricots and crush the fruit into small bits. Add to the soup as soon as the chapati noodles are soft. Serve immediately.

Recipe from: *Kyle McCarthy*

Servings: Four servings of 1¼+ cups each.

Nutritional information: 233 calories, 4 grams fat, 51 grams carbohydrate, and 2 grams protein per serving.

›› Side Dish: Chapatis

These flat breads from India and surrounding countries are essentially tortillas made of whole wheat flour. There should be enough liquid to hold the dough together, but the dough should not be soft.

At home or on trail, combine:

1½ cups whole wheat flour

¾ cup water

Stir, then knead at least 5 minutes until smooth. Divide into golf-ball-sized pieces and roll out into round, uniformly thick wafers. Chapatis should be as thin as possible. Cook chapatis on both sides in unoiled frying pan over a medium-hot stove. Keep the chapati moving constantly to prevent it from sticking and burning. The longer you cook it, the crisper your chapati will be.

Recipe from: *Kyle McCarthy*

Servings: Six chapatis, the number needed for Apricot Soup.

Nutritional information: 100 calories, 4 grams fat, 21 grams carbohydrate, and 1 gram protein per chapati.

LIQUID REFRESHMENTS

» *Hot and Spicy Nightcap*

This concoction is not for the faint-hearted. Give it a test run at home to see if you like it.

At home, combine in a zipper-lock bag:
½ cup powdered milk
1 tablespoon butter powder
2 teaspoons sugar or honey granules
½ teaspoon ground ginger
½ teaspoon ground cinnamon
3 pinches ground cardamom
3 pinches black pepper

On trail, place ingredients in a mug and add:
1 cup boiling water

Servings: One serving of 8 ounces (1 cup).

Nutritional information: 202 calories, 5 grams fat, 28 grams carbohydrate, and 12 grams protein per serving.

» *Orange Delight*

Mike Davis loves the sweet, satisfying taste of childhood Creamsicles so much that he invented this trail version.

At home, combine:
1 teaspoon orange-flavored instant drink mix
1 teaspoon powdered milk
2 teaspoons instant vanilla pudding mix

On trail, pour ingredients into a 16-ounce (2-cup) mug, add cold water to taste, and stir well.

Recipe from: *Mike Davis,* Backpacker

Servings: One.

Nutritional information: 52 calories, 0 grams fat, 12 grams carbohydrate, and 1 gram protein per serving.

PART 2

Hot Topics

WHAT KIND OF BACKCOUNTRY EATER ARE YOU?

When I was the backcountry chef for an outdoor website and fielded reader questions, I was often asked: "What food should I take camping?"

I consistently answered, "It depends on what kind of backcountry eater you are"—what you like and don't like, whether you enjoy the process of preparing food, how much energy you will be expending, and whether you have more time than money, or more money than time.

So, before you reach for the grocery list, complete the Backcountry Cuisine Questionnaire. You might also want to get your outdoor cohort(s) to answer it, too. There are no right or wrong answers—only honest ones—and they will help you figure out what to put in your pack.

Backcountry Cuisine Questionnaire

1. At home, what do you eat for breakfast, lunch, snacks, dinner, and dessert? What favorite foods give you a lift or make your day?

2. Are there any limitations to what you can eat? Are you a vegan or vegetarian? Do you have food allergies or food intolerances? Are there foods you just plain don't like?

3. What kind of a trail cook are you?

- Low-effort: You go for very minimal prep and cooking; you rely on oatmeal packets, energy bars, box pasta dishes, ramen noodles, and other quick-fix foods.

- Medium-effort: You don't want to spend a whole lot of time cooking, and you use some of the products listed above, but you vary breakfasts, add fruit and nuts to cereal, include a choice of items for lunch, and pack dried vegetables and tasty seasonings for dinner.

- High-effort: You are a gourmet. You use more complicated recipes, search for special ingredients, and devote time on trail to eating well. If you own a dehydrator, you are willing to dry food to enhance your meals.

4. Do you have any prerequisites for trail food? What items (say, breakfast coffee) are not negotiable? Do you prefer three meals a day, or consider lunch/snacks anything between breakfast and dinner? Do you want dessert? Every night?

5. Will this trip be laid back, of average difficulty, or extremely challenging? Will you will be backpacking, canoeing, kayaking, or winter camping? Will yours be a spring, summer, fall, or winter trip? What temperatures do you expect for both day and night?

6. How many cups of food do you want at breakfast and dinner?

Cups at breakfast: 1 1½ 2 2½

Cups at dinner: 1 1½ 2 2½ 3 3½ 4

If you have trouble answering this question, take a large bowl and fill it with cups of water until you have what you consider to be a trail-size portion, or measure how much you eat at breakfast and dinner.

Would you rate yourself as a light, medium, or hearty eater?

7. How much you are willing to spend on trail food?

- You're on a tight budget.

- You don't want to eat ramen noodles every day, but don't need to be extravagant, either.

- You like to eat well and are willing to pay for good food.

Answers

Question 1: If you have favorite meal types at home, such as Mexican, Thai, or Chinese, think about how you can incorporate them into your trail menu.

Question 2: If you don't eat meat, you'll need to get protein from another source. If you are allergic to nuts, you'll have to put something else in your gorp. If you don't like oatmeal, leave it at home; it won't taste better in the backcountry.

Question 3: It's useful to know your style. If you prefer simple, quick meals at home, you may not enjoy preparing complicated meals on trail. If you enjoy gourmet cooking at home, go ahead and plan elaborate meals for the nights you cook, but don't assume that your fellow adventurer(s) will want to do the same. If you are planning all the meals, include some quick ones for those days of adverse weather, steep mountains, or headwinds.

Question 4: Knowing your eating habits can help you plan appropriately.

Question 5: You'll burn fewer calories on a laid-back float trip with comfortable temperatures than you will on a skiing trip in the dead of winter, so you need to factor in the activity, expected temps, and weather. Remember, trips are no time to diet.

Question 6: You need both volume and calories. A bowl of nuts would give you enough calories, but it might not leave you feeling satisfied.

Question 7: As a fellow foodie Jean Spangenberg says, your body is your most important piece of equipment. If you are willing to invest in tents, raingear, and everything in between, why cut corners when it comes to food? You owe it to yourself to spend a little extra to eat well. What mouthwatering goodies would you buy if you took the money from dinner in a restaurant and dedicated it to trail food? This trip is your vacation. Enjoy yourself.

And here's the corollary. If you have gourmet tastes, are willing to pay for good food, and don't have the time or energy to prepare food, there's a world of backcountry products as diverse as wild rice soup, Greek pasta salad, pizza with pesto topping, and almond-fudge cake—all at your fingertips through the Internet. (See Appendix D.)

Toast nuts: Place nuts in a 350° oven for 8 minutes. Or, place nuts in a skillet (with a few drops of oil) over medium heat until they are lightly browned. Nuts will continue browning after they have been removed from the heat—either oven or skillet—so be careful not to overcook. And here's the voice of experience: Do not put nuts in a toaster oven and press the "toast" lever thinking that you'll rescue them in the nick of time. Just 10 seconds can make the difference between well-browned and burned.

Clarify butter: Clarified butter does not need refrigeration because the milk solids, which will spoil, are removed. To clarify butter, melt it over a low heat, remove from the heat, and let stand for a few minutes. The sediment will fall and the oil will rise. Pour off or skim the yellow oil, then strain into a container. Clarified butter allows you to have the smooth taste of butter without worrying about the ambient temperature. Some health food stores and international markets sell clarified butter, or ghee, as it is known in Indian cooking.

Cook instant rice: Add boiling water, cover, and let stand. When purchasing, read the directions to make sure that the brand you've chosen is really instant. Some "instant" brands tell you to boil the rice 1 or more minutes.

Make tomato powder: If you only need a little and you have tomato flakes or bits on hand, toss about ¼ cup of either into the blender and whir away to make 2 to 3 tablespoons rough powder.

Use herbs: Unless otherwise noted, measurements are for dry herbs.

Hot Tips: Choosing and Using Fresh Meat

- You've probably always dismissed meat as too much trouble for the trail. Steak (yes, that's right, steak!) should be frozen and, if possible, vacuum packed before you hit the trail. Wrap it in two or three layers of foil and a plastic bag to prevent leakage, and carry it in the middle of your pack to prevent thawing. A 1-pound piece feeds two and takes a full day to thaw, then remains fresh for a day or two if kept cool. If you use a stove for cooking, slice steaks thin so that they cook quicker. Use a little oil, any herbs you have, and a decent amount of chopped garlic.

- Smoked sausages come in all shapes, sizes, and flavors and are perfect with pasta, rice, or eggs. Sausages that are heavily smoked and spiced hold up best. Still, as with all meats, they should be packed frozen and eaten as soon as possible.

- Never take fresh chicken.

- Use common sense. Leave the meat at home if you're planning a desert hike in June. Likewise, stick to freeze-dried if you'll be in bear country.

—Toby Rowland-Jones, *Backpacker*

Make zest: Zest is the grated rind of oranges, lemons, or limes. To dry it, grate the rind on a fine grater, being careful to get just the colored outer coating and not the bitter inner layer. Spread the zest in a thin layer, and leave out overnight. It should dry easily, but if the humidity is high, or you are in a hurry, place the rind in a toaster oven set on warm and remove as soon as it is dry.

Use eggs: You don't want to get food poisoning in the backcountry (or anywhere for that matter). Unfortunately, fresh eggs—even when they are still in the shell—can harbor salmonella, bacteria that can make you very sick. Powdered eggs won't ever be confused with fresh in taste, but they have, at least, been pasteurized. When handling powdered eggs, keep a clean kitchen, because it is possible to reintroduce salmonella. Use only a clean spoon to remove eggs from the original package and place them in a new plastic bag. Do not touch the eggs with your hands.

Or, use one of the egg substitutes now available in cartons in the dairy section of the supermarket. If you freeze a container and then place it in the middle of your pack, insulated by clothing, the contents should remain cool until the next breakfast.

Substitute mayonnaise for oil: To avoid carrying a container of oil, use mayonnaise portion packs for frying pancakes, eggs, tortillas, and other items, says Jean Spangenberg, product development specialist at Adventure Foods. The mayo melts right back down to the oil and does not give the food a mayonnaise flavor.

Plan amounts for store-bought instant mixes: Use this chart to convert ounces and volume to rehydrated amount.			
MIX	**USE**	**ADD WATER**	**TO MAKE**
Black beans, instant (7 ounces/box)	1 cup (3⅓ ounces)	1 cup boiling	1 cup
Falafel, instant (10 ounces/box)	1 cup (almost 5 ounces)	⅔ cup cold	3 small burgers
Hummus, instant (6 ounces/box)	¾ cup (4 ounces)	⅔ cup boiling	1 cup
Refried beans, instant (7 ounces/box)	½ cup (2⅓ ounces)	½ cup boiling	1 cup

Hot Tips: Choosing and Using Tofu

- Tofu (also known as soybean curd) is a trusty trail staple. It is quick-cooking and convenient; you can even dehydrate it to save weight and space, then just add water in camp for dinner. It's also incredibly nutritious. But if it's that good for you, it has to taste bad, right? Wrong. Select the right kind, prepare it properly, and tofu is downright scrumptious.

- The easiest option is to buy baked or smoked tofu. These come sealed in plastic, so you can throw the package in your backpack and go. Look in the refrigerated section at a local natural foods store. The tofu will last unrefrigerated for a day or two, so it's best suited for short trips. Like most ready-made foods, both smoked and baked tofu cost more than raw tofu, but they cut prep time to as fast as you can slice. Hint: Slice and eat the tofu with a bagel for lunch, throw it into soup, or add it to pasta during the last few minutes of boiling.

- Raw tofu is available in several textures, from silken to extra-firm. Extra-firm contains less water and cooks faster than other textures.

- Tofu that's packed in an aseptic cardboard container (it looks like a juice box) is handy because it requires no refrigeration prior to opening and isn't as messy as the water-packed variety. However, it is not as firm as water-packed extra-firm.

- You can save time in camp by cooking raw tofu at home before your trip. Here's how: Slice a 1-pound block into cubes or slabs. Heat 1 tablespoon oil in a wok or skillet on the highest heat, then add the tofu. Flip and rotate the tofu frequently. When it is well browned, add a little more oil, 1 tablespoon finely chopped fresh garlic, and 1 tablespoon soy sauce or tamari. Cook for a few more minutes. Experiment with other flavors, such as a tablespoon of stone-ground mustard or grated ginger. Although you can carry tofu in a zipper-lock bag, a hard-sided container helps it keep its shape longer. Cooked tofu lasts a day or two unrefrigerated and is good hot or cold.

—Allison Carroll, *Backpacker*

Hot Tips: Choosing and Using Cheese

- Buy several small chunks rather than one large block. Exposure to air and contaminants makes cheese go bad, so keep cheese uncut in its original wrapping, whether plastic or wax, as long as possible.
- For cheese to be used at dinner, freeze it before putting it in your pack. The longer it stays cool, the longer it stays fresh. The cold treatment can make cheese crumbly and messy, however, so don't put cheese you want to slice at lunch in the deep freeze.
- Store cheese in a cool spot deep in your pack, not in a top or side pocket heated by the sun.
- Cool cheese when you reach camp by placing it in a cold stream or snowbank to slow spoilage. Temperature changes do not speed spoilage.
- After you've opened the original packaging, wrap the cheese tightly in double zipper-lock bags and suck out as much air as possible before sealing.
- Make sure your hands, knife, and wrapping materials are clean each time you handle the cheese.
- If you find suspicious green fuzz on hard cheese, trim the green and a half-inch layer around each spot. If soft cheese grows a green carpet, pack the cheese out to the nearest trash can, as mold toxins can penetrate the whole chunk by the time green shows on the surface.
- Molds and harmful bacteria, such as salmonella, E. coli, and Listeria, can multiply quickly and stealthily in unrefrigerated cheese, especially soft, high-moisture types like Brie or cream cheese. A piece of cheese may look and smell fine, yet still contain pathogens. To be completely safe, add cheese to the pot when other ingredients are done, then boil for 10 to 15 seconds.
- If you're planning a warm-weather trip (or if the mention of pathogens gives you the jitters), try cheese powder or freeze-dried cheese shreds. Both products will keep for more than a year and using them will reduce the weight and bulk of your food load.

—Cheryl Manning, *Backpacker*

What should you take with you for your kitchen-away-from-home? Camp cooking has changed considerably from the days of a tripod with a big pot hanging over a fire and a coffee pot next to the coals.

If you're backpacking by yourself and plan on using meals that need only boiling water, you can get away with one small pot that doubles as your bowl, a lid, a pot gripper, salt and pepper, a spoon, and a mug. If you're traveling with a companion, add a bowl (one of you can still use the pot), spoon, and mug.

At the other extreme—say a reunion canoe trip with no portages and no white water—you can take coolers, a cast-iron Dutch oven, and almost anything else you want.

If you fall somewhere in between, then you need to look carefully at your needs and what's available, then choose what's right for you.

Features to consider: A lock-in bail stabilizes the container for lifting and pouring; a domed lid can be used as a cover or saucepan. Note: The outside of the pot, blackened by fire, now absorbs heat rather than reflecting it.

What's Cooking in Cookware

Pots are made of aluminum, enamel-coated steel, steel, and titanium. Aluminum has been around for years, with good reason. It's light and sturdy, and it provides even heat. Its major drawback? Try scrubbing a pot with burned-on food, and you'll see why many aluminum pots are now being offered with nonstick coatings. The trouble with nonstick coatings, however, is that some are more durable than others, and all have to be treated with care. They require wooden or plastic utensils at the least, plus careful packing so that they don't get scratched.

Enamel cookware has also been around for eons. The enamel—usually bright blue with white speckles—is baked onto a lightweight steel core. The drawbacks are legion: Enamel is difficult to clean and can chip easily; the pots do not nest well; and the combo is heavier than aluminum or plain steel. Enamel cookware is a technology whose time has past, at least for trail use.

Stainless steel, on the other hand, has many advantages. You can use a metal spoon to stir, and wash a pot with a handful of sand when dinner is done. The hard surface of the steel cleans more easily than does plain aluminum. But because steel pots must be thin walled to make them light, the pots conduct heat a little too well, and there's more of a chance of burning whatever delicacy is held within.

Titanium, the latest darling of the camp kitchen, is lighter than steel and stronger than aluminum. A 2-liter titanium pot, lid, and pot gripper weigh in at a mere 8 ounces. The price, though, is positively steep—almost $70 for just those three items.

Lightweight stainless steel pot has swing-out handles that fold next to container.

Nonstick coating inside makes cleaning easy; black exterior increases heat absorption and fuel efficiency; lid has stand-up toggle that won't burn fingers, yet flattens for packing (MSR Blacklite).

When you are choosing cookware, go to a store and check out pots firsthand. Consider these features:

- Handles. Those who are particularly weight conscious prefer a single pot grip to built-in handles on each pot. This trail cook prefers pots with lock-in bales because they don't fail (my grip once did, and I dumped a quart of hot water in my mate's lap). Pots with swing-out, plastic-coated handles aren't ideal because they can be difficult to nest and the plastic tends to melt over an open fire.
- Silhouette. Some cooks prefer sides that round into the bottom (easier to clean) over straight sides that form a corner with the bottom.
- Outer finish. Pre-blackened pots absorb heat better. Pots used over an open fire acquire a patina of soot naturally; some companies give their pots a dark finish.
- Nestability. Ideally, all your pots and pans (and maybe your bowls, too) will nest into a tidy pile.
- Lids. Lids have many uses. Some double as saucepans and skillets. You can serve hors d'oeuvres or dessert on lids with a lip. You can

Sizing Pots

Ever tried to boil a bag of pasta in a pot the size of a soda can? Starch-city! Pots that are too small can cramp your cooking style, whereas jumbo cauldrons add unnecessary weight and bulk to your pack. The size pots you choose depends on the menu and the number of people in the group. If you cook a lot of pasta, for instance, you will need a pot that will let the noodles boil freely, rather than gum up into a knot of sodden flour. Here's a quick look at pots and sizes. One liter equals 1.06 quarts, so these recommendations remain true using either measuring system.

- 1-liter. A good choice for solo trips. Can handle a couple cups of hot chocolate or a small freeze-dried dinner for one.

- 1.5-liter. The most versatile size pot. Can handle a pot of pasta for two, or simmer the sauce for a larger group working with two stoves.
- 2-liter. This pot can hold enough water and pasta for a hearty feast for three.
- 3-liter. A must for groups of four or more. Can accommodate soup or spaghetti for up to six hungry hikers.

—Kristin Hostetter, *Backpacker*

Author's Note: Big eaters will require bigger pots. If these recommendations don't fit your needs, simply use the next larger size. Or, look at your recipes and calculate the volume of food you'll be cooking at any one time. Get a pot that size, plus one slightly larger or smaller for hot water.

My first personal eating utensils had character. The curve of my wooden bowl fit nicely into my hand and the horn spoon was warmer in the mouth than metal. Although the spoon was small, I always managed to eat my share. I drank from a neat little double-walled plastic cup. Assembled, the cup had its own insulation. Apart, it became two individual cups—quite handy when someone needed a dipper to serve water for hot drinks.

But the wooden bowl was a relatively heavy 7 ounces, and it didn't fit into the pot set. The spoon worked for me but couldn't double as a cooking spoon. I moved on to the utterly pragmatic—a recycled butter container and a metal spoon. I continued using my little red cup. The plastic bowl, I discovered, had a death-grip on grease, and when its thin walls cracked in the middle of a long canoe trip I ate off a pot lid for the duration.

Time for a new bowl, one of those plastic food-storage containers that are sold in the supermarket. I use the lid and bowl together when I want to rehydrate on trail; the lid holds in heat and keeps the contents from spilling. I have a Lexan spoon that's good for stirring a small pot and shoveling in food. And, finally, I moved on to the ubiquitous travel mug, which provides a hefty hot drink but alas, no spare dipper.

plunk the dripping coffee cone or set the gooey wooden spoon on a lid. A pot with a tight lid will heat faster and won't lose as much moisture through steam.

Check whether the lid fits the pot well (and whether it will fit after the pot has been mashed in your pack). Can you pick up the lid easily? One lid I used had a small, floppy, metal tab; I couldn't get at the tab with a pot gripper and so I had to use my bare fingers or try to pick up the lid with a bandanna.

Other Kitchen Utensils

- Large spoon, spatula, and knife. These will suffice for most situations, but if you've ever burned your fingers while trying to pour off the water from pasta, you'll agree that a strainer is immensely useful. Look for a specially designed folding strainer in the food section of any outdoor store.
- Coffee-making device. Everyone has his or her own preference. If you don't, see Hot Topic 12 for an overview of this important and sometimes contentious subject.

Iodine alone (small jar) does not kill all pathogens. Boil water or use a water filter with an iodine component.

What is your favorite bowl? Mine changed through the years. From right: wood bowl, mini-spoon, two-part plastic cup; plastic margarine container and thrift shop spoon; plastic food storage container with lid, Lexan spoon and travel mug.

- Trail baker. Imagine the fragrance of fresh-baked biscuits or cake. If you don't have to go super light, consider carrying one of the several bakers (see Hot Topic 11). Two bakers come with pans that can double as frying pans, so if you plan on frying anyway, the rest of the baker might not be much additional weight.
- Frying pan. If you use lids that are also frying pans, or carry a baker that serves as a frying pan, you're all set. Otherwise, a pan that nests with your pots is useful for hash browns, stir fries, and lots more.
- Bowls, spoons, mugs. One per person.
- One-cup measure. With a group, this bit of plastic is worth its weight. Not only can you add the right amount of water to the oatmeal, entree, or pudding, but you can dip hot water easily.
- Collapsible water carrier. It makes life in the camp kitchen easier all around.
- Compact, lightweight cutting board. If you've ever tried cutting vegetables on your knee or a pot lid, you know that a lightweight, compact cutting board can be pretty handy. Stiff polyethylene boards are inexpensive; a 9 x 6-inch board might weigh something like 10 ounces. If you have a closed-cell foam mat lurking in your closet, free up a section and cover one side with duct tape. My "board" weighs 1.5 ounces and it cost only a few cents for duct tape.
- Scrubby. For just two of you, it's enough. For a larger group, use biodegradable soap sparingly. Half a teaspoon bleach in the rinse water can cut down on the chances of sickness sweeping through the group.
- Spices. If you like to add a pinch of this and a pinch of that, take a spice kit with a range of seasonings: fresh or powdered garlic; an Italian mix of parsley, basil, oregano, rosemary, and sage; something fiery (chili pepper, hot oil, or hot sauce); cinnamon; salt; and pepper. Another approach is to pack spices with their accompanying

meals (for example, include a packet of ginger and lemongrass with Ginger Chicken), and carry just salt and pepper.

Whichever method you choose, throw away those empty film canisters; they can retain manufacturing chemicals that you surely don't want to ingest. Instead, use small, leakproof plastic containers available from outdoor stores.

• Kitchen organizer. Gearheads love these kitchen-organizer kits because there are lots of little plastic bottles, and a place for every utensil, condiment, and spice. Some kits come with mini-spatula, can opener, pot scrubber, and whisk, while others come with much more. If the idea appeals to you, go for it. The kits range from 10 or so ounces to a pound (empty, not stocked). If you are counting every ounce, just use a nylon bag for salt, pepper, spoon, matches or lighter, and any other essentials.

• Water purifier. Most backcountry water must now be purified. Bring water to a rolling boil or use water filter with an iodine component.

Deluxe Kitchen Set (for 6)*

Total weight: 4 pounds, 1 ounce
3-liter pot with lid
2-liter pot with nonstick coating (for baking) with lid
Pot gripper
1 Lexan spoon with handle shortened
1 plastic insulated mug with lid
1 plastic bowl
Pocketknife
Plastic/mesh coffee filter

Small scrubber sponge
Stuff sack
Lightweight trail baker
Fully stocked spice pouch including plastic bottles of olive oil, Tabasco; Italian seasonings; mixture of brown and white sugar; salt; pepper; curry powder; cayenne; zipper-lock bag of dried milk

* Each person is responsible for their own eating utensils; only mine are included here.

Dorcas's Kitchen

(For two to three on base camp hiking trips, sea kayaking trips, and canoe trips)

Total weight: 4 pounds, 9 ounces (add 7 ounces for bowl, mug, and spoon for third person, 3 ounces for 6-liter water carrier)

1½-liter pot with lid

2-liter pot with lid

3½-liter pot with lid

Trail baker/frying pan (can be used over stove or fire)

1-cup measure

2 plastic bowls

Stuff sack for pots

Pot gripper

Knife

Salt and pepper

2 spoons

Pot scrubber

Stuff sack for utensils, spices

2 travel mugs

Coffee filter cone

Closed-cell foam cutting board

Kristin's Kitchen

Basic Backpacking Kitchen Set (for two)

Total weight: 1 pound, 8 ounces

1.5-liter pot with lid and gripper

1 plastic bowl

2 plastic insulated mugs with lids

2 Lexan spoons with handles shortened to fit in the pot

Small scrubber sponge

Plastic/mesh coffee filter

Pocketknife

Stuff sack

1 small plastic bottle of Tabasco sauce (I don't leave home without it)

We expect a lot from camp stoves. We want them to work in all conditions, including wind, rain, and snow. We want them to be rugged, light, dependable, fuel efficient, and easy to use. We want them to boil water in a hurry and simmer without burning food. And of course we want them to be as inexpensive as possible.

Fortunately, there are several dozen models from which to choose. Unfortunately, no one stove is perfect for everyone, so you have to look at your needs and choose the one that's right for you. Consider these features:

Mountain Safety Research's Pocket Rocket, a cartridge stove

- Fuel source. There are two general categories of stoves—those that use a pressurized canister and those that use liquid fuel such as white gas. With canister stoves, you simply purchase a metal bottle that contains fuel under pressure. You attach a small burner, light the vapor, and boil your dinner. The advantage of canister stoves is that they are very easy to use; you don't have to fill the tank or pressurize the fuel with a pump. The disadvantage is that toward the end of the tank there is less pressure, so the stove does not burn as well. Also, you can't tell exactly how much fuel is left because you can't look inside the canister.

Some liquid-fuel stoves come with a built-in tank located just below the burner. Others use a special fuel bottle that is attached to the stove by a small hose. Either way, you need to fill the tank with fuel (usually white gas but sometimes automobile gas or kerosene), pump the tank to create pressure, and then light the burner. Alas, the top-choice white gas, often sold under the brand name of Coleman fuel, is available only in North America. If you are traveling abroad, you'll do better with a multi-fuel stove that can handle a variety of fuels.

Coleman's Peak 1, a tank-under stove

Airlines have always been touchy about stoves, but these days you can kiss your stove goodbye if it has an attached or attachable fuel tank. Not long ago, airport officials confiscated a stove from *Backpacker* editors. If it can happen to them, it can happen to you. Better to fly with the small burner for a canister stove and buy the canister at your destination.

If you are interested in buying a stove, talk with knowledgeable friends and sales personnel, but remember that people can develop brand loyalty that may color their advice. You may want to check the annual gear issue of *Backpacker* magazine, which gives information about these topics:

Fuel Efficiency

Customize Your Cookware

- To increase heat absorption, apply flat black stove paint (available at hardware stores) on the outside of cookware. The combination of a blackened pot and tight lid can reduce boiling times by 20 to 30 percent.
- A heat exchanger—an adjustable accordion of metal vents that clamps around pots to capture heat and channel it up the sides—saves roughly its own weight in fuel for two people cooking two hot meals a day for two days. Mountain Safety Research makes the only heat exchanger on the market and it is designed for the MSR Alpine pot.
- A wraparound windscreen reduces fuel consumption and boil times by 20 to 50 percent, depending on wind conditions. With integral tank stoves (like the Peak 1 or any blended fuel canister stove) be sure to monitor how much heat reflects down onto the fuel tank or cartridge to avoid dangerous overheating. A windscreen should fit snugly around the pot, with half an inch to an inch between the two.
- Harness heat released toward the ground and redirect it up to the pot with a heat reflector. You can make a heat reflector out of aluminum sheeting or heavy duty aluminum foil.

- Keep your stove in top operating condition. Sixty seconds spent futzing with a sputtering stove is a full minute spent not boiling water. One wasted minute x 2 meals per day x 7 days = 14 minutes wasted gas—enough for another meal.

Customize Your Cooking

How you cook is as important to fuel efficiency as what equipment you use.

- Rehydrate food as you walk. Pack a spare wide-mouth, screw-top water bottle that you can fill at breakfast or lunch with ingredients for the evening dinner. Lentils soaked during the day, for instance, need only minimal heating to cook.
- Heat only what you need.
- Use a tight lid.
- Use only as much heat as is required; don't boil when simmering will do.
- Plan meals with quick-cooking foods such as instant oatmeal, bulgur, couscous, instant rice, Oriental noodles, and vegetables that rehydrate quickly (dehydrated tomatoes, mushrooms, onions, mixed dried veggies–but not dehydrated chunk carrots, peas, corn, or potatoes).

—Jim Gorman, *Backpacker*, and the author

- Boil time. This number tells you how many minutes the stove needs to boil 1 quart of water at room temperature at sea level. Boil time is more useful as a relative number than an absolute one, because you'll rarely have the ideal conditions of the test. Instead, you may be contending with cooler temps, wind, and altitude.
- Burn time. These two numbers tell you how many minutes the stove will burn wide open at optimal conditions on a specified amount of fuel. If you add up the projected number of quarts you'll boil on a trip, you can fold in the boil time and get a general idea of how much fuel you'll need. Take extra, though, because both estimated boil time and burn time are under ideal conditions.
- Weight. Stove weight is important, but the real number to consider is the weight of the stove along with the fuel you'll need on your trips.
- Price. Canister stoves are less expensive than liquid-fuel stoves because they are less complicated and don't include a fuel tank. The fuel for canister stoves is more expensive because you cannot reuse the canister.
- Other considerations. Is the stove easy to set up and use? Does it shed pots or hold them in place? Is it easy to refuel? Is it stable? Does it have a self-cleaning jet? Is it field-repairable? Does it have a heat control device so you can simmer as well as blast? Does it work well in cold temps? Does it come with a carrying case or stuff sack and a repair kit?

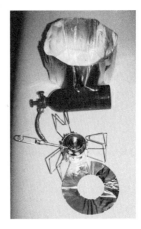

MSR's Dragonfly, which uses a fuel bottle as the tank, has a windscreen for added fuel efficiency.

Test Now, Play Later

Tucked into a campsite in the High Sierra, we pumped up the stove, put on a pot of water, and turned the setting on high. When Cashew-Ginger Chicken and Rice started bubbling, I nudged the lever to simmer. The stove kept on blasting. After I'd coaxed the meal to conclusion, my climbing partner tinkered. He managed to get it to simmer, but by then it would no longer burn hot. We left it that way, fearing that more repair might reduce it to a useless hulk of metal.

The lesson: Parts do wear out. Better to test your stove before you leave than to discover its shortcomings in the backcountry.

The inside of a pack is a hostile environment for food—it's hot, cramped, and full of hard-edged objects—so store each ingredient and meal to withstand the punishment. Here's how to get your vittles from the grocery store to the trailhead intact.

Containers

Zipper-lock bags: The genius who invented zipper-lock plastic bags has won my eternal gratitude. Before you begin packing, get an assortment of sizes from sandwich to 1-gallon size, and get the heavier-duty freezer-weight style with the write-on strip at the top. Because these bags are so strong, you can give them double-, even triple-duty by bringing them home, rinsing them, and reusing them. Generic brand bags might save you a few pennies, but if the plastic is thin and the zippers are flimsy, they aren't worth it.

Vacuum sealer: As an alternative to zipper-locks, use a vacuum sealer like the Fresh Lock II, which I purchased at a local Sears for around $40. It's effective at sealing homemade energy bars, small amounts of vinegar, even whole meals. Vacuum sealing beats zipper-locks when it comes to keeping food fresh, a decided advantage if you're packing well in advance of a trip, or if you're preparing food drops for resupplies.

Lexan bottles: Lexan is a tad more expensive than competing brands, but Lexan retains no food odor. These bottles are a good bet for olive oil, vinegar, and other strong-flavored liquids. Make sure you mark bottles with measurements on the side.

Old prescription vials: Perfect for packing special mustards and other oozy substances needed in small quantities.

Food tubes: When the weather is warm, these refillable containers do the job holding mess makers like peanut butter and cream cheese, but when it's cold the tubes split or the clip pops off. A wide-mouth, screw-top plastic bottle, such as an old peanut butter jar, is a better bet.

Cracker and bar protectors: Crackers are a treat on trail but will end up as a pile of crumbs unless you stow them in a sturdy canister such as an empty Pringles potato chip can. Several round crackers fit nicely in these cans and emerge intact. One can feeds two people for a weekend trip.

Lightweight plastic food-storage containers are useful for crackers and homemade bars. Milk containers, either cardboard or plastic, can be cleaned and lined with plastic for bars.

Duffle bag: A simple, lightweight nylon duffel bag shelters your meals from cuts and punctures within your pack and keeps food separate from your other belongings. A duffel loads and unloads more easily than a stuff sack, and it can be tied off at the handles and slung on a bear pole or in a tree.

Bear canister: In areas where bear canisters are suggested or required, ask about renting. It's an inexpensive way to safeguard your food.

Packing It Up

Start stripping: Food from the supermarket is encased in plastic and cardboard that will add bulk and weight to your pack, so strip away excess packaging and get down to the barest essentials. Or, buy as much of your trip food as possible in bulk at health food stores or other outlets.

Twist and tie: To separate two ingredients going into the same pot at different times, place the ingredient to be used second in the bag and then twist-tie off the corner. Then, add the ingredient that will be used first.

Write directions: Note name of dish and cooking directions on the bag's write-on strip or on a slip of paper tucked into every meal bag. Write legibly and make sure you can see the paper when the bag is closed. Label everything, even if you think you'll remember it.

Make meal bags: Pack every meal into its own zipper-lock bag. Preplanning, measuring, and packing complete meals consumes the better part of an evening at home, but it frees you from kitchen chores on the trail. Single bag each meal if you're using high-quality freezer bags and they're going into a nylon duffle before being packed in your backpack. Double bag meals to stave off leaks or rips if you're stuffing them directly into your pack.

Fill the food duffel: Spare yourself a lot of aggravation on long trips with a group by taking at least three duffels of different colors. Load the breakfast food in one duffel, lunch/snacks in another, and dinners in a third.

Loading your backpack: Because food is one of the heaviest and densest items you're likely to carry, it should be packed at shoulder blade level or higher in your backpack and close to your back if you'll be walking strictly on maintained trail. If you're going off trail, pack it slightly lower. If you are packing a bear canister, position it about two-thirds of the way from the bottom of the pack and closest to your back for better balance. This position also puts food in a relatively cool spot.

Cheeses and other perishable items should be tucked deep down in the pack (one-half to one-third of the way from the top) to stay cool. Snack items go in outer pockets for easy access during the day, but don't forget to include them with the rest of the food when hanging your bear bag or filling a bear canister.

—Ilo Gassoway, *Backpacker*

Of kitchen-related activities, the cooking fire has the most impact on the backcountry. Cooking fires require wood (which involves destruction of habitat), leave a scar, produce ash and partly burned wood, and can cause forest fires. Using a cookstove all but eliminates these problems. If you want to Leave No Trace (LNT), carry a cookstove and follow these other LNT guidelines:

- To minimize impact on nearby waters, set up your camp kitchen 200 feet from rivers or lakes.
- The kitchen is the social center, so place it on a durable surface that will hold up to foot traffic.
- Be a careful cook. Don't drop food onto the ground; pick up anything that you do drop.
- Eat leftovers at the next meal or carry them out; never bury them. Better still, plan carefully so you don't have unwanted leftovers.
- Instead of using soap to clean your bowl, try one of these two methods. When you've finished eating, add a few tablespoons of hot water to your bowl, swish it clean, and drink the broth; you'll get to savor every last calorie. Or, lick your bowl clean; the rules of etiquette are flexible in the backcountry. If you are carrying individual portions—say cold cereal in a zipper-lock bag—and don't mind eating out of plastic, simply add water to the bag and chow down; there's no bowl to clean.
- Wash dishes on a durable surface 200 to 300 feet from a water source and—to lessen impact on the campsite—away from the kitchen.

When to Light a Fire

Use a fire only if:

- It is legal and you have a permit when one is required.
- The danger of starting a forest fire is low.
- There is appropriate wood, that is, downed wood that is as thick as a wrist or thinner, whose removal will not change the look of the campsite.
- There is a preexisting fire scar. If there are several scars, use the one that is best situated: It's on a durable surface and not on moss, grass, or peat that could catch fire; it is in a logical place for a group to gather; it already has access trails. Dismantle the other fire circles.
- You can keep a small, controlled fire that burns as little wood as possible.
- You make sure that the fire is doused and completely out.

- Use biodegradable if you use soap at all; scrubbing well and rinsing in boiling water may suffice. Disperse soapy water on unvegetated ground.
- Use sand or snow to scour pots (but do not use sand on pots with a nonstick surface).
- Strain wash water through a small piece of screening or cheesecloth. Place the culled material in your trash bag.

Bear-bagging in Canada's Quetico Provincial Park, Ontario: Scout for the perfect site before it gets dark.

In an increasing number of national parks and wilderness areas, campsites are provided with poles for hanging food or metal bins for food storage. Ask before you go, so you'll know whether you need to take a rope, rent a bear canister, or make other provisions. When you get there, be sure to use the equipment that's available. It's there for a reason and that reason can only involve past episodes with bears or other animals.

When poles or bins have not been provided, some areas request or even require the use of specially designed plastic canisters that bears cannot open. Usually, you can rent these canisters for a nominal fee.

In areas with trees, the logical choice is to hang food, but it's not always easy to find the perfect setup, so scout early before darkness descends. Choose a location away from your kitchen, so if a bear is attracted to the food, it won't be standing in the middle of your tents. Look for a branch 8 feet or higher from the ground that's strong enough to hold your food at a distance of 4 feet from the trunk; tie your rope around a rock or other heavy object and throw the rock over the branch.

Don't Lure a Bear

Besides bacon and berry pie, there's nothing that attracts bruins quite like the aroma of fish. To protect yourself from midnight visits, follow some simple but critical rules for keeping a clean camp.

- If you've seen bears near your fishing hole or heard that they're prevalent and aggressive in the neighborhood, throw back your catch. Cooking it isn't worth the risk. You may even want to think twice about making any casts at all.
- Avoid touching your face, clothes, and any gear when cleaning and cooking fish. Clean up with premoistened towelettes (hang used ones in your bear bag), or wash your smelly hands in a pot of warm, soapy water.
- Burn the guts and carcass completely. If you can't build a fire, toss them far out into the lake, stream, or river.

- Clean your dishes and utensils in hot, soapy water. If you didn't pack soap, use sand, dirt, or ashes to scrub them, and rinse with boiling water. Don't forget to wash everything you may have touched. (Pour the rinse water through a small sieve and pack out any collected particles.) I once neglected to wipe two water bottles, and they were shredded during the night by some large-toothed animal that fancied the oil residue on the lids and sides.
- Hang all your dishes and utensils as well as any clothes stained with fish oils. In grizzly country, you may want to hang the clothes you cooked in as well.

—Jonathan Dorn, *Backpacker*

If you can't find an appropriate tree, then look for two trees about 8 feet apart that have branches at least 8 feet from the ground. String a rope between the trees, then hang your food bag using a second rope.

Whichever method you use, place all food and anything with a scent (toothpaste, hand cream, even a bandanna used in the kitchen) in the container before you hoist it and store it for the night. Take no food into the tent—no candy bars, no gorp, no midnight treat that could turn into a bruin lure.

At home, long before you set out on your trip, consider leaving sardines and other odorous snacks on the shelf.

Other Critters

If you aren't in bear country, you still need to take precautions against mice, raccoons, skunks, ringtailed cats, and other four-legged explorers. If you put all your food in one container, then place pots and pans on top, the raider will make enough noise to scare itself or wake you so you can do the scaring.

Mice are determined little creatures that are often the bane of a campsite. Hanging food in a tree safeguards it from mice as well as bears. If you are in a shelter or a hut and plan to hang your food from a beam, make this modification in your line: Tie a knot halfway between the two ends and slip on a can lid. Tie the lower end to the food and upper end to the beam; the order is food, knot, lid, beam. If a mouse runs down the cord, it cannot get around the lid to the food bag.

Catching dinner on Markham Lake, Northwest Territories: When you go to shore, keep a clean camp.

DRYING FOOD FOR THE TRAIL

Anyone with an oven can put together meals that are light, reasonably priced, simple to prepare on trail, and tailored to your tastes and appetite. All you have to do is dry "real food" and then reconstitute it at your convenience.

Just about anything can be dried, from individual ingredients (cooked beans and grains, fruits, vegetables, and meat) to whole meals (check out Southwestern Pasta, Quick Seafood Capellini, Quick Hoppin' John, and other recipes in the Dinner section). Yes, it takes time, but once you get used to whipping fruit or veggie slices into the dryer, or doubling your favorite dinner and drying half for a trip, you may find that the effort is less burdensome than you expected.

Drying isn't difficult—after all, people have been doing it in the sun for thousands of years—but it helps to follow some general guidelines:

- Choose fruits and vegetables that are at the height of their flavor. Wash, then remove bruised areas, stems, cores, and pits. Peel if you wish; skin has vitamins, but it also increases drying time.
- Slice, dice, shred, or blend, depending on the food and the desired product. Most fruits and vegetables should be dried in ¼- to ⅜-inch slices. Using a uniform thickness ensures even drying within a batch.

Anasazi granary

Drying Times

Here's how long it'll take you to drive the moisture out of some pack favorites. For foods not listed, compare with an item of comparable texture and consistency. Drying times will vary with the amount and type of food being dried, the type of dryer, the humidity, and other factors.

Fruit	Preparation	Drying Time	Consistency
Apples	Pare; core; slice ⅜" thick. Dip helps retain color.	4 to 14 hours	Leathery, pliable
Apricots	Slice in half; pit; dry in halves or quarters. Dip helps retain color.	8 to 20 hours	Leathery, pliable
Bananas	Peel; slice ⅛" to ¼" thick. Dip helps retain color.	5 to 24 hours	Crisp
Cherries	Slice in half; pit; place skin side down.	6 to 20 hours	Leathery, tacky
Peaches	Pit; slice ⅜" thick circles. Dip helps retain color.	5 to 24 hours	Leathery, pliable
Pears	Peel; remove core; cut into thin wedges. or ⅜" circles. Dip helps retain color.	5 to 24 hours	Leathery, pliable
Pineapple	Core; peel; slice ¼" to ⅜" thick.	8 to 20 hours	Leathery, sticky
Strawberries	Remove stem; slice ⅜" thick. Dip helps retain color.	5 to 24 hours	Leathery, crisp
Vegetables			
Beans, green	Cut into 1" pieces; steam blanch until almost done; cool.	4 to 14 hours	Brittle
Broccoli	Chop or cut in thin strips; steam until nearly done; cool.	5 to 15 hours	Brittle
Cabbage	Chop or cut in ⅛" strips.	4 to 12 hours	Leathery
Carrots	Slice ¼" thick; steam* until nearly done; cool.	4 to 12 hours	Dry but pliable
Carrots	Grate; steam briefly*.	2 to 4 hours	Dry but pliable
Corn	Use straight from freezer.	4 to 9 hours	Brittle
Mushrooms	Slice ⅜" thick. Lemon dip helps retain color.	3 to 10 hours	Leathery
Onions	Slice ⅜" to ¼" thick.	4 to 12 hours	Brittle
Peas	Use straight from freezer.	4 to 9 hours	Brittle
Peppers, bell	Remove seeds and membranes; slice in ⅜" strips or rings, or chop.	6 to 12 hours	Slightly pliable
Potatoes	Slice ⅛" thick or dice; steam 5 minutes; cool.	5 to 12 hours	Brittle
Tomatoes	Remove skin; slice ¼" to ⅜" thick.	4 to 16 hours	Leathery
Zucchini	Slice ⅛" thick for chips, or dice.	4 to 15 hours	Leathery

*Skip steaming if carrots are to be used in near future.

Note: Most drying times are from *The Complete Guide to Food Dehydrating,* a booklet that accompanies the Harvest Maid dehydrator.

Approximate Yield from 1 Pound Produce	
Fruit	
Apples	1.9 to 2.5 ounces
Apricots	2.5 ounces
Cherries	3.2 ounces
Peaches	1.9 to 2.5 ounces
Pears	3.2 ounces
Prunes	4.8 ounces
Vegetables	
Beans	1.9 to 2.5 ounces
Beets	1.9 to 2.5 ounces
Cabbage	1.3 ounces
Carrots	1.9 ounces
Celery	1.3 ounces
Corn	5.1 ounces
Onions	1.6 ounces
Peas	3.2 to 3.8 ounces
Potatoes	3.2 to 5.1 ounces
Spinach	1.3 ounces
Squash	1.3 ounces
Tomatoes	0.6 to 1.6 ounces

• Set your dehydrator or stove 10 degrees higher than you will eventually want it, and turn it on several minutes before you start putting in trays. These two steps help compensate for the drop in temperature that occurs when you add food. Remember to reduce the temperature in an hour or so. If you are making jerky from uncooked beef, start the temperature at 145° and keep it there.

Approximate Yield from Individual Fruits and Vegetables

The actual yield depends on the size of the produce, how thin you slice the pieces, how dry they get, and how tightly you pack them in the cup. Use these numbers as a guide.

Fruits	Preparation	Yield
Apple, medium	Sliced	7 rings; ¾ cup
Pear, medium	Sliced	5 to 7 rings
Pineapple, crushed, 20 ounces	1 cup drained, packed	1 cup loosely packed
Vegetables		
Beans, green	1 cup sliced	3 tablespoons
Carrot, medium	1 cup shredded 1 cup sliced	¼ cup Scant ½ cup
Celery, 2 ½ large stalks	1 cup chopped	1½ to 2 tablespoons
Corn	1 cup	½ cup
Cucumber, medium	Sliced	About 60 chips
Mushrooms, 7 medium	1 cup sliced	¼ cup
Onion, 1 medium	Chopped	⅓ cup
Peas, green	1 cup	Scant ½ cup
Pepper, bell, medium	1 cup chopped	2½ to 3 tablespoons
Potato, medium	1⅓ cup diced Sliced	½ cup dried 20 to 25 slices
Spinach	1 cup	½ cup packed
Tomato, medium	Sliced	8 to 12 chips
Zucchini, medium	Sliced	About 60 chips

Drying fish the Cree way, Coldwater Lake, Quebec, Canada

- Spread food on racks or sheets. Slices can touch one another but should not overlap.
- Dry herbs at 95° to 105°, vegetables at 130°, fruits at 135°, and meat, chicken, and fish at 145°. If food is dried at too high a temperature, the outside will dry but the inside will not—this is called case hardening—and the food will eventually spoil.
- Drying time varies greatly depending on the type of dryer, number of trays, thickness of slices, humidity, amount of moisture in the food, and so on. Check food after 3 or 4 hours, then check periodically. Remove samples from the dryer and let them cool for a few minutes before you test for dryness.
- Label dried food and store it in a cool, dark, dry place in moisture-proof and insect-proof containers. Glass jars and thick, heat-sealed plastic bags work best. Food stored in plastic bags should be placed in a rigid container.
- After a couple of days, check food for dryness. Any bags that show moisture should be removed. Either continue drying or, if mold has taken hold, discard.
- Because regular plastic bags allow some moisture to enter and escape, store plastic-wrapped fruit, vegetables, and meat in their own metal or glass containers. When stored together long-term, moisture will migrate from the higher-moisture foods (fruits) to the lower-moisture foods. Home-sealed boiling pouches are heavier duty, allowing foods to be stored together.
- Shelf life depends on the food and whether it was blanched or pretreated. Dried food will lose color and taste over time, especially if it has not been treated. Shelf life at 34° is at least a year for most fruits and vegetables; for broccoli it is 4 months, for tomatoes it is 8 to 12 months, and for bananas and onions it is 8 to 16 months. Shelf life at 0° is at least 2 years for everything.
- Rehydrate using 1 cup of water for every cup of vegetables and 2 cups water for every cup of fruit compote. Allow ample time for rehydration. Dense foods like peas, corn, green beans, and chunks of meat take more time than do thin slices of vegetables. Salt slows rehydration, so add it (or salty sauces) 5 minutes after starting to soak food.
- To rehydrate food slowly, cover the food with cold water and let stand; this process may take from 1½ hours to 8 hours. This length

of time works well when you are preparing food for a later meal. To rehydrate food in 30 minutes or so, start with boiling water. To rehydrate food in 5 to 20 minutes, place food in boiling water and simmer.

- Always check the densest pieces to see if they are soft. If they aren't, keep soaking or cooking. A chunk of chicken that is still dry is more like a small pebble than an edible—and you can do damage to your teeth when you chomp down.

Fruit

- Cut fruit into slices ¼- to ⅜-inch thick.
- For apricots, cherries, and prunes, simply cut in half, remove the pit, and pop the backs by turning the skin side in, leaving the flesh side exposed.
- Grapes, blueberries, and prunes have a waxy coating that must be removed before they can be dried. Dip the fruit into boiling water for 1 to 2 minutes to remove the wax, a process called "checking" the skins.
- Plums should be halved, cooked for 5 minutes, and put through a colander to remove pits and skins. Dry the flesh as fruit leather.
- Dried fruit naturally browns with age. To slow this process—and to protect vitamins—place fresh slices in a bowl with lemon juice, pineapple juice, or an ascorbic acid–citric acid bath for 2 minutes. To make the bath, stir 1½ teaspoons citric acid and the same amount of ascorbic acid into 1 quart water.
- Dry fruits at 135°.

Vegetables

- Vegetables that have a relatively long cooking time should be steam-blanched or microwaved to preserve color, stop the process of ripening, and decrease the potential for spoilage. These vegetables include beans, broccoli, carrots, cauliflower, corn, peas, and potatoes. Steaming or microwaving is preferable to boiling because vitamins are lost when produce is covered with water.
- To microwave, place veggies on the outer circle of the tray and run the oven for about three-quarters of the time it would take to cook.
- To steam-blanch, pour an inch or two of water in a large pot and place a colander with produce above it. Blanch until veggie is about three-quarters done.

Waiting for dinner to rehydrate: soup, veggies and wild rice

- Blanching softens the skin, so most blanched vegetables do not need to be peeled.
- After heat treating vegetables, cool them quickly to prevent further cooking. Drain and towel to remove moisture.
- Beets should be completely cooked before being dried.
- Mushrooms, onions, bell peppers, zucchini and other summer squash, carrots that will be used within a month or two, and tomatoes do not need to be heat treated; with celery, treatment is optional.
- Mushrooms can be dipped in lemon juice to preserve their light color.
- Removing skin on tomatoes is optional; tomatoes dry more quickly without skins.
- Dry vegetables at 130°.

Fruit and Vegetable Leathers

- Leather is made from fruit or vegetables that have been blended into a homogenous liquid.

- Most fruit is sweet enough that it does not need sugar added; tart fruits such as rhubarb do need sugar. Fresh fruit, at the peak of its ripeness or a little overripe, produces better flavor than canned fruit.
- Spaghetti sauce and salsa can be dried straight from the pan or jar. Brands with chunks of vegetables will take longer to dry than those without. Dry these leathers in a fixed amount (say, 1 cup sauce or ½ cup salsa) so that you will have useful portions when you are packing food. Label contents and note how many cups water to add. If you dehydrated a cup of sauce, add a cup of water to the sauce leather.
- Even if you have a dehydrator with solid trays, line the trays with plastic wrap; otherwise the leather will stick to the trays. When the leather is dry, you can let it cool and roll it or fold it using the same wrap.
- Dry fruit leather at 135° and vegetable leather at 130° until leather is no longer tacky (although cherry leather does remain sticky).

Cooked Beans, Grains, and Pasta
- Place canned beans in a colander, rinse well, then spread on fine mesh or solid trays. After 3 hours, check the beans every half hour; time will vary according to the size of the bean. Beans are dry when they are brittle.
- Place cooked rice or other grain on solid trays in a thin, even layer.
- Place cooked pasta on fine mesh or solid trays in a thin, even layer. Time will vary according to type and thickness of pasta.
- Dry beans, grains, and pasta at 130° until food is brittle.

To Dry or Not to Dry

Sometimes it doesn't pay to dry things yourself. It's easier and more cost-effective to buy raisins than to dry grapes, and if I need a lot of onion, I'm happy to let someone else suffer the tears.

On the other hand, it takes almost no work to pour frozen corn or peas onto a dehydrator tray and turn on the machine. (I use extra-sweet corn and tender petit peas for better flavor.) On trail, after they've been soaked, these veggies are as tasty as if I were eating them in my kitchen.

I also dry food that I can't get elsewhere, such as spaghetti sauce leather or salsa leather made from my favorite home brand. And although I can purchase almost any dried fruit at my local grocery store, the one that I like best—dried kiwi—isn't available, so if I want it, I dry it.

Meat

- Cook meat until it is done but still tender; overcooked meat becomes tough when rehydrated. Trim away fat. Cut into small chunks or slices ⅜-inch thick. Dry at 145° for 8 to 15 hours. Use a paper towel to absorb any fat that comes to the surface while drying. Meat will be dry-leathery or partly brittle when done.
- To make jerky, see JERKY in Lunch and Snacks section.
- To make dried ground beef, buy the leanest beef available and brown in a skillet. Break into fine pieces and cook until there is no pink meat remaining. Drain fat. Place on solid trays lined with paper towel (to absorb fat) and dry for 2 to 4 hours at 145°. Meat is done when it is brittle. One pound of ground beef yields about 3 cups cooked, which dries to about 1½ cups. Store in refrigerator or freezer. To make seasoned ground beef, add herbs when cooking. To make ground beef with built-in gravy, add a tablespoon or so flour when cooking, and when you later rehydrate the beef, there will be gravy.

Eggs

- Do not dry eggs. Raw eggs may contain pathogens or pick up pathogens when you dry them.

Do you have a favorite recipe that you'd like to adapt to trail fare? One option is to make the dish at home and then dehydrate it. A second is to pack all of the ingredients and then cook them later, on trail. Here are some tips for both methods:

- Cut vegetables, tofu, and meat into pieces no larger than ½-inch cubes for longer rehydration and ¼-inch slices (or thinner) for shorter rehydration.
- After you have dehydrated the ingredient or dish, add a label that says what's inside, how much water to add, and the date.
- As a rule of thumb on trail, cover the dehydrated mixture with water and—to cut cooking time—soak until individual ingredients have all rehydrated; then heat. If you are in a hurry, simply bring to a boil and simmer until done. Add water as necessary.

Dehydrating a Meal or Salad

- Choose recipes that have relatively small amounts of fat. High-fat foods are more likely to go rancid with time.
- Use eggs as an ingredient only if they will be cooked thoroughly before drying.
- Look at how recipes in this book have handled whole-meal or whole-dish dehydration—check out Fish Chowder, Tofu Vermicelli, Quick Seafood Capellini, One-Step Lasagna, Southwestern Pasta, Black Bean Chili Mac, Quick Hoppin' John, Sweet and Sour Pan-Fried Noodles, Mexican Corn Pie, Vegetable Frittata, Mexi-Bean Salad, Carrot-Pineapple Crunch, Packer's Coleslaw, Zucchini-Apple Salad, and Chinese Cabbage Salad.

Using Dehydrated Ingredients

- Become familiar with the many dehydrated items available at stores and websites. You can get anything from dehydrated tamari to sour cream powder to instant wild rice to precooked bacon.
- In general, vegetables shrink by one-fourth to one-half (see Hot Topic 8 for more details).
- If you use jerky instead of meat, cut down on the amount of salt in the recipe because jerky is salty. Also, jerky doesn't rehydrate completely, so it will be chewier than cooked meat.
- For 1 tablespoon fresh herbs, substitute ⅓ teaspoon powdered or ½ teaspoon crushed (or more to taste).
- For quicker rehydration, use precooked or fractured grains, such as bulgur or couscous.

Buying Dried and Freeze-Dried Foods

Companies generally sell dried and freeze-dried ingredients by some multiple of an ounce. Use this chart to convert from ounce to volume.

FOOD	DRY WEIGHT	MAKES
Beans, cooked, freeze-dried	1 ounce	½ cup
Beef, cooked, freeze-dried	1 ounce	⅔ cup
Bell peppers, dried	1 ounce	1 cup
Broccoli, freeze-dried	1 ounce	2 cups
Cabbage, diced, dried	1 ounce	⅞ cup
Carrots, dried	1 ounce	⅔ cup
Celery, dried	1 ounce	1¾ cups
Cheese powder	1 ounce	¼ cup
Chicken, cooked, freeze-dried	1 ounce	⅔ cup
Corn, freeze-dried	1 ounce	⅔ cup
Couscous, white	1 ounce	⅓ cup
Couscous, whole wheat	1 ounce	½ cup
Egg powder	1 ounce	2 eggs
Lentils, freeze-dried	1 ounce	½ cup
Maple syrup granules	1 ounce	3+ tablespoons
Mushrooms, dried	1 ounce	1 cup
Onions, chopped, dried	1 ounce	⅔ cup
Pasta, no-cook, no-boil	1 ounce	¾ cup
Potatoes, instant hash brown	1 ounce	⅜ cup
Rice, brown, cooked, freeze-dried	1 ounce	½ cup
Rice, wild, instant	1 ounce	½ cup
Shrimp, freeze-dried	1 ounce	½ cup
Sour cream powder	1 ounce	¼ cup
Tomato powder	1 ounce	¾ cup
Tomatoes, dried	1 ounce	1 cup
Tuna, freeze-dried	1 ounce	½ cup
Turkey, freeze-dried	1 ounce	⅔ cup
Vegetables, mixed dried and freeze-dried	1 ounce	⅔ cup

- Keep an eye on the approximate nutrient count. If there is very little protein, consider adding some to the recipe or serving a side dish with protein.

Example 1

Consider how this recipe for Buck's Couscous with Feta Cheese from *Backcountry Cooking* was converted to dry ingredients; because the feta cheese is so much better in its original form, carrying fresh feta does limit the pack life of this recipe.

Original ingredients	Backcountry ingredients
1 cup couscous	Same
⅔ cup sun-dried tomatoes	Same
½ cup fresh peas	¼ cup dried or ½ cup freeze-dried peas
1 red bell pepper	2½ to 3 tablespoons dried
⅓ cup raisins	Same
4 ounces feta cheese	Same; fresh cheese better than dried
1 clove garlic	⅛ teaspoon powdered garlic
3 slices fresh ginger	⅛ teaspoon ground ginger

Example 2

The editors at *Backpacker* converted this recipe submitted by reader Carol Donaldson. Because instant soup doesn't thicken like canned soup, they have added instant potatoes.

Original ingredients	Backcountry ingredients
1½ pounds venison	½ to ¾ pound jerky, chopped into tiny pieces
1 medium onion, chopped	⅓ cup home dried or 1½ tablespoons flakes
1 tablespoon paprika	Same
1 can (4 ounces) mushroom pieces	2 ounces (¼ cup) dried mushrooms
1½ tablespoons tomato paste	1½ teaspoons tomato powder
1 can (10½ ounces) cream of mushroom soup	two 1-cup serving packages instant cream of mushroom soup plus ½ cup instant potatoes
1½ tablespoons fresh parsley	1½ teaspoons dried parsley
1 pint sour cream	¾ cup sour cream powder
2 tablespoons butter	Skip
Salt to taste	Skip

COOKING WITH FRESH FOOD

Biting into something juicy and fresh enhances your physical and emotional well-being—never mind all the vitamins, minerals, antioxidants, and micronutrients found in fresh fruits and vegetables.

The downside to fresh food, of course, is its short shelf life. Take away refrigeration and factor in a cramped pack, and you have a recipe for an unhealthy mess. There are, however, some ways around this dilemma.

- Choose recipes and fresh foods appropriate for your trip. Here are some general rules for how long fresh foods will last in 70° weather.

  One to two days: asparagus, bananas, broccoli, cucumbers, green beans, green onions, and pit fruits such as peaches and plums.

  Three to five days: avocados, cauliflower, celery, mushrooms, pears, peppers, snap peas, zucchini, yellow summer squash, and underripe tomatoes. (When the accordion-like flesh on the underside of the mushroom cap is open, the mushrooms are mature and flavorful, but they don't travel well.)

  Six or more days: apples, cabbage, citrus fruits, garlic, onions, potatoes, and root vegetables such as carrots, beets, and turnips.

- Buy only unblemished, brightly colored fruits and vegetables that are heavy for their size. Yes, they add weight to your pack, but they're the foods bursting with flavor.
- Smaller fruits and vegetables were harvested younger and will be superior in flavor, texture, and durability. Look for dense broccoli and cauliflower heads, and select root vegetables with healthy, fresh-looking greens.
- Experiment with different varieties to find sturdy, long-lasting fruits and veggies. Braeburn, Fuji, and Granny Smith apples, for instance, withstand the rigors of packing. So do Yellow Finn, red, and Yukon Gold potatoes. Plum or Roma tomatoes, with their thick, meaty, almost dry flesh, are also excellent; salad tomatoes are a good runner-up. D'anjou pears stay firm when ripe and provide a juicy, sweet change of pace from dried fruit. The tight, strong flesh of fresh shiitake mushrooms holds up better to pack abuse than the more common white button variety. Even a small, tight head of iceberg lettuce or Romaine hearts can last up to four days in the backcountry.

Using Fresh Instead of Dried or Freeze-Dried

If the recipe calls for dried or freeze-dried, and you prefer fresh or (for meat) canned, use this substitution chart.

	FOR	SUBSTITUTE
Vegetables		
Bell peppers	1 tablespoon dried	About ⅓ fresh pepper; about ¼ to ⅓ cup chopped
Carrots	1 tablespoon dried	⅛ medium carrot
Corn	1 tablespoon freeze-dried	1 tablespoon frozen corn
Corn	1 tablespoon dried	2 tablespoons frozen corn
Mushrooms	1 tablespoon dried	2 tablespoons sliced mushrooms; 2 medium sliced
Onions	1 tablespoon dried	⅕ medium onion; about 2 tablespoons chopped
Peas	1 tablespoon freeze-dried	1 tablespoon frozen peas
Peas	1 tablespoon dried	2 tablespoons frozen peas
Tomato bits or flakes	1 tablespoon	About 3 tablespoons fresh tomato
Other Ingredients		
Butter powder	1 teaspoon	1 teaspoon clarified butter
Cheese powder	1 tablespoon	1 slice (½ ounce) cheese
Eggs, powdered	1½ or 2 tablespoons	1 egg
Garlic powder	⅛ tablespoon	1 small clove
Ginger powder	½ teaspoon	1 teaspoon minced fresh
Meat, freeze-dried	½ cup	½ cup cooked
Shortening, powdered	1 teaspoon	2 teaspoons shortening

- You can extend the pack life of some foods by buying them when they're almost ripe. Try slightly green and firm avocados, tomatoes, pears, and pit fruits. The caveat: Keep your menus flexible because when something ripens, you have to use it.
- Don't wash or cut food until you're ready to prepare the meal. Once they have been cut, many fruits and vegetables discolor. Spoilage accelerates, and flavor and nutritional values suffer.
- Remove excess greens, but leave an inch of stem to help retain moisture in root veggies like beets, carrots, and radishes.
- Experiment with the exotic. Try chayote (a light green, pear-shaped vegetable) diced and boiled with pasta; fennel (which looks like flattened celery) raw in salads or cooked into pilafs; or kohlrabi (which looks like a green turnip) shredded and added to salad.

Cooking Time

Sometimes no cooking is best. After all, you've gone to the trouble of hauling weighty produce, so why not enjoy it raw when it's at its peak of flavor? Grate beets into a salad. Eat baby carrots with lunch. Try thin-sliced turnips as a refreshing mid-afternoon snack.

Potatoes are too starchy to eat raw, and like all root vegetables, they are slow to cook. Save them for campfires, when you can prepare them slowly while you enjoy the sunset. If you're using a stove, you don't have to use all the fuel in the tank to cook potatoes. Dice, cover with water, and bring to a boil while keeping the pot covered. Remove from the heat and let the pot stand for 15 minutes; cover it with a spare layer of clothing to retain heat.

Add diced zucchini to noodles about 5 minutes before the pasta is ready, and the squash and pasta will be done at the same time. Ditto for broccoli or asparagus.

Weight

This is where most backpackers balk, because not only does fresh food weigh more than its dried or freeze-dried counterparts, but if you want to cook it, you have to carry about 25 percent more fuel. Personally, I'm willing to carry a slightly heavier pack on shorter trips if it means eating "real" food at the end of the day. I make every ounce count by going for as much flavor, texture, and substance as possible.

The only time I stick to dried or freeze-dried is in bear country. The weight and volume of fresh grub makes it tough to hang in a bear bag or cram into slender bear proof canisters.

Waste

To reduce waste, consider produce that's entirely edible, like sugar snap or snow peas, zucchini, or carrots, rather than weighty and wasteful foods like artichokes. Some people eat the entire apple, core and all, while others cook bell peppers with the seeds and membranes.

Try to use everything that you carry. The dark green portions of leeks and green onions are edible and visually enhance the meal. Thin-sliced broccoli stems add texture and zing to salads and replace water chestnuts in a stir fry. Even orange peels can be grated into pancakes, desserts, and salads for a flavorful twist.

If you buy organic, you can use the skin of apples and cucumbers without worrying about pesticides or the wax coating that is applied to retard spoilage.

How to Grow Trail Greens

If you crave green stuff on backpacking trips, there's a simple way to turn your pack into a garden: Grow sprouts. Bean sprouts add a fresh, nutty crunch to pasta, salads, and sandwiches (peanut butter, hot sauce, and sprouts on pita is one of my favorites). Time it right and you can harvest fresh greens every day of your trip. As you grow your greens, use purified water at each step.

Materials:
- Plastic 1- or 2-liter wide-mouth bottle
- 2 x 2-inch swatch of cheesecloth or mosquito netting
- Rubber band
- 1 cup dried beans or lentils, or radish or alfalfa seeds

Step 1: Wash the beans or seeds, then place them in the bottle with enough water to cover. Screw on the cap and keep the bottle in a warm, dark place until they begin sprouting, usually one to two days.

Step 2: Once the beans have sprouted, drain the water and cover the bottle opening with the cheesecloth or netting; secure with the rubber band. Now air can circulate, so the sprouts shouldn't rot. Keep the bottle in the sun; fasten it to the outside of your pack if you can.

Step 3: Twice a day, rinse the sprouts by pouring water into the bottle, shaking gently, and then draining. In about three days the sprouts are ready to eat. Rinse and drain every day, and your sprouts will last up to a week.

—Kristin Hostetter, *Backpacker*

Packing Produce

Once you're jazzed about fresh fruits and veggies, how do you avoid making fruit salad inside your pack?

- Store easily bruised or squashed items in hard-sided cooking pots and mugs. I carry lettuce and tomatoes in a 1-quart plastic container that I also use as my plate and bowl.
- Wrap items in loose clothing or bubble wrap (the latter provides entertainment if you become tent bound).
- Pack apples and oranges near the top of your pack or in side pockets, and don't overfill or cinch too tightly.
- Pack fresh foods in a paper bag or perforated plastic vegetable bag. They need to breathe, and should be kept out of the sun. A light cotton pillowcase allows ventilation, and in camp you can plop it in a stream or snowbank. Or, simply douse the pillowcase with water, wring out the excess, and let evaporation keep your food cool.

—Jasmine Star, *Backpacker*

See Jasmine's fresh-produce recipe Breakfast Potatoes.

Probably not packing produce on this trip. © David Getchell

Heading into the backcountry doesn't mean that you have to forgo biscuits, cakes, or other mouthwatering goodies. There are several ways to bake on trail, so you can choose the method best suited to your style and trips.

The BakePacker, a boil-in-a-bag type baker, is a lightweight aluminum grid that conducts heat from the stove burner through aluminum cells filled with boiling water and into a special plastic bag filled with your favorite dough or batter. This baker is well loved for good reason: It is light (8 ounces for the Standard and 4 ounces for the smaller Ultra-Light model), inexpensive, and easy to use. There is no cleanup because food is mixed and baked in an oven bag. Best of all, you cannot burn your food. I have loaned my BakePacker to friends who had little camping experience, and they came back raving about the chocolate cake that they baked. The only drawback is that with the BakePacker, you never get a browned crust. As for the heat source, a stove is better than a fire; a fire that becomes large and hot can melt the plastic, with unappetizing results. Another caveat is that you must use an oven bag (look in the aisle with plastic bags) because with a regular plastic bag, there can be a transfer of plastic molecules from the bag to your food.

The Outback Oven is a lightweight, portable convection oven that is easier to carry and use than it sounds. A reflector collar channels heat up into the oven; a diffuser plate moderates the heat from the flames; a fiberglass cloth dome holds in the heat; a small vent in the dome lets hot air circulate; and a thermometer on the lid of the baking pan provides a temperature gauge. You can purchase this oven complete with a lid and nonstick pan, or use your own pot. I've made superb pizza, cinnamon rolls, and other goodies in this baker, and my gearhead friends love its high-tech detailing. You can get a lovely, browned crust. I recommend giving the Outback Oven a test run at home to get the hang of using it. You need to monitor the thermometer closely because heat can build up and burn your goodie. Also, make sure you get all the pieces back in the bag when you're done; losing the heat diffuser would seriously affect future baking efforts. The Outback Oven is designed to be used over a camp stove. If you buy the entire outfit, you will find that the nonstick pan can be used as a frying pan, although you have to treat it gently because it's easy to scratch the surface. Even when you're not baking, the dome comes in handy; if you park it over your pot (and use a reflector collar), you'll conserve heat and therefore fuel.

The Banks Fry-Bake Pan is a modern-day equivalent of the cast-iron or cast-aluminum Dutch oven. At 10 ounces (Alpine model) and 29 ounces (Expedition model), it is far, far lighter than traditional Dutch ovens that weigh 4 to 7 pounds or more. The Fry-Bake Pan is made of tough, scratch-resistant anodized aluminum. You can use the pan as you would a Dutch oven, placing coals below and above (the lid is designed to accommodate embers).

Or, you can place the pan on a cookstove and build a small, twiggy fire on top of the lid to achieve the oven effect. Because of the heat source from above, you get a nicely browned crust. The Fry-Bake Pan serves as a frying pan and is a worthwhile investment for backpackers and paddlers alike.

The key is to monitor the heat. If you use the pan over coals, use your hand as a temperature gauge. If you can't get your hand anywhere near the coals, they are too hot, and you'll burn the bottom crust. (Of course, don't burn your hand, either.) Wait until things have cooled a bit, or put some of the coals back in the fire. Think about how hot a 350° oven feels in your kitchen—that's what you're trying to achieve.

High-Altitude Baking

As altitude goes up, leavening agents like baking powder and baking soda become more potent, making air pockets in the batter larger than they would be at lower altitudes. Larger air pockets mean thinner walls, which in turn can cause a cake to fall. A rise in altitude also increases evaporation, which makes a cake dry.

To counteract these effects, it is necessary to adjust the ingredients. Because it is impossible to reduce the amount of baking powder in a commercial mix, cake mix manufacturers direct users to add 4 tablespoons flour for every 3 cups cake mix when above 3,500 feet. (For 1 cup cake mix, add 1 tablespoon plus 1 teaspoon flour.)

Directions that come with the Outback Oven recommend adding 3 tablespoons flour and 3 tablespoons water for every 2 cups commercial cake mix when above 5,000 feet. If you are making cakes from scratch, also decrease the baking powder by ½ teaspoon at 5,000 feet, another ½ teaspoon at 7,500 feet, and so on. (For 1 cup commercial cake mix, add 1½ tablespoons flour and 1½ tablespoons water. When baking from scratch, also decrease baking powder by ¼ teaspoon at 5,000 feet and every increment of 2,500 feet thereafter.)

Because evaporation is not a problem when using the BakePacker, and the liquid/flour balance is tightly prescribed, the manufacturer simply recommends increasing the cooking time 1 minute for every 2,000 feet of gain in elevation.

Set the pan on three small rocks that will hold the pan above the coals by an inch or so, put coals on the lid, and start baking. If you are using a gas stove, use the lowest setting. If the lowest setting is too hot, buy a heat diffuser such as the one sold with the Outback Oven. (Again, it's worth experimenting at home, so you can get a heat diffuser if you need one.) Position the flame under one quarter of the pan, then shift to the next quarter, and so on to prevent burning. If you do happen to burn the bottom of your bake, be assured that the pan is amazingly easy to clean; just let it soak, and the burned-on crust comes right off.

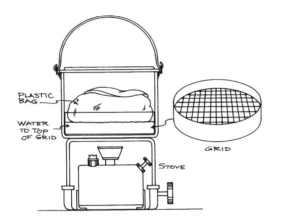

The BakePacker, which comes in two sizes, is a boil-in-a-bag type baker.

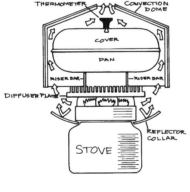

The Outback Oven, which can be used with your own nonstick pot or with a special baking pan, is a portable convection oven.

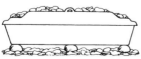

The Banks Fry-Bake Pan, which comes in two sizes, is a lightweight, scratch-proof Dutch oven that uses coals above and below or a twiggy fire above and a stove below.

It was our late-night camping routine. Last thing, right before we slid into the sleeping bags, we'd fill the three-cup perker with water and put grounds in the basket. Then we'd set the stove at the door of the tent, place the perker on top of the stove, and lay the lighter beside it. In the morning one of us would sit up, flick on the flame, and lie back down. Pretty soon the pot would be making that morning sound, the aroma of coffee would rise up and grab us by the sensory organs, and we'd be nursing that first hand-warming cup before we unzipped our sleeping bags.

Java rituals come in many guises, but they never fail to elicit intense opinions. Each method has its virtues and drawbacks.

Cowboy coffee: For years all I ever made was cowboy coffee, and it's still the best method for a big, bleary-eyed group. My formula goes like this: Fill a good-sized pot with water and add 3 to 5 handfuls of grounds right off the bat. Heat to a rolling boil, then immediately remove the pot from the flame.

If it's a leisurely morning, I let the pot quiet down on its own, covering it while I tend to chores for a few minutes. Then I take a large utensil and give the side of the pot three sharp whacks. The grounds drop immediately as if stunned.

If I'm surrounded by a ring of bloodshot eyes, I used the cold water trick: about ⅓ cup poured in right away, followed by a tap or two on the side of the pot, then pour.

Filter cones: For those occasions when I'm traveling with non-java-drinkers, I generally opt for either a plastic filter cone with a reusable silk liner, or a single-cup aluminum or plastic cone filter that has an insert for the grounds. In either case, perch the filter over the cup (or over a pot if you're using a large filter), dump grounds, and douse with boiling water. The trouble with drip filters is that they are notoriously slow.

Percolator: While my perk method is expedient, it's not the best way to brew the perfect cup of percolator coffee. By putting the coffee in at the start, you risk overcooking it and making it bitter and cloudy. Ideally, you want to bring the water to a boil in the perker, add the basket with the grounds, then perk for 6 to 8 minutes. The big drawbacks to a percolator are the weight and bulk; you're packing a contraption that isn't good for anything but a few cups of coffee.

Single-brew bags: These seem like a great idea, allowing coffee drinkers to pour boiling water over the little bag and be done with it. Trouble is, the ones I've tried yield a cup of tawny brew more closely resembling dishwater than good, strong coffee. Adding a second bag doesn't seem to help much.

Espresso maker: If you want to juice up your java, try one of the two-piece aluminum espresso makers that are available in one-cup and three-cup sizes. They brew that midget cupful in 90 seconds, once they start sputtering. The three-cup model weighs less than a pound, and the one-cup version is 7 ounces. The cup is sold separately.

—Alan S. Kesselheim, Backpacker

Top to Bottom: Coffee press for travel mug; basket (coffee sits rather than filters); cone with built-in compartment for coffee (very slow draining)

If it's just you and your buddy for a weekend, it's relatively easy to plan the food. But when you factor in more people and a longer trip, figuring out what you will need quickly gets more complicated. If you're planning to hike one of the long national trails, you will be going through towns where you pick up your resupplies and can purchase food. In small towns, though, you're at the mercy of the store, where prices are higher and choice is restricted. If you really want something other than milk and ice cream, then plan ahead.

I'll walk you though how I planned and packed for an 18-day canoe trip in northern Canada. You can use the same process for backpacking, sea kayaking, or winter camping. If what I'm describing seems like a pile of work, you're right. It takes a lot of planning and packing to feed six people for 18 days, especially when it's prohibitively expensive to charter a resupply and the nearest store is 300 miles away.

Step 1. Count the number of meals you need in each category—breakfast, lunch, and dinner. Then, recount to make sure you have it right. A mistake at home is not a big deal, but in the backcountry it could mean that you run out of food.

Step 2. Poll trip members about what kinds of foods they like. I had traveled with four out of five of my paddling partners before, so I knew likes and dislikes: hot cereal (though not oatmeal), granola, bulgur and cheese, and pancakes for breakfast; lots of variety—including three pieces of hard candy per person and a big chocolate bar—for lunch and snacks; dinners that included pasta, rice, and other grains; and a dessert every third night.

Step 3. Ask trip members how much food they want. Some people eat more than others. My goal is to provide enough food for everyone to have ample firsts and seconds if desired. People who have bigger appetites can clean up the pot. But I do want the pot to be clean; I don't want to waste food or have to deal with unwanted, cooked food.

Sometimes I ask people directly: "How much hot cereal, etc., do you want?" Other times I go with an educated guess. Because I knew the average amount we consumed at a meal to be a mere 1¼ cups each, I used that guideline in packing. Generally, ½ cup dry grain turns into 1 cup cooked. Fruit, vegetables, meat, and/or cheese rounded up the per-person serving to the desired amount.

Step 4. Draw up a preliminary plan. With this baseline information, I made a menu, giving the per-person amount, amount for six, and amount per trip (see chart page 204–205).

Step 5. Send this draft menu and a questionnaire to all group members.

I had three goals. I wanted feedback about meals, amounts, and preferences. I wanted team members to sign off on amounts; if there wasn't enough, I'd rather know during the planning process instead of in the backcountry. And, I wanted input regarding hot and cold beverages and condiments.

In the questionnaire, I asked: Are the amounts for meals and pantry items okay? Are there too many meals of one type? Do you have suggestions for other meals? Other comments? Regarding the beverages, I wanted to know how many cups coffee, caffeine tea, herbal tea, orange breakfast drink, and lunch fruit drink people wanted, as well as how much sweetener and powdered milk they used.

This was their chance to say, "Would love a little beef jerky" or "I like the boxed mac and cheese, but I can eat a whole box myself," which was exactly what people said. I made adjustments in the menu, adding jerky and increasing the pasta portion.

Preliminary Food List for an 18-Day Trip

MEAL	PER PERSON	FOR 6	MEALS/TRIP	AMT/TRIP
Breakfast: 17 meals				
Granola	1 cup	6 cups	3	18 cups
Bulgur & Cheese	½ cup	3 cups	3	9 cups
Pancakes	1 cup mix	6 cups	3	18 cups
Creamy Rice	½ cup	3 cups	3	9 cups
7-grain cereal	½ cup	3 cups	2	6 cups
Lunch: 18 meals				
Dried fruit	⅓ cup	2 cups	18	36 cups
Mixed nuts	⅓ cup	2 cups	18	36 cups
Cheese	⅙ pound	1 pound	18	18 pounds
Peanut butter	¾ T	4½ T	18	3 pounds
Jam	¾ T	4½ T	18	3 pounds
Hard candy	3 pieces	18 pieces	18	306 pieces
Bread/crackers				
Dense bread	⅙ loaf	1 loaf	4	4 loaves
Pilot crackers	3	18	4	72
Bannock mix	½ cup	3 cups	5	15 cups
Cornbread mix	½ cup	3 cups	5	15 cups
Dinner: 17 meals				
Burritos	2	6	1	1 recipe
Mac & Cheese	—	4 boxes	2	8 boxes
Fettucini	—	4 boxes	1	4 boxes
Brown Rice	½ cup	3 cups	3	18 cups
& Dried Veggies	—	⅔ cup	3	2 cups
Tortellini	—	3¾ cup	2	7½ cups
& Pesto	—	1 cup	2	2 cups

Tamale Pie	—	1	1	recipe
Spaghetti	¼ lb	1½ lb	2	3 lbs
& Sauce (to be dried)	⅔ cup	1 quart	2	2 quarts
Parmesan	—	⅔ cup	2	1⅓ cup
Pizza	—	2 pizzas	2	2 mixes
Wild Rice	⅓ cup	2 cups	2	4 cups
& Dried Veggies	—	⅔ cup	2	1⅓ cups
Red Lentil Stew	½ cup	3 cups	1	3 cups
& Dried Veggies	—	⅔ cup	1	⅔ cup
Dessert: Every third night,				
Fig Bars	—	—	2	1 package
Banana Nut Bread	—	—	1	1 mix
Fudge Brownies	—	—	2	2 mixes
Coffee Cake	—	—	1	1 mix
Hot drinks:				
Cocoa	1 packet	6 packets	17	102 packets
Other hot drinks*: coffee, tea, orange breakfast drink, lemonade, instant soup Pantry: cornmeal, flour/Biscuit Mix, margarine, cooking oil, honey, white sugar, brown sugar, lemon juice, powdered milk, spice kit, supplements (multipurpose vitamin, calcium) *Amount to be determined				

Step 6. With the general menu and amounts in mind, use recipes to pack individual meals. Lots of bags, lots of work—but this is your way to ensure that you'll have food every day of the trip.

Step 7. Get all the food in one place and pack it in a way that gives you access to what you want. I organized the food into 6-day batches. We had variety within a batch, so we could choose what appealed according to our hunger and available energy. In each sack, there were quick-prep meals as well as slow-prep meals. I also packed a pantry bag that allowed

Overall Organization

Tasty food in just the right quantity on trail means careful planning and packing at home.

If you pack the food, make sure that you include instructions. Otherwise, you'll become the camp cook.

Week #1

Breakfast sack
Granola
Creamy Rice
Bulgur & Cheese
Pancakes
7-grain cereal
Eggs, spuds, refries

Lunch sack
6 days, lunch items
Crackers, bread

3 days, lemonade
Peanut butter, 3 lb
Jam, 3⅓ lb
Some jerky, fruit roll-ups

Dinner sack
Burritos & cheese
Tortellini & Pesto
Spaghetti
Mac & Cheese
Brown Rice & Veggies
Red Lentil Stew

Dessert sack
Fig Bars
Banana Nut Bread

Pantry
Biscuit Mix, 4 cups
Cornmeal, 3 cups
Margarine, 3½ cups
Oil, 2 cups
Honey, 1 pound

Week #2

Breakfast sack
Granola
Creamy Rice
Bulgur & Cheese
Pancakes
7-grain cereal
Eggs, spuds, refries

Lunch sack
6 days, lunch items
Leftover crackers/bread
2 bags Biscuit Mix
1 bag cornbread mix
3 days, lemonade
Leftover from Week 1
Leftover from Week 1
Leftover from Week 1

Dinner sack
Pizza
Tortellini & Pesto
Spaghetti
Fettucini
Brown Rice & Veggies
Wild Rice & Veggies

Dessert sack
Fudge Brownies
Coffee Cake

Biscuit Mix, 4 cups
Leftover
Leftover
Leftover
Leftover

Week #3

Breakfast sack
Granola
Creamy Rice
Bulgur & Cheese
Pancakes
7-grain cereal

Lunch sack
6 days, lunch items
—
4 bags Biscuit Mix
2 bags cornbread mix
3 days, lemonade
Leftover from Week 2
Leftover from Week 2
Leftover from Week 2

Dinner sack
Tamale Pie
Holiday Dinner
Spaghetti
Mac & Cheese
Curried Brown Rice
—

Dessert sack
Fudge Brownies
—

Leftover
Leftover
Leftover
Leftover
Leftover

White sugar, 3 cups	Leftover	Leftover
Brown sugar, 1 pound	Leftover	Leftover
Maple syrup, 1 quart	Leftover	Leftover
Lemon juice, ½ cup	Leftover	Leftover
Powdered milk, 4 cups	Powdered milk, 4 cups	Powdered milk, 3 cups

Beverage bag*   **Beverage bag***   **Beverage bag***

Spices

Salt, pepper, tamari, ginger, curry, cinnamon, Italian herbs, garlic

Supplements

Daily vitamins, calcium

*coffee, tea, soup, breakfast orange drink

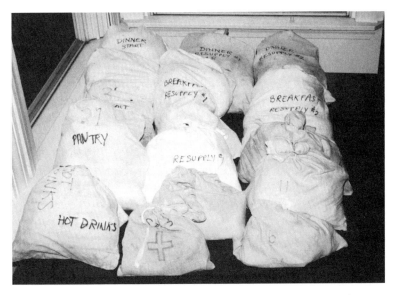

Organize food any way you want, but make sure you know where everything is and can get to it when you need it.

people to be creative if the spirit moved. (We had marvelous cinnamon rolls one rest day, thanks to the extra Biscuit Mix and some leftover nuts and raisins.)

We ate our way through the bag marked Week 1, then broke into Week 2, and cleaned out Week 3 by the end of the trip. If you are backpacking, you can use resupplies to limit how much food you carry, and you'll need to organize the food differently so that pack weights are equitable among group members as the days pass.

Step 8. Unless you want to be the camp cook, make sure that each meal has complete directions, and put a copy of the food organization plan in each food pack.

If everything is perfectly clear, then you won't have to answer questions when you'd rather be exploring, photographing, or catching some zzzzzz's. Making a list of who has what is particularly important when backpacking, when "Who has the—" is the most common food question.

Step 9. On the trip or immediately after you get home, write on an extra copy of the menu what worked and what didn't. Too much or too little food at certain meals? Favorite meals? Least favorite meals? Write it down—you won't remember—so next trip you're halfway there in the planning division.

Just the girls on the Harricanaw River, Quebec

In our at-home lives, food is everywhere we turn—in the refrigerator, in our lunch bags, at take-out and fast food restaurants, at the corner market. On trail, with the exception perhaps of berries and fish, we have only the food we take with us. There's no convenience store around the corner in case we get the munchies for something not in the pack. The obvious challenge is how to pack enough calories to get you through each day. The hidden challenge is how to pack calories from the appropriate sources (and with sufficient flavor) to get you through each day happily. We get calories from three sources: carbohydrates, protein, and fats, so let's start with carbos.

Carbohydrates. Carbohydrates are the mainstay of our diet because they supply calories in a quickly usable form. When you eat carbohydrates, they are promptly broken down into glucose that fuels muscles. Muscles and the liver store extra glucose in the form of glycogen and release the glycogen when you need it. Nutritionists recommend getting 60 to 65 percent of our calories from carbos; there are 4 calories per gram (113 calories per ounce).

There are two types of carbohydrates: simple, such as the sugars in fruits and sweeteners; and complex, such as the starches in grains, pasta, bread, and beans. Simple carbos are burned very quickly, while complex carbos provide energy for one to two hours. Sugar does not contain vitamins and minerals that your body needs, but fruits and complex carbohydrates do. It follows, then, that candy bars are a poor way of getting energy (they have calories, but they are otherwise empty) while fruits and especially complex carbos are better sources.

Protein. The body uses protein to rebuild body tissue; protein also serves as a catalyst for metabolic functions. If there is extra protein, the body burns it for energy. The body cannot use a full day's worth at one time, so protein intake must be spread over the course of a day. Protein provides only 4 calories per gram (113 calories per ounce). Nutritionists recommend getting 15 percent of a day's calories from protein.

Fats. Fats are a concentrated source of calories. There are 9 calories in each gram fat (255 calories per ounce). Fats release energy over three to four hours and are particularly important in long-term strenuous activity and in cold weather. They also supply fat-soluble vitamins. Although fats should contribute only 20 to 25 percent of the calories at home (compared to the 35 to 40 percent that is common in the American diet), some authorities suggest that strenuous outdoor activities and activities done in cold-weather conditions merit an increase in the percentage as long as a minimum for carbohydrates and proteins is met.

Calories per Day

So how many calories will you need each day in the backcountry? It depends on your size and weight, the activity at hand, and the temperature (both day and night). The National Outdoor Leadership School (NOLS), which has provided food for thousands of students in its programs, uses this simple guide:

Going for the Glycogen

For a sustained, moderate-intensity exercise like backpacking, some fats and protein are necessary for normal body functions, a pleasantly full feeling, and, in the case of fat, as a concentrated fuel source. However, too many calories from either or both can leave you feeling sluggish. "Protein and fat take longer to digest than carbohydrates—three to four hours versus one to two hours—so some of your blood supply is shunted toward the stomach instead of taking oxygen to the legs," says Jacqueline Berning. Berning teaches biology at the University of Colorado in Boulder and wrote *The Diet and Nutrition Guide for Peak Performance*.

Also, protein and fat aren't the fuels of choice for hard-working muscles, which are hungry for the glycogen your body manufactures from carbohydrates. According to Kris Clark, director of sports nutrition at Penn State University's Center for Sports Medicine, each of us stores between 1600 and 1800 calories' worth of glycogen in muscle tissue and the liver. Without replenishment in the form of simple and complex carbohydrates, that supply will quickly disappear as you continue to exercise, and you'll become exhausted.

As glycogen levels head toward empty, your body begins tapping its nearly inexhaustible store of fat as a fuel source (even skinny hikers have an immense supply). Here again, carbohydrates are vital. "Without high-firing carbohydrates, fat doesn't burn effectively," says Clark.

Hikers who view a lengthy trip as a great opportunity for dropping a few pounds of unwanted fat may be in for a cruel surprise. If you starve yourself of calories, especially calories from carbohydrates, your body will fuel the burning of released fat by converting the amino acids found in muscle tissue into glucose. It's a very inefficient and costly process that can tip your body fat/muscle balance in the wrong direction. "You may end up losing weight, but it'll be a whopping load of water and lean tissue," says Berning.

—Jim Gorman, *Backpacker*

- For normal backpacking, ski touring, and paddling: 2500 to 3000 calories/day
- For strenuous activities, including winter camping: 3000 to 3700 calories/day
- For extreme mountaineering: 3700 to 4500 calories/day

If you want to be more exact, check out the Nutrition Analysis Tool (http://www.nat.uiuc.edu/) that the Food Science and Human Nutrition Department at the University of Illinois provides as a public service. In the Energy Calculator section, the program asks you to enter weight, height, and age, then choose levels of activity in a 24-hour period. The calculator is both very easy to use and very useful.

According to the calculator, for a day that includes 8 hours sleep, 8 hours light activity, 4 hours moderate exercise, and 4 hours heavy exercise, a 30-year old female who is:
- 100 pounds and 60 inches tall will use about 2500 calories;
- 120 pounds and 60 inches tall, about 3000 calories; and
- 150 pounds and 68 inches tall, about 3500 calories.

A 30-year old male who is:
- 150 pounds and 69 inches tall will use about 4000 calories;
- 180 pounds and 72 inches tall, about 4800 calories; and
- 200 pounds and 72 inches tall, about 5300 calories.

If you just want to know the number of calories you will expend in an hour of a particular activity, check the Calorie Burn Calculator (internetfitness.com). A 120-pound person, for example, will use about

Consuming glycogen in Crystal Rapids on the Colorado River

Time for a snack in the Talkeetna Mountains, Alaska

350 calories per hour hiking, 460 calories cross-country skiing or snowshoeing, and 290 calories whitewater kayaking.

Crunching the Numbers

So do you have to haul out a calculator and add up every calorie from all of the carbohydrate, protein, and fat that you put in your pack? Only if you want to. NOLS uses a simple system slightly modified from the rule of thumb that says take 2 pounds per person per day:

- for an average outdoor day: 1½ to 2 pounds food;
- for heavier workdays: 2 to 2¼ pounds food;
- for extreme mountaineering: 2¼ to 2½ pounds food.

These pounds represent a combination of some grocery-store foods and some dried foods. Diligent use of dried and freeze-dried food, say NOLS food planners, might cut weight by 20 to 25 percent.

The other option is to become acquainted with calorie sources and keep a general eye on the ratios. Recipes in this book provide nutritional information, and packaged foods are required to provide these numbers as well. The University of Illinois's Nutrition Analysis Tool has a program

The 60/15/25 Percent Ratio			
It can be helpful to add up the numbers on a sample day or two in order to become more familiar with the system. Over time, you can develop an eye for balancing fat-rich, carbohydrate-rich, and protein-rich foods. These target amounts can help you get started.			
	25% FATS	**60% CARBOHYDRATES**	**15% PROTEIN**
3000 calories	750 calories (83 grams)	1800 calories (450 grams)	450 calories (113 grams)
3500 calories	875 calories (97 grams)	2100 calories (525 grams)	525 calories (131 grams)
4000 calories	1000 calories (111 grams)	2400 calories (600 grams)	600 calories (150 grams)
4500 calories	1125 calories (125 grams)	2700 calories (675 grams)	675 calories (169 grams)

in which you can learn how many calories and how many grams fat, carbohydrate, and protein are in a recipe that you enter. This part of the site is not as easy to use but is worth exploring if you have a particular interest in the topic. You can also get information from the U.S. Department of Agriculture Nutrient Database (www.nal.usda.gov/fnic). If you'd rather consult a book, Jean Pennington's *Bowes & Church's Food Values of Portions Commonly Used* (17th edition) is the most user-friendly.

No Calories but Still Important

Vitamins and Minerals. Various vitamins and minerals are essential for the body to function properly. Adequate amounts can be obtained through a balanced diet. On long trips, when fresh fruits and vegetables are not as plentiful, a combination vitamin and mineral tablet may be the easiest way to ensure getting enough of these essential nutrients.

Water. Don't forget to drink plenty of water, the amount of which depends on your size and the day's activities. If you are not taking regular pit stops; if your urine is yellow and smells concentrated; or if you feel tired, have a headache, feel nauseous, or have muscle cramps, drink water immediately and increase your overall intake of liquids.

Sweet, Salt, and Fat?

According to Dr. Richard Mattes, a professor of foods and nutrition at Perdue University, fat may carry a flavor all its own. Just as the mouth can differentiate salt and sweet, it may be able to taste fat. Of course, trail cooks and trail eaters have always known that fat feels good in the mouth.

It's challenge enough to provide tasty, nutritionally balanced food on a backcountry trip, but it's an even greater challenge if you don't eat dairy or red meat. Protein is the main problem.

Protein Complementarity

Protein is composed of building blocks called amino acids. There are 22 amino acids, 8 of which the body cannot manufacture. These essential amino acids must be obtained through food. The body needs these building blocks in specific ratios: 3 units of A must be present with 2 units of B, 4.3 units of C, and so on. Meat and dairy products most closely duplicate the protein pattern that humans need. Your body can use:

- more than 94 percent of the protein in eggs;
- more than 80 percent of the protein in milk;
- more than 80 percent of the protein in fish;
- 70 to 75 percent of the protein in cheese;
- 65 to 70 percent of the protein in meat and poultry.

The extra building blocks cannot be stored for future needs, so they are burned for energy.

Grains, legumes, nuts, and seeds also contain protein, though they are each deficient in one or more of the essential amino acids. You body can use only 42 percent of the protein in peanut butter, for example, and 30 percent of the protein in lentils.

If you drink a glass of milk when you eat half a cup of rice, the milk will supply the missing building blocks in the rice and increase its usable protein by almost a third. This principle holds true for other foods as well. By matching the amino acid strengths and weaknesses of various foods, you can use complementary relationships to increase the overall amount of usable protein.

For those who eat dairy products, it's fairly easy to complement grains. If you add 3 tablespoons powdered milk or 3 tablespoons grated cheese to 1 cup cooked grain or 2 cups flour, you'll gain an extra gram or 2 of protein. Over the course of a weekend the amount is relatively small, but over the course of a long trip, the grams add up. Many complements—such as cereal and milk, pasta and cheese—are already paired in the American diet.

Beans show a much greater gain. For each 1 cup cooked beans, lentils, or peas, the addition of ¼ cup powdered egg, 6 tablespoons grated cheese, or ⅓ cup powdered milk yields an extra 4 or 5 grams protein.

Non-Dairy Complements

½ cup rice : 3 tablespoons beans, split peas, or lentils

½ cup rice : 1 tablespoon soy grits

½ cup rice : ⅜ cup bulgur and ⅓ cup soy grits

½ cup rice : 1½ tablespoon sesame or sunflower butter

½ cup bulgur : 2 scant tablespoons beans

½ cup bulgur and 2 tablespoons soy grits

½ cup bulgur 1 tablespoon soy grits : 2 tablespoons sesame seeds

½ cup wheat flour : 1 tablespoon soy grits

½ cup wheat flour : 1 tablespoon peanut butter

¾ cup peanuts : ¼ cup soybeans and ½ cup sesame seeds

¾ cup peanuts : 1 cup sesame or sunflower seeds

1 cup cornmeal : ¼ cup beans

⅓ cup beans : ½ cup sesame seeds

Note: Beans, rice, soy grits, and bulgur are given as cooked portions.

Equivalent Quantities

Use this chart to substitute one form of food for another.

½ cup soybeans	=	½ cup soy grits
	=	1 scant cup soy flour
	=	17 ounces tofu
⅓ cup powdered milk	=	1 cup liquid milk
	=	⅓ cup grated cheese (packed)
	=	1 ounce cheese
2 tablespoons peanut butter	=	¼ cup peanuts
1 cup whole wheat flour	=	¾ cup bulgur
	=	½ cup wheat berries
	=	1 cup rolled grain
	=	5 slices commercial bread
	=	1 cup pasta (uncooked)
½ cup sesame seeds	=	¼ cup sesame butter
1 cup cornmeal	=	6 to 7 corn tortillas

If you don't eat dairy products, then you have to work harder at matching foods. Certain combinations of grains, beans, and seeds produce extra usable protein. Simply by adding a tablespoon of soy grits to each half cup of rice, or 2 tablespoons soy grits to each half cup of bulgur, you will increase the amount of protein available to you.

Nutritional Yeast

At 55 to 60 percent protein by weight, nutritional yeast—also called brewer's yeast—can add welcome protein to the backcountry diet. Two heaping tablespoons contain 110 calories, less than 1 gram of fat, 8 grams carbohydrate, and whopping 17 to 18 grams protein. Nutritional yeast also contains hefty amounts of the B vitamins and iron.

You can drink nutritional yeast that has been dissolved in a glass of water, use it in one-pot grain and bean meals, or add it to sauces. It does have its own flavor, which some describe as "cheeselike" and others say is unique.

Nutritional yeast is entirely different from baker's yeast, which is used as a leavening in breads. You can't substitute one for the other. Nutritional yeast can be found in health food stores and some supermarkets. Be prepared for sticker shock, though, as it is expensive.

Snacks with Non-Milk, Non-Red-Meat Sources of Protein		
Almond butter	2 tablespoons	4 grams protein
Cashew butter	2 tablespoons	6 grams protein
Egg, hard-boiled	1 large	6 grams protein
Hummus, instant	2 tablespoons (powder)	3 grams protein
Peanut butter	2 tablespoons	8 grams protein
Soy nuts	¼ cup	8 grams protein
Tofu jerky	4 slices	7 grams protein
Tuna	2 ounces (about ¼ cup)	13 grams protein

If you have diabetes, can you engage in outdoor activities in the backcountry? In a word, yes. "With proper education and within the context of healthy eating, a person with diabetes can eat anything a non-diabetic eats," says Karen Chalmers, Director of Nutrition Services at Joslin Diabetes Center in Boston. The fat/carbohydrate/protein percentages that apply to the general population of hardworking backpackers also apply to diabetic hikers. Maintain those ratios in the 20 percent/50 percent/30 percent range, and you should get the energy you need. But that's not quite the end of the story.

While diabetes experts agree that there is no such thing as a "diabetic diet," there are guidelines to help the insulin-impaired maintain healthy blood sugar levels when engaging in backpacking, paddling, or other activities:

- First, and most important, find a registered dietitian who can help you develop a diet that suits your weight, insulin requirements, and activity level. Menu planning for diabetics must be individualized. Only you and your health-care professionals can determine what will work best. If your hiking partner is a diabetic, ask him or her to plan the menu or take your menu to a dietitian.

- Ration carbohydrates throughout the day so your blood sugar doesn't spike too high—or, even more important, drop too low—at any one time.

- Always carry a low-fat, high-carbohydrate snack for quickly treating low blood sugar. A bag with a couple handfuls of raisins is ideal.

- Don't focus so much on carbos that you ignore fats, protein, and total calories. A medium banana and a chocolate bar both contain about 30 grams of carbohydrates, for example, but the chocolate also packs 15 grams of fat. Maintaining a healthy weight is critical to controlling diabetes.

- Bulk up on fiber. A recent study published in the *New England Journal of Medicine* suggests that people with Type II (adult onset) diabetes can lower their blood sugar significantly by increasing the amount of soluble fiber in their diets. The most effective foods in the study included oat and rice bran, apples, dried peas and beans, barley, fruits, and vegetables. Just make sure you introduce fiber gradually and drink plenty of water to keep things moving through your system.

• Finally, remember to test your blood sugar frequently both during and after your activity, because extended or intensive exercise can lower your blood sugar for hours after you've taken off your boots in the evening.

—Michele Morris, *Backpacker*
See Michele's recipes for Wheat Bagel
with Mushroom Omelette.

FOR PEOPLE WITH FOOD ALLERGIES OR FOOD INTOLERANCE

Food allergy reactions vary by the person. Some people experience annoying chronic ailments like nervous jags, fatigue, heart palpitations, brain fog, canker sores, eczema, jumpy stomach, congested or runny nose, headaches, tension, and nausea. Others suffer show-stopping symptoms like migraine headaches, severe depression, panic attacks, and difficulty breathing. The most allergenic foods are almonds, walnuts, and other tree nuts, peanuts, shellfish, fish, eggs, and milk.

While more than a quarter of American adults suspect they have a food allergy, the fact is that only about 1 percent are truly allergic. It's more likely that they have food intolerance, which tends to show up through digestive and intestinal problems. Of course, other medical complications could be behind any of the aforementioned symptoms, and only your doctor can say for sure.

If it sounds as though I know a bit too much about food allergies, that's because I learned about them the hard way. Two years ago my doctor pronounced me allergic to just about every staple in the American diet.

Hold the Milk, Please

For lactose-intolerant folks like me, cheese is a double-edged sword. We love the taste but our bodies can't handle it because we don't produce the enzymes needed to digest milk sugar. Sure, we can take over-the-counter lactase supplements to help reduce symptoms (abdominal cramps, bloating, and diarrhea), but I'd just as soon not tempt the gastric gods when I'm miles from modern plumbing. So what's a fat-craving outdoor adventurer to do if string cheese, Cheddar on a bagel, and mac 'n' cheese are off the menu? Try these substitutes.

Instead of . . .	Try . . .
Cheddar and salami on a bagel	Soy cheese* or instant hummus on a bagel
Alfredo sauce on pasta	Pasta tossed with olive oil and bacon bits or toasted pine nuts
Monterey Jack on quesadillas	Tortillas with grilled onion and portobello mushrooms
Cheesy tuna, rice, and peas	Tuna, rice, and peas with mayo and a pinch of flour

*Many soy cheeses are made with casein, which is not lactose but is a dairy product.

—Stern Dixon, BACKPACKER

Try Stern's Ersatz Eggs and Cheese.

Once the initial shock wore off, I faced the task of feeding myself on a daily basis without triggering an allergic reaction. It was difficult. Supermarkets and restaurants were suddenly like minefields. Then there was the even more important matter of how I was going to fuel my body on six-day backpacking trips.

I couldn't take chances with the mystery ingredients in somebody else's campstove creations. That's when I decided to become chief camp chef within my circle of outdoor friends.

It took a lot of experimenting and more than a few culinary disasters, but I managed to build a repertoire of trail recipes that gets a thumbs up from allergic and allergy-free backpackers alike. All of my recipes are free of milk, corn, wheat, egg, and citrus. If you're allergic or intolerant to nuts, shellfish, or soy, then simply omit that ingredient from the recipe.

Shopping for some of the offbeat ingredients in these trail recipes isn't as hard as it might seem. If you live in a metropolitan area, specialty food stores should carry the ingredients you need. Or check out your local health food stores, foreign food outlets such as Asian markets, and farmer's/gourmet food markets. Mail-order suppliers are another good source.

—Carol Steinberg

See Carol's recipes for Teff Pancakes with Applesauce; Hot Buckwheat Cereal with Bananas, Nuts, and Honey; Curried Chicken and Barley; Hearty Miso Soup with Shrimp; and Chickpea Fritters.

Appendices

Appendix A: Conversion Tables

Volume

1 teaspoon = ⅓ tablespoon = ⅙ fluid ounce
3 teaspoons = 1 tablespoon = ½ fluid ounce
2 tablespoons = ⅛ cup = 1 fluid ounce
4 tablespoons = ¼ cup = 2 fluid ounces
5⅓ tablespoons = ⅓ cup = 2⅔ fluid ounces
8 tablespoons = ½ cup = 4 fluid ounces
10⅔ tablespoons = ⅔ cup = 5⅓ fluid ounces
12 tablespoons = ¾ cup = 6 fluid ounces
14 tablespoons = ⅞ cup = 7 fluid ounces
16 tablespoons = 1 cup = 8 fluid ounces
2 cups = 1 pint
2 pints = 1 quart
4 quarts = 1 gallon

Weight

1 gram = 0.35 ounces
1 ounce = 28.4 grams
16 ounces = 1 pound = 454 grams

Volume of Containers

Spoon, dessert = 1 teaspoon
Spoon, Lexan = 1 tablespoon
Spice container lid = 1½ teaspoons
Bowl, small plastic storage = 2 cups
Bowl, large plastic storage = 3 cups
Travel mug, medium = 1½ cups
Travel mug, large = 2½ cups

Enlarging Recipes						
ORIGINAL AMOUNT	**X 1½**	**X 2**	**X 3**	**X 4**	**X 5**	**X 6**
pinch (less than 1/32 t)	1½ pinches	2 pinches	3 pinches	⅛ t	more than ⅛ t	almost ¼ t
1/16 teaspoon	less than ⅛ t	⅛ t	more than ⅛ t	¼ t	more than ¼ t	less than ½ t
⅛ teaspoon	more than ⅛ t	¼ t	more than ¼ t	½ t	more than ½ t	¾ t
¼ teaspoon	⅜ t	½ t	¾ t	1 t	1¼ t	1 ½ t
½ teaspoon	¾ t	1 t	1½ t	2 t	2½ t	1 T
¾ teaspoon	1⅛ t	1½ t	2¼ t	1 T	1 T + ¾ t	1 T + 1½ t
1 teaspoon	1½ t	2 t	1 T	1 T + 1 t	1 T + 2 t	3 T
1½ teaspoons	2¼ t	1 T	1 T + 1½ t	2 T	2 T + 1½ t	3 T
2 teaspoons	1 T	1 T + 1 t	2 T	2 T + 2 t	3 T + 1 t	¼ c
1 tablespoon (3 teaspoons)	1 T + 1½ t	2 T	3 T	¼ c	about ⅓ c	¼ c + 2 T
1½ tablespoons	2¼ T	3 T	¼ c + ½ T	¼ c + 2 T	½ c - ½ T	½ c + 1 T
2 tablespoons	3 T	¼ c	¼ c + 2 T	½ c	½ c + 2 T	¾ c
3 tablespoons	¼ c + ½ T	¼ c + 2 T	½ c + 1 T	¾ c	1 c - 1 T	1 c +2 T
¼ cup (4 tablespoons)	¼ c + 2 T	½ c	¾ cup	1 c	1¼ c	1½ c
⅓ cup (5⅓ tablespoons)	about ½ c	⅔ c	1 c	1⅓ c	1⅔ c	2 c
½ cup	¾ c	1 c	1½ c	2 c	2½ c	3 c
¾ cup	1 c + 2 T	1½ c	2¼ c	3 c	3¾ c	4½ c
1 cup	1½ c	2 c	3 c	4 c	5 c	6 c

Converting Pounds to Cups

These foods are often sold by the pound. Here's how to convert to cups, uncooked.

Almonds	1 pound	3⅓ cups
Apples, dried, packed	1 pound	4 to 5 cups
Apricots, dried, loosely packed	1 pound	3½ to 4 cups
Barley	1 pound	2½ cups
Beans, dry (small, such as navy)	1 pound	2⅓ cups
Beans, dry (large, such as kidney)	1 pound	2½ to 2¾ cups
Beans, black, instant	1 pound	4¾ cups
Beans, refried, instant	1 pound	3½ cups
Biscuit Mix	1 pound	4 cups
Bulgur	1 pound	2½ cups
Cashews	1 pound	3⅓ cups
Cheese, Cheddar, grated	1 pound	4 to 5⅓ cups
Cheese, Parmesan, grated	1 pound	5⅓ cups
Cheese, powdered	1 pound	4 cups
Chili mix	1 pound	3¾ cups
Chocolate chips	1 pound	2⅔ cups
Cocoa mix, commercial	1 pound	6 cups
Cocoa mix, homemade	1 pound	4½ to 5
Coconut	1 pound	5 to 6 cups
Cornmeal	1 pound	3¼ cups
Couscous	1 pound	2⅔ cups
Dates, dried, pitted, loosely packed	1 pound	2½ cups
Eggs, powdered	1 pound	4 cups
Falafel, instant, powdered	1 pound	3¼ cups
Farina (creamed wheat)	1 pound	3 cups
Flour, unsifted	1 pound	3½ cups
Fruit drink powder, with sugar	1 pound	3 cups
Gemelli (a type of pasta)	1 pound	4½ cups
Honey	1 pound	1⅓ cups
Honey granules	1 pound	2⅔ cups
Hummus, instant	1 pound	4 cups
Kasha	1 pound	3⅓ cups

Lentils, dry	1 pound	2⅔ cups
Macaroni elbows	1 pound	4 cups
Macaroni, instant	1 pound	8 cups
Margarine	1 pound	2 cups
Milk, powdered	1 pound	6 cups
Millet	1 pound	2½ cups
Molasses	1 pound	1⅓ cups
Molasses granules	1 pound	2⅔ cups
Noodles, egg	1 pound	7 to 9 cups
Nut butters	1 pound	1⅔ cups
Oatmeal	1 pound	5 cups
Oil	1 pound	2¼ cups
Onion flakes	1 pound	5½ cups
Peaches, dried, loosely packed	1 pound	3 cups
Peanut butter	1 pound	1⅔ cups
Peanuts	1 pound	3½ cups
Peas, split, dry	1 pound	2¼ cups
Pecans	1 pound	3½ cups
Popcorn	1 pound	2¼ cups
Potato flakes	1 pound	8 to 10½ cups
Prunes	1 pound	2½ to 3 cups
Raisins	1 pound	2¾ to 3 cups
Rice, brown	1 pound	2⅔ cups
Rice, creamed	1 pound	2½ cups
Rice, instant	1 pound	5 cups
Rice, wild, quick	1 pound	4 cups
Rotini (pasta spirals)	1 pound	6 cups
Rye flakes	1 pound	5 cups
Sesame seeds	1 pound	3¼ cups
Sour cream powder	1 pound	4 cups
Sugar, granulated	1 pound	2⅓ cups
Sugar, brown, packed	1 pound	2½ to 3 cups
Sunflower seeds	1 pound	3½ cups
Tahini	1 pound	1⅔ cups
Tortellini	1 pound	4 cups
Vegetables, mixed, dried	1 pound	6 cups
Walnuts	1 pound	3½ cups
Wheat germ	1 pound	4 cups

Converting Ounces to Cups

These products are often sold by ounces. Use this chart to convert to cups.

	Dry weight	Cups
Butter powder	2 ounces	⅔ cup
Buttermilk powder	2 ounces	½ cup
Cheese powder	2 ounces	⅔ cup
Shortening, powdered vegetable	2 ounces	¼ cup plus 2 teaspoons
Tomato flakes	2 ounces	1⅓ cups
Tomato powder	2 ounces	⅓ cup

Appendix B: Nutritive Values

All values have been rounded to the nearest whole number.
*May vary according to brand
Abbreviations: t = teaspoon; T = tablespoon; c = cup; oz = ounce(s);
pkt = packet

FOOD	AMOUNT	CALORIES	FAT (GRAMS)	CARBOHYDRATE (GRAMS)	PROTEIN (GRAMS)
Almond, butter	1 T	101	9	3	2
Almond, paste	2 T	133	7	14	3
Almonds, sliced	1 T	32	3	1	1
Almonds, sliced	⅓ c	170	15	5	7
Apples, dried	5 rings	84	0	20	1
Apples, dried	¼ c	120	0	28	1
Applesauce (from jar)*	1 c	100	0	26	0
Apricots	4 small	77	0	18	0
Apricots	¼ c	110	0	26	0
Bacon, cooked	3½ slices	70	5	0	5
Bacon-flavored bits	1 T	20	1	1	2
Bacon bits, lowfat	1 t	10	1	0	1
Bacon bits, lowfat	1 T	30	1	0	3
Bagel, cinnamon-raisin	1	336	3	65	12
Banana chips, sweetened	¼ c	180	15	9	5
Beans, black, powdered	⅓ c	160	2	29	10
Beans, black, cooked	¼ c	57	0	10	4
Beans, kidney, cooked	¼ c	56	0	10	4
Beans, navy, cooked	¼ c	65	0	12	4
Beans, instant refried	1 T powder	23	0	6	2

FOOD	AMOUNT	CALORIES	FAT (GRAMS)	CARBOHYDRATE (GRAMS)	PROTEIN (GRAMS)
Beans, instant refried	¼ c powder	90	0	23	8
Beans, instant refried	⅓ c powder	120	1	30	11
Beans, instant refried	½ c powder	180	1	45	17
Beans, instant refried	1 c powder	360	2	90	33
Beef, freeze-dried	½ oz	60	2	0	11
Beef, ground, cooked/dried	1 T	10	1	0	1
Beef, ground, uncooked	1 lb	1086	74	0	129
Biscuit mix, commercial	1 c (4 oz)	480	16	74	8
Biscuit Mix, from recipe	2⅓ c	756	16	93	18
Blackberries, fresh	1 c	74	1	18	1
Blueberries, raw	1 c	82	1	21	1
Bouillon	1 t/1 cube	5	1	0	0
Bulgur, uncooked	¼ c	150	0	33	4
Bulgur, uncooked	⅓ c	200	0	44	5
Bulgur, uncooked	½ c	300	0	66	8
Bulgur, uncooked	1 c	600	0	132	16
Butter	1 T	108	12	0	0
Butter powder	1 t	16	2	0	0
Butter powder	1 T	48	5	1	0
Buttermilk powder	1 T	40	2	3	1
Cabbage, dry	2 T	8	0	2	0
Cabbage, raw	½ c shredded	8	0	2	0
Cake mix, yellow*	1 c (¼ pkg)	540	12	108	6
Carrots, dried	1 T	4	0	1	0
Carrots, raw	1 medium	31	0	7	1

FOOD	AMOUNT	CALORIES	FAT (GRAMS)	CARBOHYDRATE (GRAMS)	PROTEIN (GRAMS)
Cashew butter	1 T	167	8	5	3
Cashews	1 T	49	2	3	4
Cashews	½ c	393	32	21	12
Cashews	1 c	785	64	41	24
Celery	1 medium stalk/ 2 t dry	6	0	2	0
Cheese, Cheddar	1 cubic inch (1 oz)	115	7	1	9
Cheese, Cheddar, powdered	1 T	38	2	2	3
Cheese, cream	1 T (½ oz)	50	5	1	1
Cheese, feta	1 oz	80	6	0	5
Cheese, Parmesan	1 T	38	2	0	3
Cheese, string (mozzarella)	1 piece (1 oz)	80	6	0	7
Cheese, Swiss	1 oz	95	7	1	7
Cherries, dried	¼ c	140	0	31	3
Chicken, canned	⅓ c	75	1	0	15
Chicken, canned	1 can (10 oz)	404	10	0	76
Chicken, freeze-dried	⅓ c	60	2	0	13
Chickpea flour (besan)	1 c	339	6	53	21
Chilies, green	8 T (4.5 oz)	5	0	1	0
Chips, corn	6 chips	130	6	19	2
Chocolate chips	1 T	80	4	10	0
Chocolate chips	1 c	1280	64	160	0
Coconut, dry/sweetened	1 T	29	4	3	0
Coconut, flaked	¼ c	140	12	4	2

FOOD	AMOUNT	CALORIES	FAT (GRAMS)	CARBOHYDRATE (GRAMS)	PROTEIN (GRAMS)
Coconut cream powder	1 T	99	10	2	1
Coconut ginger soup mix	1 envelope	60	4	8	0
Corn chips	1 oz	153	9	17	2
Corn, freeze-dried	1 T	10	0	2	0
Corn, freeze-dried	¼ c	40	1	9	2
Corn, freeze-dried	½ c	80	1	17	3
Corn, frozen	½ c	67	0	17	3
Cornmeal	1 T	30	0	7	1
Cornmeal	¼ c	117	1	27	3
Couscous	¼ c	165	1	35	6
Couscous	⅓ c	220	1	46	8
Couscous	1 c	660	3	138	24
Crabmeat	½ c	68	0	2	14
Crabmeat	1 c (6 oz)	135	0	3	27
Cracker, graham	2 crackers (⅔ c crushed)	66	2	111	1
Cranberries, dried	1 T	26	0	7	0
Cranberries, dried	⅓ c	130	0	33	0
Cranberries, raw	1 c	46	0	12	0
Dates	¼ c	130	0	31	1
Dates	5 to 6	120	0	31	1
Eggs, powdered	1½ to 2 T (1 egg)	62	4	0	5
Fig	1 medium	37	0	10	0
Flour, white	1 T	26	0	6	1
Flour, white	¼ c	105	0	22	3

FOOD	AMOUNT	CALORIES	FAT (GRAMS)	CARBOHYDRATE (GRAMS)	PROTEIN (GRAMS)
Flour, white	1 c	420	1	88	12
Flour, whole wheat	1 c	400	16	85	2
Flour, tapioca	1 c	482	0	118	0
Flour, teff	1 c	455	3	103	12
Fruit, mixed dried	¼ c	150	1	39	1
Fruit, tropical, mixed dried	¼ c	100	0	23	1
Garlic	1 clove	4	0	3	1
Ginger, candied	1 T	13	0	4	0
Ginger, candied	¼ c	54	0	14	0
Gravy, brown	1 T powder	20	1	3	0
Gravy, brown	½ pkt (2 T)	40	1	6	0
Gravy, brown	1 pkt (makes 1 c)	80	2	12	0
Grits, instant	1 T	17	0	4	0
Grits, instant	1 pkt (6 T)	100	0	22	2
Ham, lean	½ c (½ can)	113	8	0	11
Hash browns, dried	¼ c	65	0	15	2
Hash browns, dried	⅓ c	87	0	20	2
Hash browns, dried	½ c	130	0	30	3
Hash browns, dried	1 c	260	0	60	6
Honey	1 T	65	0	17	0
Hummus, powdered	1 T	30	1	5	2
Hummus, powdered	2 T	60	2	9	3
Hummus, powdered	¼ c	120	4	18	6
Hummus, powdered	½ c	240	8	32	12
Hummus, powdered	1 c	480	16	64	24

FOOD	AMOUNT	CALORIES	FAT (GRAMS)	CARBOHYDRATE (GRAMS)	PROTEIN (GRAMS)
Jam, raspberry	1 T	40	0	10	0
Jerky, commercial	7 oz	70	1	3	13
Linguini, uncooked	4 oz	420	2	82	14
Macaroni, uncooked	½ c (2 oz)	210	8	42	1
Mango, dried	¼ c	32	0	9	0
Margarine	1 T	100	12	0	0
Marshmallows	4 large	100	0	25	1
Mayonnaise	1 T	100	11	0	0
Milk, evaporated	½ c (4 oz)	169	10	13	9
Milk, powdered	1 T	15	0	2	2
Milk, powdered	¼ c	60	0	9	6
Milk, powdered	⅓ c	80	0	12	8
Milk, powdered	½ c	120	0	18	12
Mincemeat, condensed	¼ c	400	1	76	0
Mussels, smoked	1 (1.65-oz) tin	90	5	3	9
Mushrooms, dried	1 T	8	0	2	0
Mushrooms, dried shiitake	⅓ c (4 mushrooms)	44	0	11	1
Noodles, Chinese	¼ c	100	0	23	3
Noodles, Chinese	⅓ c	133	0	30	3
Noodles, Chinese	½ c	200	0	45	5
Noodles, Chinese	1 c	400	0	90	10
Oatmeal, instant	½ c	140	3	26	5
Oil, vegetable	1 t	42	5	0	0
Oil, vegetable	1 T	125	14	0	0
Oil, vegetable	¼ c	500	52	0	0

FOOD	AMOUNT	CALORIES	FAT (GRAMS)	CARBOHYDRATE (GRAMS)	PROTEIN (GRAMS)
Onion, dried	1 t	4	0	1	0
Onion, dried	1 T	11	0	3	0
Onion, dried	¼ c	45	0	12	1
Onion, raw chopped	½ c	27	0	6	1
Orange	1	65	0	16	1
Orange, powdered	1 T	38	0	10	0
Orange, powdered drink	1 T	50	0	12	0
Orzo, uncooked	½ c	316	1	64	10
Oysters, smoked	1 (3-oz) tin	170	9	10	12
Pasta, shells, uncooked	½ c	210	1	41	7
Peaches, dried	1 half	31	0	8	1
Peaches, dried	¼ c	110	0	25	2
Peanut butter	1 T	95	8	4	4
Peanuts, dry roasted	½ c	354	29	12	21
Pears, dried	1 half	46	0	12	0
Pears, dried	¼ c	110	0	26	0
Peas, freeze-dried	1 T	10	0	2	1
Peas, freeze-dried	¼ c	40	0	7	3
Peas, freeze-dried	½ c	80	0	14	5
Pecans	1 T	36	4	1	0
Pecans	⅓ c	190	19	5	2
Penne, uncooked	¾ c (2 oz)	200	1	40	7
Pepper, green, raw	1	29	0	6	1
Peppers, green, dried	1 T	9	0	2	0
Peppers, green, raw	½ c	12	0	3	0

FOOD	AMOUNT	CALORIES	FAT (GRAMS)	CARBOHYDRATE (GRAMS)	PROTEIN (GRAMS)
Pesto, fresh	¼ c	144	21	2	6
Pesto, packet	2 t	15	0	2	0
Pie crust, graham cracker	1 (3½-inch) crust	120	6	15	1
Pineapple, canned	½ c	60	0	15	0
Pineapple, dried	½ c	119	0	30	0
Pineapple, dried at home	½ c loose	60	0	15	0
Pine nuts	¼ c (1 oz)	190	17	2	7
Pistachios, shelled	¼ c	190	14	9	6
Pita bread	1 (8" diameter)	120	1	23	5
Poppy seeds	1 T	45	4	2	2
Potato with skin, cooked	1	220	0	51	5
Potatoes, instant mashed	¼ c	53	0	13	2
Potatoes, instant mashed	⅓ c	70	0	17	2
Potatoes, instant mashed	1 c	210	0	51	6
Pudding, instant chocolate	3 T	100	1	25	0
Pudding, instant coconut	2 T	100	2	21	0
Pudding, instant vanilla	2 T	90	1	23	0
Quinoa, uncooked	¼	159	2	28	5
Raisins	1 T	33	0	8	0
Raisins	¼ c	130	0	31	1
Raspberries, fresh	1 c	61	1	14	1
Rice, brown, uncooked	½ c	232	1	50	5
Rice, creamed	5 T	200	4	46	0
Rice, long-grained, uncooked	½ c	170	0	38	4

FOOD	AMOUNT	CALORIES	FAT (GRAMS)	CARBOHYDRATE (GRAMS)	PROTEIN (GRAMS)
Rice, uncooked, instant*	½ c	150	1	33	4
Rice, uncooked, instant*	1 c	300	2	66	8
Salsa	2 T	10	0	2	0
Sardines, in oil	1 tin (3.75 oz)	210	16	0	16
Sesame seeds	3 T	161	14	7	5
Sesame sticks	¼ c	160	11	13	3
Shortening	1 t	35	4	0	0
Shortening	1 T	93	10	0	0
Shortening, powdered	1 t	31	3	0	0
Shrimp	¼ c	45	0	0	10
Sour cream powder	1 T	35	3	1	1
Sour cream powder	¼ c	140	12	4	5
Soy nuts	⅓ c	140	7	9	11
Spaghetti, uncooked	4 oz	420	2	84	15
Spaghetti sauce*	½ c	60	2	9	2
Strawberries, fresh	1 c	45	1	11	1
Stuffing, cornbread	1 c	221	3	43	5
Sugar, brown	1 t	17	0	4	0
Sugar, brown	1 T	51	0	13	0
Sugar, granulated	1 t	13	0	4	0
Sugar, granulated	1 T	40	0	11	0
Textured vegetable protein	½ c	120	0	14	23
Tofu, fresh	16 oz	371	19	5	37
Tomato, fresh	1	24	0	5	1
Tomato bits, dried	1 T	6	0	1	0

FOOD	AMOUNT	CALORIES	FAT (GRAMS)	CARBOHYDRATE (GRAMS)	PROTEIN (GRAMS)
Tomato bits, dried	2½ T	15	0	3	1
Tomatoes, dried	5 pieces	55	1	10	3
Tomato powder	1 t	20	0	5	0
Tomato powder	1 T	60	0	15	0
Tortellini, cheese, dry	⅔ c	240	8	32	8
Tortilla, corn	1	67	1	13	2
Tortilla, flour	1 (7½ inch)	150	4	25	4
Tuna, from foil package	about ¼ c (2 oz)	60	1	0	13
Turkey, canned	½ c (½ can)	157	10	0	16
Turkey, cooked	3.5 oz	170	5	0	29
Turkey, freeze-dried	½ oz (makes ⅓ c)	240	7	34	11
Vegetable mix, dried*	¼ c	24	0	7	0
Vegetable mix, dried*	½ c	47	0	14	1
Vegetable mix, dried*	1 c	94	0	28	3
Walnuts	1 T	49	5	2	2
Walnuts	¼ c	197	18	7	6
Walnuts	½ c	394	38	14	13
Wheat germ	1 t	8	0	1	1
Wheat germ	1 T	25	1	3	2
Wheat germ	1 c	400	12	48	36
Whipped topping*	1 envelope	240	8	16	0

Appendix C: Ingredients

The variety of ingredients for outdoor cooking is truly impressive. Whereas campers a hundred years ago took flour, lard, sugar, rolled oats, dried fruit, rice, potatoes, bacon, condensed milk, tea, coffee, and similar staples, we now have access to items as intriguing as coconut cream powder, freeze-dried corn, sun-dried tomatoes, and tamari powder. (Some ingredients not called for in the recipes are listed here to show the wide variety of available ingredients.)

Grains and Grain Products

Bulgur is wheat that has been cracked, steamed, and dried. Commonly used in Middle Eastern dishes, it has come into its own in the United States as a convenience food in the form of wheat pilaf. Bulgur is available in three sizes—largest for pilaf, midsized for cereal, and smallest for tabouli. Buy the smallest grain for quick cooking and use the midsized and large grain in recipes that call for simmering or overnight soaking.

Couscous is wheat or millet that has been cracked, steamed, and dried. It is usually white, though several companies market brown (whole wheat) couscous. This versatile food comes to us from North Africa, where it is a staple. Its small size allows it to rehydrate quickly with the addition of boiling water, or more slowly with the addition of cold water.

Instant grits are grits (granular pieces of hulled corn from which the germ has been removed) that have been cooked and dried. They are about the same size as grains of couscous. Instant grits are sold packaged in individual portions (use two per person) or in a box with a pour spout.

Oat flakes or rolled oats are oats that have undergone processing that includes removing the hull, rolling the groats, then steaming and drying the resulting flakes. Thin oat flakes cook faster than thick ones.

Quick oats are oats that need to be simmered in water for 1 minute to make oatmeal.

Instant oats, available in boxes or single-serving packages, require only the addition of boiling water to make oatmeal.

Instant rice, or one-minute rice, is a common ingredient in backcountry food bags. Add boiling water, let the rice stand 10 minutes, and you have a cup of rice. Instant rice is available in white and brown forms.

Freeze-dried brown rice retains some texture when reconstituted. It works in no-cook dishes and can be rehydrated between breakfast and lunch for a cold salad.

Basmati rice is used regularly in Indian food. If you are willing to take along rice that needs to be cooked, then this is a good choice because it requires only 10 to 15 minutes of simmering, rather than the 25 to 40 minutes required for some other types of rice.

Freeze-dried or quick-cooking wild rice—sure, it's expensive, but wild rice has a great nutty flavor that's even better on trail. For freeze-dried rice, all you need to do is add boiling water. For the quick-cook kind, cook about 7 minutes (or according to package directions).

Creamed rice, which is generally used as a hot cereal, is white rice that has been granulated.

Pasta and Noodles

Chinese (instant ramen) noodles have been precooked and dried. This ingredient has become a mainstay of outdoor adventurers. Most meal-sized packages of ramen noodles come with a seasoning packet that is heavy on salt and monosodium glutamate (MSG). Even if you do not have to restrict your salt intake or are not allergic to MSG, you may want to use only part of the packet. As an alternative, look for Chinese noodles (or curly Japanese noodles) without seasoning packets in the Asian food section of your grocery store. One ounce equals about ½ cup.

Pasta is usually made from wheat, although increasingly other ingredients—including spinach, tomato, mushrooms, chilies, lemon, and even smoked salmon—are being added. Pasta comes in dozens of shapes, from tiny stars that cook in a few minutes to larger tubes, spirals, and strips that take 8 to 10 or 11 minutes. Shells and rotini are convenient because you can eat them with a spoon. Spaghetti, a traditional favorite, is a challenge to manage even when broken into pieces. It is worth experimenting with different shapes, colors, and flavors to add welcome variety to your meals.

The chief drawback to pasta is that, in most recipes, you're instructed to heat a large pot of water, cook the pasta, and then drain off the water. A lot of gas is used to heat a lot of water that is then thrown away—a fairly inefficient process. In contrast, with grain-based meals all of the water heated is consumed.

No-cook (no-boil) pasta is available through mail order. Just add a small amount of hot water and let the pasta stand—but don't throw away the water that is not absorbed. Dried vegetables and seasonings can turn the unused water into a savory broth that will help you stay hydrated.

Egg noodles come in several sizes, from thin, narrow noodles that cook in about 4 minutes to wider noodles that cook in 7 to 9 minutes. The smallest size, with noodles about 1½ inches long, works well with a bowl and spoon; you don't have to slurp as you do with spaghetti.

Potatoes

Freeze-dried potatoes are useful because they are quick cooking, but they taste like and have the consistency of instant potatoes. With some doctoring, they can be used in hash browns, and their lack of texture is masked somewhat when they are used with other ingredients in a stew or one-pot meal.

Instant hash browns are a boon for backcountry campers because crispy, golden hash browns are so wonderful and because whole potatoes are so heavy. There are other dehydrated potato products, including julienne potatoes and scalloped potatoes, both of which take about 15 minutes to rehydrate and cook. To make sure you buy hash browns, check the directions. They should tell you to add boiling water to the spuds, rather than directing you to simmer them. Instant hash brown mixes include dried onion flakes and other seasonings, so they're all set to go.

Instant mashed potatoes or potato flakes are a great base upon which to build a meal. By themselves, they have that "instant potato" taste and texture, which some people find more objectionable than others. Instant potatoes can be improved with seasoning and a dab of margarine or a teaspoon of butter powder.

Beans and Other Legumes

Instant refried beans and black bean powder greatly simplify Mexican cooking. Just add water and you have seasoned refried beans, a key element in burritos, dips, and other dishes. These box mixes are widely available in supermarkets and health food stores.

Bean flakes come in several varieties (I've found black bean and pinto bean so far in various health food stores). The flakes contain salt but no other seasonings. Other than having to spice them up yourself, you can use them as you would the instant bean powder described above—just add boiling water and let the flakes stand for 5 minutes.

Freeze-dried beans and lentils are available through mail order. Choices include pinto, navy, black, and kidney beans, plus lentils. In testing these foods (I added boiling water and let them stand for 10 minutes in an insulated mug), I found that some beans cooked/rehydrated all the way through while others retained a tiny powdery core. Those with the powdery core are edible, though they have an odd texture. When they're mixed with other ingredients, the texture problem is less noticeable.

Fruits and Vegetables

Dried fruits of many kinds are available in supermarkets and specialty stores. Apples, apricots, pears, raisins, mangoes, papaya, cherries, pineapple, peaches, cranberries, cherries, blueberries—take your pick. The more exotic fruits may be expensive, but you only need a handful to get a delightful burst of flavor some afternoon when the miles are long and the pack is heavy.

Freeze-dried fruit, including blueberries, peaches, pineapple, and strawberries, is available through mail order. Freeze-dried blueberries look great, but no one is likely to mistake them for fresh. (But then, if you knew there were going to be fresh blueberries along the trail, you wouldn't take along their freeze-dried cousins.) The virtue of freeze-dried fruit is that it is extremely light and provides a taste of something that wouldn't otherwise be available. This type of fruit is best used in something, rather than by itself.

Orange powder gives a nice flavor to cereal and desserts. Orange-flavored breakfast drink, the taste of which I find somewhat artificial, can be substituted for orange powder.

Coconut cream powder, an ingredient in Asian cooking, is very rich and flavorful. Powdered coconut can be used as a substitute, but it's not as tasty.

Dried vegetables, including carrots, bell peppers, cabbage, celery, corn, mushrooms, onions, tomatoes, and mixed veggies, are available in supermarkets and health food stores and through mail order. Before you bag up a big pile of instant meals, though, test a few pieces of each dried vegetable you plan to use to make sure that they will all rehydrate per recipe instructions. Celery, in particular, may take a while to return to the land of the edible, so it may require extra soaking time. Carrot flakes, shredded carrots, and carrots that have been sliced very thin will work in instant recipes.

If you are putting together the ingredients for an instant dish, do not use a vegetable mix that includes dehydrated peas or corn, or square chunks of carrots or potatoes, because these vegetables take more than 10 minutes (it may take 20+ minutes) to rehydrate. Dehydrated corn and peas can be used in the backcountry if they're presoaked.

Freeze-dried vegetables, including asparagus, broccoli, corn, green beans, peas, potatoes, and vegetable flakes are available through mail order, and many backpacking stores sell individual portions of corn and peas.

Corn, green beans, and peas rehydrate very well and with a little butter powder make up nicely as individual side dishes. The other freeze-dried vegetables vary—generally either texture or taste suffers. These vegetables are useful when combined with other ingredients in instant soups, stews, and one-pot dishes. While dehydrated corn and peas are hard as rocks, freeze-dried corn and peas (and some of the other freeze-dried vegetables) crumble easily. Use them early in the trip or pack them carefully for the long haul.

Tomato powder and spinach powder can add flavor to one-pot meals and soups. Although these powders are usually only available by mail order, stores that carry fixings for homemade pasta may have them in stock for use as pasta ingredients—it's worth calling if there's such a store nearby.

Eggs, Egg Replacers, and Dairy Products

Eggs: Salmonella are bacteria that can wreck your gastrointestinal system. Because eggs are a terrific medium for growing salmonella, it's important to handle raw eggs and egg products carefully. Do not carry raw eggs in any container except their own shells. Even breaking them into a clean container may expose them to salmonella. An egg with a broken shell should not be used. Cartons of "fat-free egg product," which contain egg whites and other ingredients but no egg yolks, are useful only for the first morning out, because for longer-term storage they must be refrigerated, or they, too, can harbor salmonella. Pasteurized powdered eggs are light and easy to pack, and they work well in baking. Doctored up, they make tolerable scrambled eggs. Pasteurized powdered eggs are germ free when you buy them, but they can easily be contaminated with salmonella. (See Hot Topic 2: How To— for how to handle powdered eggs.)

Egg substitute or replacer contains leavening plus potato starch, tapioca flour, and carbohydrate gum. Directions call for using 1½ teaspoons plus 2 tablespoons water to replace one egg. If cholesterol is a concern, this is a good substitute for eggs in baked goods.

Buttermilk powder used in combination with baking soda provides leavening and flavor. Use ¼ cup powder to make 1 cup buttermilk.

Cheese is available fresh and powdered. The real stuff is vastly superior when you are eating cheese and something (crackers, tortillas, et cetera), but cheese powder works well as an ingredient in egg dishes, soups, stews, and one-pot meals.

Parmesan and Romano have been around as shake-ons for years, but recently both white Cheddar and orange Cheddar have become available in powdered form—the same powders that are used in macaroni and cheese box mixes.

Blocks of hard cheeses like Parmesan are a good choice for warm-weather outings because they will not weep as much oil as softer cheeses like Cheddar. Although people think of pasta when they think of Parmesan, in fact thin-sliced Parmesan is quite tasty with crackers or tortillas. Individually packaged servings of string cheese, which is actually part-skim mozzarella, last well.

Sour cream powder makes up rather nicely. Be wary of buying this powder from a bulk container at a health food store; you don't know how long the powder has been sitting around unrefrigerated. Sour cream powder that has gone bad is really bad, so buy fresh and store it in the refrigerator or freezer. You can substitute (real) cream cheese, though it is heavier because it has more moisture.

Butter powder can be found in the baking section of the supermarket or purchased through mail order. I am unimpressed with the supermarket version, but the pure butter powder sold by mail has a mild butter flavor that enhances chowder, vegetable side dishes, one-pot meals, and baked items. Unlike powdered shortening, powdered butter does not revert to oil, so you cannot use it for frying.

Powdered vegetable shortening isn't a dairy product but is included here anyway. Powdered shortening can be used for frying (it turns to liquid oil as it heats up), baking, and boosting calories. Powdered shortening is handy if you aren't using regular oil or shortening in any other recipes and aren't planning on carrying a container. Powder is, however, far more expensive than oil or shortening, so you have to evaluate whether the ease is worth the cost. It is concentrated; if the recipe calls for 1 teaspoon of oil or shortening, use ½ teaspoon powder.

Meat and Seafood

Canned chicken and turkey have long been used by outdoor folk to add heft and flavor to a one-pot meal.

Freeze-dried chicken and turkey rehydrate tolerably well with the addition of water, boiling or otherwise. A little can go a long way when used as an ingredient rather than as a main course. Comparison shopping is in order when considering freeze-dried versus canned. A 1-ounce package of freeze-dried chicken makes ⅔ cup chicken; a 5-ounce can of chicken (meaning 5 ounces of chicken not including the can) holds ⅔ cup. Freeze-dried costs almost twice as much as canned. The decision, then, involves a trade-off between weight and cost—in other words between knees and wallet.

Dried chicken and turkey are not, to my knowledge, commercially available. To dry poultry yourself, see the sections about drying foods and making jerky. Some folks say that rehydrated poultry has great flavor and texture, while others say it tastes like cardboard. One's reaction doubtless depends on a combination of drying technique, hunger, and personal preference.

Freeze-dried beef, when reconstituted, comes close to the real thing. Like freeze-dried chicken and turkey, it is exceedingly light and an excellent choice when weight is a major concern.

Dried beef—the kind used in creamed chipped beef—contains enough moisture that it must be refrigerated after the jar has been opened. You can easily dry it a little more to make a handy addition to one-pot meals.

Dried ground beef is not available commercially, but you can make your own (see Hot Topic 8). Dried ground beef can be used in instant meals; it costs about one-fifth as much as freeze-dried beef. The dried version, however, does weigh more. One-half cup dried ground beef, made from 1 cup cooked ground beef, weighs just under 2.5 ounces. One-half cup freeze-dried, cubed beef, by comparison, weighs 0.75 ounce, or one-third of its dried counterpart.

Freeze-dried ground beef rehydrates well.

Bacon is a potent ingredient that adds a meaty taste and salt, even when used in small quantities. Crumbled bacon and low-fat bacon morsels are available in plastic pouches that, once opened, should be used promptly. Because of bacon's high fat content, dry mixes containing it should be refrigerated or frozen until it is time to take them on trail.

Cooked bacon strips packaged in an oxygen-free pouch will keep well without refrigeration for several months. All bacon should be eaten soon after the package has been opened.

Imitation bacon-flavored morsels offer an alternative to real bacon. The brands that are low in fat don't require subsequent refrigeration.

Freeze-dried shrimp are wonderful, delightful, scrumptious—and very expensive. They rehydrate quickly in hot or cold water and have the taste and feel of fresh shrimp. If money was not a consideration, freeze-dried shrimp would be at the top of my shopping list.

Canned shrimp are heavier than freeze-dried shrimp but not nearly as expensive.

Dried shrimp, which are available at Asian food markets, are small whole shrimp, shell and all. Dried shrimp are used in Asian cooking to make a shrimpy broth, but they cannot be substituted for either the freeze-dried or canned varieties. I find the flavor to be a little off, and the shells make the shrimp very chewy indeed.

Freeze-dried tuna fish rehydrates well and tastes more or less like canned tuna. Be aware that a pungent fishy odor does emanate from the used plastic bag, even when it's placed inside another plastic bag. The smell is one more reason to bear-bag your trash.

Foil-wrapped tuna is lots lighter than canned because you don't have to carry the can or excess water. Take some mayonnaise packets and some relish packets (or fresh or dried vegetables) to make tuna salad.

Soup

Instant soups of all varieties—ranging from black bean soup to corn chowder—are available at the supermarket in envelopes as well as paper cups. All you have to do is add boiling water. Because these soups usually contain freeze-dried beans, veggies, and other ingredients, they can be combined with a quick-cooking carbohydrate like bulgur or couscous to fill out a meal. However, because the soup is spiced for one cup of food, if you add a carbohydrate, you'll need to add more seasonings.

Dehydrated soups also come in many flavors and can be very handy when you want to add flavor and body to a dish. But let the user beware: Some dehydrated soups contain a whopping amount of salt—as high as two-thirds of the daily recommended amount. (For comparison, one cube of bouillon may contain 40 percent of a day's worth of salt, and low-salt alternatives ring in at 1 percent.) If you need to watch your salt intake, be careful with dehydrated soups. Also, people with a sensitivity to monosodium glutamate (MSG) should probably avoid prepared soups. Several brands use MSG as an ingredient, and many others use ingredients such as autolyzed yeast and yeast extract that contain MSG.

Bouillon is available in supermarkets in both powder and cube forms and in regular and low-salt versions, though I've not found an MSG-free version. Bouillon is beef-flavored, chicken-flavored, or vegetable-based.

Sauces

Gravy mixes are available at supermarkets. One packet generally makes 1 cup.

Cheese sauce mix is available from supermarkets. In a pinch, though, you can combine cheese powder and powdered milk.

Sweet and sour sauce mix purchased in the supermarket contains vinegar powder. If you want to make this sauce from scratch, check out the Internet backcountry food providers.

Pesto can be found in glass or a metal tube in the pasta section of the supermarket or fresh in the produce or deli sections. Fresh pesto should be used within 24 hours if carried at room temperature. Dried pesto is available in packets in the supermarket and health food stores. Though not as tasty as fresh pesto, dried pesto is easier to carry.

Condiments

Ketchup, mustard, mayonnaise, relish, lemon juice, and other condiments are widely available in small packets at fast food restaurants and supermarkets. If you have extra left over from your order, save them; if not, negotiate with the management for a small supply. Mayo packets are useful because you use the entire contents at once. Do not take a jar of mayonnaise on trail unless you can keep it chilled in a cooler; mayo contains raw eggs, so once the jar has been opened, it can be a breeding ground for salmonella.

Salsa is available in small packets (see above) as well as in dehydrated form at some health food stores. It's also easy to dry salsa at home.

Tamari or soy sauce is a salty seasoning brewed from soybeans. It is usually sold as a liquid, but is available in powdered form.

Wasabi is a very strong Japanese horseradish powder. This slightly greenish condiment can be used to spice up grain and potato dishes.

Salad sprinkles, which generally contain such ingredients as sunflower seeds, sesame seeds, some form of soy, and dehydrated vegetables, can be used to flavor eggs, cold lunch salads, and all manner of dinner meals.

Seasonings

Herb blends allow you to experiment without buying so many individual ingredients. Some—such as curry and garam masala—are traditional, while others—including Mediterranean and Thai seasonings—have been created for the convenience of shoppers. All herbs, blends or not, should be stored in a cool, dry place to maintain freshness. The usual site, above the stove, is not a good storage area.

Chinese five-spice seasoning—or at least one version of this seasoning—contains anise, cinnamon, star anise, cloves, and ginger. Another brand contains fennel, anise, cinnamon, black pepper, and cloves. Use ¼ to ⅓ teaspoon per serving.

Creole seasoning may contain chili powder, salt, cumin, coriander, paprika, and cloves; other versions contain chili powder, garlic, parsley, salt, thyme, and cayenne pepper. Because brands may vary, test first, starting with about ½ to ¾ tablespoon for every ½ cup tomato sauce or ½ cup uncooked grain.

Curry powder in the supermarket represents only one of the many possible configurations of spices that form curry bases. Some curries are very hot, some quite mild; different types are used for different foods. The amount to use depends on the age of the mix (fresher is stronger) and how many other spices the recipe calls for. Start with ¾ teaspoon per ½ cup uncooked grain, and work upward to your level of comfort.

Herbs de Provence, a blend that takes its name from Provence, France, includes rosemary, marjoram, thyme, sage, anise seed, and savory. Use ¼ teaspoon per serving.

Mediterranean seasoning may include salt, onion, spices (including chili pepper, oregano, fennel seed, cumin seed, red pepper, and garlic), red and green peppers, carrots, parsley, and turmeric. As with any seasoning mix, check for additives such as autolyzed yeast extract, which often contains MSG. Use 1 to 1½ tablespoons of Mediterranean seasoning for every ½ cup uncooked grain.

Garam masala is a hot spice mixture from India that is made from black pepper, coriander, cumin, cloves, cardamom, and cinnamon. It is usually used with other seasonings, and the amount of garam masala depends on the amounts of those other seasonings.

Lemon pepper contains garlic, pepper, onion, citric acid, lemon crystals and oil, turmeric, and other spices and herbs; some brands are salt free.

Thai seasoning may include chili pepper, ginger, coriander, red pepper, cumin, cinnamon, star anise, salt, garlic, lemon peel, shallots, cornstarch, jalepeno peppers, and other flavors. Use ¼ to ½ teaspoon per serving.

Appendix D: Sources of Ingredients

"Where do I find —?" is the most common trail cooking inquiry after "What food should I take?" The key to a business may be location, location, location, but in backcountry cuisine is ingredients, ingredients, ingredients.

The number and variety of ingredients available today are no less than phenomenal, but it's up to you to look for them. Check your local supermarket, health food store, and Asian food store if there is one nearby. The benefit to buying locally is that you save on shipping and don't have to wait for an order to arrive. Then, let your fingers slide along the keyboard and check online offerings.

As you shop, keep these tips in mind:
- Read the fine print about shipping costs.
- Factor shipping into the cost of the product.
- It's a deal only if you need it—all of it.
- If the smallest size is too much for you, encourage friends to join the order; if you do, get everyone's money up front.
- Offerings may change over time, so ingredients listed here may not be available later.

The following companies sell products of particular interest to the outdoor adventurer:

Adventure Foods (www.adventurefoods.com): This company offers a huge line of bulk ingredients that will answer almost any cooking need. Looking for powdered tamari, Worcestershire sauce, or honey? You'll find them all here. (828) 497-4113

AlpineAire (www.alpineaire.com/Pouches-bulk.html): AA offers the ever-popular staples in dehydrated or freeze-dried form. (800) 322-6325

The Baker's Catalog (www.KingArthurFlour.com): Although geared to bakers rather than backpackers, this company does offer some interesting flavor powders—such as espresso, orange, and spinach—not available elsewhere. The nut flours can add interest and calories to bakes and desserts. (800) 827-6836

The Internet Grocer (http://internet-grocer.com): These folks sell in bulk. Their smallest container, a #2½ can, holds 3¼ cups. The cans weigh between ½ pound and 2 pounds, depending on content. There is no minimum order; you can order just one can, but the cost of shipping is proportionately higher. (972) 288-0262

Just Tomatoes (www.justtomatoes.com): This company, which specializes in dried fruit and vegetable snacks, offers a line of organic products. Because the emphasis is on snacks, foods are not available in large amounts; 8 ounces in the maximum size container. (800) 537-1985

Abbreviations: AF = Adventure Foods, AA = AlpineAire, BC = The Baker's Catalog, IG = Internet Grocer, JT = Just Tomatoes

Beans
Black, precooked: freeze-dried, AF; dehydrated, AF, AA
Kidney, precooked: freeze-dried, AF; dehydrated, AF, AA
Lentils, precooked: freeze-dried, AF; dehydrated, AF, AA
Navy, precooked: dehydrated, AA
Pinto, precooked: dehydrated, AA; flakes, AF

Dairy
Butter powder: AF, IG, BC
Butter-flavored sprinkles: supermarkets
Buttermilk powder: IG, BC, supermarkets
Cottage cheese: AF
Cheese, Cheddar: powdered, AF, AA, IG, BC; freeze-dried grated, AF
Cheese, Monterey Jack: shreds, AF
Cheese, mozzarella: freeze-dried grated, AF
Cream cheese: powder, AF
Eggs, whole: powdered, AF, IG, BC; scrambled freeze-dried, AA
Eggs, whites only: powdered, AF, IG, BC
Milk powder, whole milk: AF
Milk powder, low fat: AF, AA
Sour cream powder: AF, AA, IG

Fruits
Apples, dehydrated: diced AF, AA; flakes, AA; nuggets, BC; sliced, IG, supermarkets, health food stores
Applesauce: powdered, AF, IG

Apricots, dehydrated: AF, BC, supermarkets, health food stores
Bananas, dehydrated: sliced, IG; crunches, JT; sweetened slices, super-
    markets
Blackberries, dehydrated: JT
Blueberries: dehydrated, AF, JT, BC; freeze-dried, AA
Cherries, dried: AF, JT, BC (both sour and sweet), supermarkets
Coconut, toasted, dehydrated: AF, health food stores
Cranberries, dehydrated: JT, supermarkets
Mango, dehydrated: JT, BC
Peach slices, dehydrated: IG
Peach-apple flakes, dehydrated: IG
Persimmons, dehydrated: JT
Pineapple, dehydrated: JT, BC, supermarkets, health food stores
Raspberries, dehydrated: JT
Strawberries: dehydrated, JT, BC; whole freeze-dried: AA
Strawberry-apple flakes, dehydrated: IG

Grains and Grain Products
Barley, quick-cooking: AF, supermarkets
Couscous: regular and whole wheat, AA, supermarkets, health food stores
Flours, almond, hazelnut, and pecan: BC
Macaroni: whole wheat and vegetable, AA
Rice, brown, precooked: 5-minute, AF; instant, AA, supermarkets
Rice, white, precooked: 3-minute, AF; instant, AA, supermarkets
Rice, wild, precooked: 7-minute, AF; instant, AA

Meat, Seafood, and Meat Replacers
Bacon, precooked: strips and crumbles, supermarkets
Beef extract: AF
Beef, precooked: diced dried, AF; freeze-dried, AA; sliced, supermarkets
Beef, ground, precooked and freeze-dried: AF
Chicken, precooked, diced and freeze-dried: AF, AA
Ham, freeze-dried diced: AF
Meats, various dehydrated: Asian food stores
Shrimp, freeze-dried: AF
Surimi (whitefish and crab), freeze-dried: AF
TVP (textured vegetable protein): beef-flavored, AF, IG; chicken-flavored,
    AF, IG; Canadian bacon–flavored, AF; ham-flavored, IG;

Italian beef–flavored, AF; regular, AF; taco-flavored, IG; sausage-flavored, IG; various types, supermarkets, health food stores
Tuna chunks, cooked and freeze-dried: AF, AA
Turkey, cooked, diced, freeze-dried: AA

Vegetables
Asparagus: dehydrated, AF; diced freeze-dried, AA
Beans, green: dehydrated, AF, IG; freeze-dried, AF
Broccoli, freeze-dried: AF, AA; dehydrated, IG
Cabbage, dehydrated: AF, AA, IG
Carrots, dried: diced, AA, IG; puffed, AF; shoestring, AF, BC; pieces, JT
Celery, dried: AF, AA, IG
Corn: dehydrated, IG; freeze-dried: AF, AA, JT
Garden vegetable mix: AA
Mushrooms, sliced dehydrated: AF, IG, JT, supermarkets, Asian food stores, health food stores
Onions, dehydrated: chopped, AF, AA, IG, JT; minced, BC; baking, BC
Peas: dehydrated, AF, IG; freeze-dried, AF, AA, JT
Pepper, bell: green, dehydrated, AF; red, freeze-dried pieces, AF; mixed dehydrated, IG, BC, health food stores; pieces, JT
Potatoes: instant: AF, AA; shreds, AF; slices: AF; diced, IG; instant hash browns, supermarkets
Salad blend vegetables (pepper, onion, celery): AF
Scallions, dehydrated: JT
Spaghetti sauce: AF
Spinach flakes: AF
Stew blend, dehydrated: IG
Stewed tomato blend of mixed vegetables: AF
Tomatoes, dehydrated: flakes, AF, AA, BC; pieces, JT; julienne, BC; sliced, supermarkets
Vegetable blend: European, mild: AF; mix, AA
Vegetable soup blend: AF

Powders, Granules, and Crystals (also see Dairy)
Apple powder: AF
Chicken powder: AF
Chocolate, ground: AF
Coconut cream powder: Asian food stores

Espresso powder: BC
Honey powder: AF
Leek powder: AF
Lemon powder: BC
Lemon juice powder: AF
Malted milk powder: BC
Maple sugar granules: AF, AA, BC
Margarine powder: IG
Molasses powder: AF
Orange powder: BC
Peanut butter powder: IG
Potato granules: IG
Salsa powder: AF
Shortening powder: AF, IG
Soy sauce powder: AF
Spinach powder: BC
Sweet potato crystals, instant: AF
Tomato powder: AF, IG, BC
Vanilla powder: BC
Vanillin crystals: AF
Vinegar powder: AF
Wine powder: Chablis, Burgundy and sherry, AF
Worcestershire sauce powder: AF

Take-Out

Everyone likes a day off. If you want to abandon planning and home prep for a meal (or two or three), you have lots of options. Here are some sites to get you started. Be sure to look at the volume—how many cups—that each package produces as well as the nutritive values. Adventure Foods offers mixes for the BakePacker, and Backpacker's Pantry offers mixes for the Outback Oven.

- Adventure Foods (www.adventurefoods.com) (828) 497-4113
- AlpineAire (www.alpineairefoods.com) (800) 322-6325
- Backpacker's Pantry (www.backpackerspantry.com) (303) 581-0518
- Mountain Gourmet (www.msrcorp.com) (800) 877-9677
- Mountain House (www.mountainhouse.com) Does not sell mail-order.
- Natural High (www.richmoor.com) (800) 423-3170

Index

About the Author

Dorcas S. Miller has worked as an Outward Bound instructor, a whitewater rafting guide, a canoe trip leader, a teacher, an environmental advocate, and a freelance writer.

After she ate neon macaroni and cheese most of one summer, she developed a lively interest in eating well on trail and has written four camping cookbooks, including *Backcountry Cooking* and *More Backcountry Cooking*.

She has canoed wilderness rivers in Quebec and the Northwest Territories in Canada, rock climbed in areas throughout the United States, and sea kayaked extensively along the Maine coast. She is the author of nine other nonfiction books, which cover topics as varied as sea kayaking, adventurous women, animal tracks, and constellations. She edited *Rescue,* an anthology of epic tales of survival from land and sea.

She lists climbing the Standard Route on Fairview, helping stop a dam on the Penobscot River, writing a mystery novel even though it never got published ("it was a challenge to make things up"), climbing and paddling amicably with her husband ("separate boats are key on water"), and listening well among personal accomplishments. She lives near the Kennebec River in Maine.